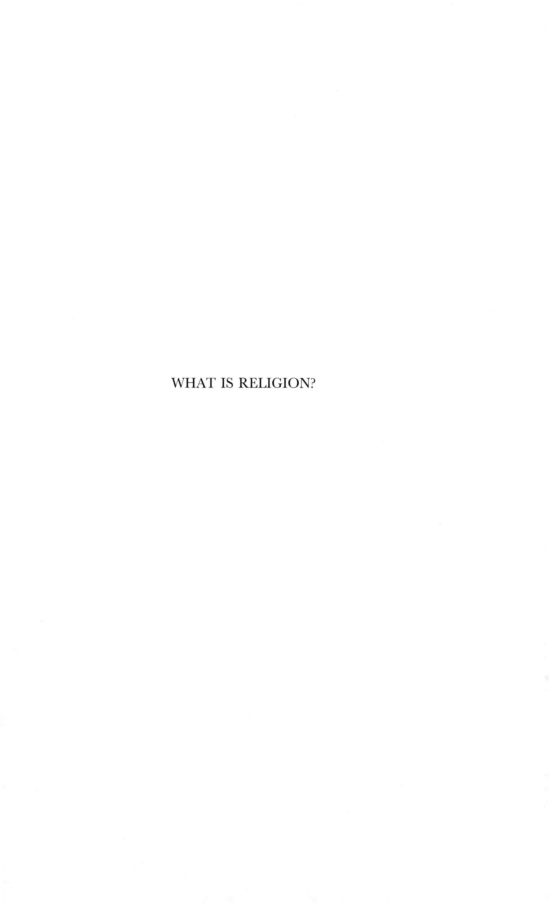

WHAT IS RELIGION?

STUDIES

IN THE HISTORY OF RELIGIONS

(*NUMEN* BOOK SERIES)

EDITED BY

H.G. KIPPENBERG · E.T. LAWSON

VOLUME LXXXI

WHAT IS RELIGION?
ORIGINS, DEFINITIONS, AND EXPLANATIONS

EDITED BY

THOMAS A. IDINOPULOS

AND

BRIAN C. WILSON

BRILL

LEIDEN · BOSTON · KÖLN

1998

This book is printed on acid-free paper.

Library of Congress Cataloging-in-Publication Data

What is religion? : origins, definitions, and explanations / edited by
  Thomas A. Idinopulos and Brian C. Wilson.
      p.   cm. — (Studies in the history of religions, ISSN
  0169–8834 ; v. 81)
    Includes bibliographical references (p.   ) and indexes.
    ISBN 9004110224 (hardcover : alk. paper)
    1. Religion.   I. Idinopulos, Thomas A.   II. Wilson, Brian C.
  III. Series: Studies in the history of religions ; 81.
  BL48.W342   1998
  200—dc21   98-34512
                                                                    CIP

Die Deutsche Bibliothek - CIP-Einheitsaufnahme

What is religion? : origins, definitions, and explanations / ed. by
Thomas A. Idinopulos and Brian C. Wilson. – Leiden ; Boston ; Köln
: Brill, 1998
  (Studies in the history of religions ; Vol. 81)
  ISBN 90–04–11022–4

ISSN   0169-8834
ISBN   90 04 11022 4

PRINTED IN THE NETHERLANDS

CONTENTS

LIST OF CONTRIBUTORS

Clayton Crockett

Department of Religion
Syracuse University
Syracuse, NY 13244

James J. DiCenso

Department for the Study of Religion
University of Toronto, Ontario
Toronto, Ontario
Canada M5S 2E8

Thomas A. Idinopulos

Department of Religion
Miami University
Oxford, Ohio 45056

E. Thomas Lawson

Department of Comparative Religion
Western Michigan University
Kalamazoo, MI 49008

Russell T. McCutcheon

Department of Religious Studies
Southwest Missouri State University
Springfield, MO 65804

Dan Merkur

630 Vesta Drive Apt. 103
Toronto, Ontario
Canada M5N 1J1

William E. Paden

Department of Religion
University of Vermont
Burlington, VT 05403

Robert Segal

Department of Religious Studies
Lancaster University
LA1 4Y6 United Kingdom

Ivan Strenski

Department of Religious Studies
University of California
Riverside, CA 92521

James Wiggins

Department of Religious Studies
Syracuse University
Syracuse, NY 13244

Brian C. Wilson   Department of Comparative Religion
                                 Western Michigan University
                                 Kalamazoo, MI 49008

Charles E. Winquist   Department of Religious Studies
                                 Syracuse University
                                 Syracuse, NY 13244

PREFACE

This volume continues the series in the methodology of religious studies. The series began with the earlier publication of two books: *Religion and Reductionism* (E. J. Brill, 1994) and *The Sacred and Its Scholars* (E. J. Brill, 1996).

We have prepared the new volume in response to a professional concern. Today, increasingly, professors of religious studies are in a quandary not only as to how to approach their subject matter, but even as to what is or should be their subject matter. It is our hope that this anthology of essays will work to ease the quandary.

Like the earlier publications, our aim is to raise fundamental questions about how best to study religion. We invited our contributors to respond to any of a number of questions: What is the origin or origins of religion? How does one explain religion? How does one explain its appearance, meaning, purpose, duration, future? Some scholars contend that religion is woven into the fabric of human culture. How does one identity the religious strand as contrasted with economics, politics, and other strands? Finally, can religion be defined? What is a proper definition of religion?

The authors who appear in this volume vary widely in their answers to these questions and even in the formulation of the questions. In the spirit of open inquiry, we may even find them posing their own questions. One thing they share is the confidence that religion cannot be adequately studied and understood if the central methodological questions are ignored and left unanswered.

We take pleasure in acknowledging the assistance of several people who helped in the preparation of this book, including Vickie Dearwester of Miami University and Gwen West of Western Michigan University. We are especially grateful for the patience and enthusiasm of Mattie Kuiper, Desk Editor for Religious Studies at Brill Academic Publishers.

This book is dedicated to Lea Mindo Spector Idinopulos and Cybelle Shattuck.

THOMAS A. IDINOPULOS
BRIAN C. WILSON

CHAPTER ONE

ON THE DISORIENTATION OF THE STUDY
OF RELIGION

Clayton Crockett

In his book, *Significations*, the historian of religion Charles H. Long defines religion as orientation. "For my purposes," he writes, "religion will mean orientation—orientation in the ultimate sense, that is, how one comes to terms with the ultimate significance of one's place in the world."[1] To simplify matters, I shorten Long's phrase, "ultimate significance of one's place in the world," with the term, "reality." Religion can be understood as orientation to reality. Every entity in the universe possesses a certain orientation to reality, but for self-conscious human beings, the issue of orientation becomes important when reality does not appear self-evident, or is considered problematic.

According to the philosopher Jürgen Habermas, one can divide the history of philosophy into three periods or types: philosophies of being, philosophies of consciousness, and philosophies of language.[2] Habermas associates the transition from philosophies of being to philosophies of consciousness with Descartes, and the transition from philosophies of consciousness to philosophies of language with Nietzsche. What is significant in such a progression or development is the notion that simple access to reality becomes more and more problematic, while more and more attention is paid to the medium or means of orientation. This development could also be viewed as a movement from objectivism to subjectivism, but it is an over-simplification to claim that consciousness and language are "merely subjective."

One of the most profound moments in this philosophical drama occurs with Kant, who divides human experience and knowing into phenomena and noumena. This "Copernican revolution" restricts human knowledge to appearances and leaves unknown objects as

---

[1] Charles H. Long, *Significations* (Philadelphia: Fortress Press, 1986), p. 7.
[2] Jürgen Habermas, *Postmetaphysical Thinking: Selected Essays*, translated by William Mark Hohengarten (Cambridge: MIT Press, 1992), p. 12.

they are in themselves.[3] The only way that Kant can secure objectivity of knowledge of phenomena is to restrict it to things as they conform to human understanding. "Thus the order and regularity in the appearances," Kant writes, "which we entitle nature, we ourselves introduce" (A125). The securing of knowledge in the phenomenal realm comes at the expense of any definite knowledge of things in themselves, or reality. Of course, Kant claims that humans can have access to the realm of things in themselves through the willing of the moral law, but this moral law lacks any determinate content, and cannot be known except in a purely formal way.

In his essay, "What is Orientation in Thinking?," Kant grapples more explicitly with the issue of orientation, and suggests that the idea of God provides subjective orientation in thinking. Written in 1786, this piece represents Kant's intervention into the dispute between F. H. Jacobi and Moses Mendelssohn regarding the legitimacy and claims of faith and reason, respectively. Kant endorses the late Jewish philosopher, whose demise some contemporary intellectuals attributed to the unfair attacks of Jacobi and others, but in doing so he also modifies Mendelssohn's consistent rationalism. Although he affirms that "reason alone" is the "necessary means of orientation," Kant emphasizes that all of our rational concepts need certain "figurative notions" to make such concepts "suitable for use in the experiential world."[4] That is, rational concepts do not provide knowledge of themselves, but their actualization depends on "a felt need of reason" in order to provide orientation for human beings in thinking and living. There exists within reason, in a practical or heuristic sense, a "feeling of a need" which is a "subjective distinction" enabling judgment to occur.[5]

Reason cannot claim to provide knowledge of the world in any objective sense. Reason itself, however, according to Kant, is the only means of orienting human beings in the world, despite the arguments of fideists like Jacobi that God provides an objective center for orientation. Kant therefore concludes that reason provides subjective orientation based on a felt need for orientation to reality. Despite skepticism regarding the objective nature of the world,

---

[3] See Immanuel Kant, *Critique of Pure Reason*, translated by Norman Kemp Smith (New York: St. Martin's Press, 1965), p. 22. Henceforth, I will cite the page number of the German A or B edition in parentheses; for this reference, Bxvi.

[4] Immanuel Kant, "What is Orientation in Thinking?" in *Kant: Political Writings*, edited by Hans Reiss and translated by H.B. Nisbet (Cambridge: Cambridge University Press, 1990), p. 237.

[5] Ibid., p. 240.

> the right of the need of reason supervenes as a subjective ground for presupposing and accepting something which reason cannot presume to know on objective grounds, and hence for orientating ourselves in thought—i.e. in the immeasurable space of the supra-sensory realm which we see as full of utter darkness—purely by means of the need of reason itself.[6]

From this premise Kant concludes that there is an unconditional need of reason to assume that God exists in the practical realm.

Kant uses the example of a person groping around in a dark room for direction; she is able to find her way around if she can locate a familiar object and orient herself practically by means of it. The disoriented person does not require a map of the room, only the ability to orient herself subjectively. Additionally, for an astronomer or stargazer, "in spite of all the objective data in the sky, I orientate myself geographically purely by means of a subjective distinction."[7] What becomes central in this brief essay is the importance of subjective orientation, rather than objective data. If access to reality as it is in itself is severely problematized, then one's orientation to that reality takes on greater importance.

What does this understanding of orientation in Kant have to do with the study of religion? The fact that reality is not given to human understanding implies that any data which is described as religion or religious can claim only phenomenal status. This means not only that religion cannot be known immediately as a thing in itself, but also that it is at least partially constructed as an object by the observer, interpreter, or scholar. I am not dealing with the notion of God here, I am simply grappling with the notion of religion as an object of study. And after Kant, any definition of religion must be seen as constructed by human knowing rather than simply given to or imposed upon an observer. Every scholar possesses her own subjective orientation.

In this vein, one can read Jonathan Z. Smith's claim that "there is no data for religion. Religion is solely the creation of the scholar's study....Religion has no independent existence apart from the academy."[8] I want to qualify Smith's striking assertion, because in a Kantian sense, one cannot claim that religion has no independent existence outside the academy, or apart from the imaginative analyt-

---

[6] Ibid., pp. 240-41.
[7] Ibid., p. 239.
[8] Jonathan Z. Smith, *Imagining Religion: From Babylon to Jonestown* (Chicago: University of Chicago Press, 1982), p. xi.

ic constructions of it. The case is rather that scholars simply do not know what religion is in itself, apart from their phenomenological characterizations of it. In the First Critique Kant makes a refutation of idealism (B274-79), claiming that objects do possess independent existence, even if that independent existence cannot be known.

So intellectual honesty demands that scholars of religion recognize their self-implication in the formation of meaningful patterns which are deemed religion or religious. Scholars should also leave an open space for the possibility of what religion in itself might be apart from and independent of their own interpretations, that is, what religion might be apart from any orientation. The otherness of religion, however, does not occur above or beyond the interpretations of religion and the empirical manifestations of religion, but is rather part and parcel of expressions of and about religion. In Kantian terms, religious expression is interrogated and understood in phenomenal, rational and immanent terms, which relate to experience, rather than in noumenal, fideistic and transcendent terms, which presuppose direct knowledge of the object of faith.

According to the theologian Paul Tillich, religion means ultimate concern, that is, what concerns human beings ultimately to the exclusion of conditional concerns.[9] Any finite concern, such as another person, a nation, or money which is elevated to the status of an ultimate concern, constitutes for Tillich idolatry.[10] I have suggested above, in my discussion of Long, that the term "reality" can be substituted for the term "ultimate concern," because an ultimate concern for Tillich is not one concern among others. It is the horizon or worldview which constitutes one's orientation in the largest sense. Tillich argues that every human being is religious, in the sense that everyone possesses an ultimate concern, or an orientation to reality. One's orientation to reality matters or is concerned with existence, for Tillich, because it concerns one's being and non-being.[11] In his *Systematic Theology, Volume One*, Tillich claims that theoretical reflection about religion is theological. To interpret or to understand in intellectual self-expression the implications of being ultimately concerned, or of being oriented to reality, involves one in theological

[9] Paul Tillich, *Theology of Culture* (London: Oxford University Press, 1959), pp. 7-8. "Religion, in the largest and most basic sense of the word, is ultimate concern."

[10] Paul Tillich, *Dynamics of Faith* (New York: Harper & Row, 1957), p. 44.

[11] See Paul Tillich, *Systematic Theology*, Volume One (Chicago: University of Chicago Press, 1951), p. 14. "Our ultimate concern is that which determines our being and non-being." This is Tillich's "second formal criterion of theology."

discourse. The "first formal criterion of theology," according to Tillich, reads: "The object of theology is what concerns us ultimately."[12]

This is a formal criterion which implicates a thinker in terms of her own orientation to reality, whenever she enters into reflective discourse. Therefore, the study of religion necessarily possesses a theological component or moment, even if only in a formal sense. That is, understood broadly as the intellectual sense-making or self-expressions of religious believers, theology articulates an existentially concerned orientation to reality. This acknowledgment has two foci. On the one hand, the scholar or religion cannot study religion or religions without taking into account the theoretical self-understandings of religious adherents and practitioners. To restrict the study of religion merely to observable behavior or rituals overlooks the point of view of the persons engaged in that practice, and ignores the fact that every interpretation is contested. If theology is abolished from religion as an object of study, then the interpreter reserves the right to herself to impose meanings and categories, and deprives the peoples, texts and traditions of any self-description.[13]

On the other hand, along with the inclusion of theology as a viable area of study within the academic study of religion, scholars of religion should recognize the implication of their own orientation to reality (existentially, economically, etc.) in the construction of their data and interpretations. This is the formal theological component of the study of religion, which does not have to be a confessional theology, especially in terms of any particular religious tradition or community (although this too cannot be excluded). An understanding of the formal nature of theological expression as it relates to religion is contrasted with any necessary content of theological commitment or belief. Theology here means the reflexive theoretical

---

[12] Ibid., p. 12.

[13] On the implicit and unacknowledged reading of intellectual dichotomies into the study of ritual behavior, see Catherine Bell, *Ritual Theory, Ritual Practice* (New York: Oxford University Press, 1992), p. ix: "Most simply, ritual is so readily cast as action in opposition to thought and theory that the structuring effect of assumptions about thought and action can be traced with great clarity." The reader might suspect that I am contradicting what was said earlier, concerning the constitution of religion as an object of study by the scholar of religion, which has no simple access to religion in itself. This is a valid criticism only if one considers that religious believers and practitioners are not and cannot be scholars, that is, cannot interpret and examine their behaviors and beliefs analytically in any way. Such a viewpoint would be open to charges of imperialism, in which only "natives" practice religion and only objective scholars observe and record and interpret religion.

reflection upon one's own concerned orientation to reality, and attention to how such an orientation distorts and disturbs, in both negative and positive ways, the results of one's study.[14]

The notion of orientation presupposes at least the possibility of disorientation. Despite Kant's anxiety regarding disorientation in "What is Called Orientation in Thinking?," he introduces a profound sense of disorientation in the sublime. The analytic of the sublime occurs in the "Critique of Aesthetic Judgment," following the analytic of beauty. Kant's aesthetic theory is related to feeling, and his teleology builds upon a felt analogy between human thinking and natural processes. Remember that it is a "felt need of reason" which provides subjective orientation. In the *Critique of Judgment*, Kant develops a theory of reflective judgment which lacks the objectivity of the determinative judgment of the First Critique, because in the feeling of beauty understanding and imagination work together in a free play which produces accord. This free play lacks objective content, however, because even though a judgment of beauty refers to all rational observers as a subjective claim or demand, no object can be described objectively as beautiful. A judgment that something is beautiful is a judgment of taste, which is a judgment "whose determining basis cannot be other than subjective."[15]

Although it is subjective, a judgment of taste or beauty is pleasurable because it is based upon a certain purposiveness which is recognized in the object and related to the human powers of thinking. This purposiveness is a felt sense of purpose in the *form* of the object.[16] The felt purposiveness is also an expression of the subjective

---

[14] Of course, this conclusion may seem anathema to scholars concerned with preserving the academic study of religion in a threatened educational environment, where to acknowledge complicity with theology would seem to render the study of religion subjective, confessional, and irrelevant to the production of academic knowledge. Some of these pressures arise from social scientific perspectives, which desire to promote the acceptance of the study of religion by making it more objective, i.e. more scientific. Unfortunately, not only does this represent a sacrifice of intellectual honesty, but it in no way safeguards the academic study of religion in higher education. Disciplines thrive, I suggest, based on their generation of theories, or new ways of looking at phenomena. This can be most creative at the intersection of theology, philosophy, and methodological aspects of the history of religions. Theoretical paradigms should be concrete, embodied, practical, and constantly pressured by the empirical manifestations of religious experience and behavior. But if the study of religion ceases to generate new ways of thinking about religious phenomena, then it in no way justifies its uniqueness and separation from departments of history, anthropology, philosophy, etc., or area studies programs.

[15] Immanuel Kant, *Critique of Judgment*, translated by Werner Pluhar (Indianapolis: Hackett Publishing Co., 1987), p. 44.

[16] Ibid., p. 66.

orientation which Kant describes in "What is Called Orientation in Thinking?" In the sublime judgment, however, a contrapurposiveness enters into consideration, because the object is perceived now as formless. This apprehension of formlessness comes about, as Jean-François Lyotard points out, as a result of a proliferation of forms by the faculty of a productive imagination which cannot be comprehended or conceptualized by the understanding.[17] Kant stresses that sublimity is properly located not in the object of nature, which prompts the imagination to produce forms in its striving toward infinity, but in the mind itself.[18] The feeling of the sublime is the result of a struggle between imagination, which outstrips the ability of the understanding to comprehend its apprehension or proliferation of forms to infinity, and reason, which steps in to contain, control and redirect the brutal and disturbing power of imagination.

> What happens is that our imagination strives to progress toward infinity, while our reason demands absolute totality as a real idea, and so the imagination, our power of estimating the magnitude of things in the world of sense, is inadequate to that idea. Yet this inadequacy itself is the arousal in us of the feeling that we have within us a supersensible power.[19]

Reason checks imagination's progression to infinity, and demands the presentation of the totality which the imagination attempts to grasp in one single idea, which the imagination is unable to perform.[20]

The sublime therefore produces a negative pleasure, negative because of the disorientation produced by the formlessness seen in the object and ascribed to the mental faculties of representation, but ultimately pleasurable in that it is the human being which is the source of that power, and it is human reason which possesses the strength to contain and control it. Here Kant values disorientation in a forceful way, although questions can be raised regarding the confidence contemporary intellectuals and others possess in the ability of human reason to control the brutal power of imagination and to di-

---

[17] Jean-François Lyotard, *Lessons on the Analytic of the Sublime*, translated by Elizabeth Rottenberg (Stanford: Stanford University Press, 1994), pp. 74-75.

[18] Ibid., p. 99.

[19] Ibid., p. 106.

[20] In the *Critique of Pure Reason*, however, it is the understanding which is charged with conceptually comprehending what the imagination apprehends. Kant blames imagination for the failure of the understanding, because otherwise questions would be asked about the objectivity of the concepts of understanding not only in reflective judgments, but also and more importantly, in the determinative judgment of the First Critique.

rect it toward moral ends. In this century, the Holocaust or *Shoah* represents the extreme case of an irruption of irrational force which calls into question reason's ability and right to play judge and law-giver in relation to imagination and understanding.[21]

In the *Critique of Judgment*, Kant states that "sublime is what even to be able to think proves that the mind has a power surpassing any standard of sense."[22] The question immediately arises, is the sublime able to be thought? Or is it rather that which disrupts our ability to think anything at all? In the *Critique of Pure Reason*, Kant restricts pure reason to the standards of sense. He writes that "it must be possible for the 'I think' to accompany all my representations; for otherwise something would be represented in me which could not be thought at all..." (B131-32). Judgment is defined as the subsump-tion of intuitions under a concept according to a rule, in the First Critique. This notion of judgment becomes most compromised in what is called alternately the Schematism of the Pure Concepts of the Understanding and the Transcendental Imagination.

The schematism represents a process or an act of representation which cannot itself be represented. Therefore I call it a sublime as-pect of thinking. In the First Critique, imagination is defined as "the faculty of representing in intuition an object that is not itself pre-sent" (B151), while the sublime is the unrepresentable in and of rep-resentation in the Third Critique. A transcendental schema, which is a product of the transcendental imagination, is defined as a "third thing" which mediates between the intellectual category and the sensible appearance (A138/B177). The schematism, or the transcen-dental imagination, is that process or ability which actualizes the concepts by fusing them to intuitions by means of schemata. A schema cannot be an image, because it abstracts from sensory con-ditions. The schema represents a rule or pattern which cannot be represented fully. Despite Kant's talk of rules, however, the tran-scendental imagination itself cannot be given a rule. "This schema-tism of our understanding," he writes, "in its application to appear-ances and their mere form, is an art concealed in the depths of the human soul, whose real modes of activity nature is hardly likely ever to allow us to discover, and to have open to our gaze" (A141/B180).

Although he calls this process the transcendental imagination, Kant ascribes its working to the understanding, in order to preserve

[21] See Jean-François Lyotard, *The Differend: Phrases in Dispute*, translated by Georges Van Den Abbeele (Minneapolis: University of Minnesota Press, 1988).
[22] Kant, *Critique of Judgment*, p. 106.

the objectivity of human knowledge of phenomena. But he highlights the failure of imagination in the Third Critique at the same time as he backgrounds imagination in favor of understanding in the First Critique. When Kant wrote the *Critique of Pure Reason*, in 1781, he believed that aesthetic feelings were purely subjective, and could involve no critique. In 1787, however, he experienced a "breakthrough" towards a "Critique of Taste." This Critique of Taste eventually became the *Critique of Judgment*. The critique of taste constitutes an awareness of the interworking or "free play" of imagination and understanding in the feeling of beauty, which is universally communicable, but lacks any objective content. Around the same time, in 1787, Kant rewrites part of the First Critique, especially the Transcendental Deduction, in order to more fully separate imagination from the objective work of the conceptual understanding.[23]

Kant "shrinks back" from the awareness that the interplay of imagination and understanding compromises the objectivity of determinative judgment. And he neglects to realize the connection between the negative pleasure and purposiveness of the sublime and the epistemological wound that the transcendental imagination inflicts on thinking. Writing about the "epistemological conception of the transcendental imagination," Charles E. Winquist claims that "to understand the significance of the transcendental imagination, the mind would have to have an immediate knowledge of itself as it contributes to the total act of knowing."[24] This immediate knowledge of itself is impossible for the transcendental imagination, but as a demand it represents a condition for knowing in general, and the activity of the schematism is necessary for any phenomenal knowing to occur.

As what makes possible the actualization of concepts and intuitions, the transcendental imagination allows representation to happen, but at the same time the transcendental imagination itself cannot be represented. The inability to represent the capacity to represent objects pressures any and every representation, and calls into question (although it does not deny) our ability to think and know at a basic level. The sublime, understood as the formless, or

---

[23] On the difference between the two editions of the First Critique, see Martin Heidegger, *Kant and the Problem of Metaphysics*, translated by Richard Taft (Bloomington: Indiana University Press, 1990), pp. 110-17. On the composition of the Third Critique, see John H. Zammito, *The Genesis of Kant's "Critique of Judgment"* (Chicago: University of Chicago Press, 1992), p. 46.

[24] Charles E. Winquist, *The Transcendental Imagination: An Essay in Philosophical Theology* (The Hague: Martinus Nijhoff, 1972), p. 14.

the unrepresentable as such, names the difficulties involved in human attempts to represent and know sensible objects. Sublimity is not simply a quality of objects, however, but is part and parcel of human faculties of thinking, feeling and willing. Human knowing involves a formal moment of disorientation or dizziness which takes it to the limits of form and what is formed, even as it allows or provides orientation in the same process.

Although absolute disorientation is impossible, because it would then be completely incoherent, absolute orientation is likewise impossible, because otherwise orientation would not even be an issue. Orientation would be reality, totally and completely. In his book, *The Creation of Chaos*, Frederick J. Ruf examines the notion of chaos in the writings of William James, and he also revaluates chaos as an important religious symbol and conceptual tool. The concept of chaos is related to that of disorientation, and "for a long tradition of religious people, disorientation is a critical religious experience."[25] Ruf distinguishes between "soft" and "hard" chaos. Soft chaos is threatening, but can ultimately be domesticated or tamed, and serves as a positive challenge to human exertion. The disorientation induced by soft chaos easily inclines one toward reorientation. This is what Kant wants the sublime to be. He wants the sublime to provide an invigorating challenge and a worthy opponent for reason to reassert its power, but the sublime must not be allowed to break free and radically disrupt reason's ability to function. Hard chaos, on the other hand, is so radically terrifying that it cannot be assimilated, and therefore it is purely destructive. This is the sort of chaos that Ruf identifies with religious experience and particularly with *The Varieties of Religious Experience*.

I am not attempting to affirm a purely destructive chaos or disorientation, but rather I want to propose a notion of disorientation which would not be caught between the either/or of hard and soft chaos. Such a disorientation would not simply provide a challenge that is not really a challenge, or an opposition that is posited to be overcome simply and easily. On the other hand, it would not be understood as a disorientation which absolutely precludes any meaning or identity.[26] This is my constructive reinterpretation of

---

[25] Frederick J. Ruf, *The Creation of Chaos: William James and the Stylistic Making of a Disorderly World* (Albany: State University of New York Press, 1991), p. 130.

[26] Such a notion of disorientation is hinted at by Gianni Vattimo in his book, *The Transparent Society*, translated by David Webb (Baltimore: Johns Hopkins Press, 1992). Vattimo combines Heidegger's notion of a work of art delivering a blow, with Benjamin's notion of shock, in order to elaborate an aesthetics of disorientation. For Vattimo, "aesthetic experience is directed toward keeping the disorientation alive" (p. 47).

the Kantian sublime, where to recognize the sublime as a problematic wound of thinking is also to recognize the sublime as an opportunity for thinking. Here disorientation is posited as a condition for the possibility of any orientation or reorientation at all. This notion of the sublime avoids positing it as a stimulant for the exercise of reason's might, as well as the obverse, which is the reaction against an irrational rationalism, a purely destructive annihilating imagination. What would such a revaluation of disorientation look like, conceptually employed in the study of religion? If the sublime can be understood in this way, might it not then function as the religious *par excellence*? Alternative or striking forms of religion and religious expression could then be valued without being appropriated, or simply reduced to previous understandings. On the other hand, strange or unfamiliar ways of thinking and living could be marked as different without thereby being seen as immediately threatening or destructive.

By way of conclusion, I want to consider the attempt, ever since Kant wrote his three critiques, to demarcate a special sphere for religion. As is well known, Kant understands religion primarily in ethical terms, and essentially appends *Religion Within the Limits of Reason Alone* to the Second Critique. This essay, on the other hand, suggests that it is a more fruitful and interesting undertaking to consider religion from the vantage point of the Third Critique, in a trajectory that runs from Kant through Schleiermacher to Otto and Tillich.[27] Although Schleiermacher tries to carve out a place for religion in the realm of feeling, following the *Critique of Judgment*, Tillich complicates any attempt to situate religion in relation to science, philosophy or reflective thinking, ethical or moral willing, and artistic or aesthetic feeling.

In his *Theology of Culture*, Tillich considers the attempts to locate religion in various domains of human spiritual life. He relates the story, ever since Kant's critiques laid the groundwork for intellectual categorization, "of how religion goes from one spiritual function to the other to find a home, and is either rejected or swallowed by

---

[27] For Otto, the Holy, or numinous, understood as *mysterium tremendum*, captures the power of the Kantian sublime, although Otto ascribes numinousity or sublimity to the object rather than to the power of one's own mind, which Kant would call superstition. See Kant, *Critique of Judgment*, p. 123. In her book, *Religion as a Province of Meaning: The Kantian Foundations of Modern Theology* (Minneapolis: Fortress Press, 1993), Adina Davidovich understands religion in terms of a relation from Kant's Third Critique to Otto and Tillich, but she completely overlooks the sublime, focusing on the teleology of the "Critique of Teleological Judgment."

them."[28] Religion turns from the moral to the cognitive to the aesthetic function, and then to feeling. Finally,

> religion suddenly realizes that it does not need such a place, that it does not need such a home. It is at home everywhere, namely in the depth of all functions of man's (sic!) spiritual life. Religion is the depth dimension in all of them.[29]

Religion does not have a home or a place in any one of the commonly demarcated spheres of human activity, which is why the attempt to locate a determinative space for religion has become impossible. As the depth dimension of any or all of these functions of human living, however, religion represents the limits of each function. As the depth dimension of individual faculties or functions, religion appears as sublime, because one can identify a sphere or phenomenon as religious only when its self-representation breaks down.

For Tillich, the metaphor "depth" drives his theology. It is the depth of reason, not the structure or logos of reason which breaks through to revelation and God as being-itself.[30] Tillich also calls this depth aspect of reason the "abyss," which must be understood in relation to the Kantian sublime, where the struggle between reason and imagination sets up a vibration (*Erschütterung*) which consists in "a rapid alternation of repulsion from, and attraction to, one and the same object." This vibration is caused by the proliferation of forms of an imagination striving for infinity, and it creates "an abyss in which the imagination is afraid to lose itself."[31] The abyssal or depth aspect of reason is more profound than the structure of reason for Tillich, because it is in the depth of reason that the possibility of being and non-being of an object or person resides.

In his book, *Kant's Critical Philosophy*, Gilles Deleuze points out the two distinct senses of the word faculty in Kant. Faculty can mean those faculties or capacities of the mind which contribute to thinking, or sources of representation, such as imagination, reason, understanding, and intuition. Deleuze also understands faculties to mean those areas which are represented by the relationships among faculties of mind: knowledge, desire and feeling.[32] The latter three correspond to the three critiques, and also to Tillich's spiritual func-

---

[28] Tillich, *Theology of Culture*, p. 6.
[29] Ibid., p. 7.
[30] See Tillich, *Systematic Theology*, Volume One, pp. 79-81.
[31] Kant, *Critique of Judgment*, p. 115.
[32] Gilles Deleuze, *Kant's Critical Philosophy*, translated by Hugh Tomlinson and Barbara Habberjam (Minneapolis: University of Minnesota Press, 1984), pp. 3-10.

tions of cognition, morality, and aesthetic or artistic feeling. For Deleuze, the relationship among these faculties in each of the three critiques is significant. In the *Critique of Pure Reason*, the understanding legislates in place of reason in the interests of phenomenal knowledge. In the Second Critique, reason legislates for itself in the interests of law and desire. Finally, in the *Critique of Judgment*, most notably in the sublime, there exists a "discordant accord" of the faculties, which are intended to produce harmony, but one faculty does not reign over all the others.[33]

What is specifically important in the reading of Kant by Deleuze, in relation to Tillich and the determination of religion, is that Deleuze in each of the critiques asks whether there is a "higher faculty" of knowledge, desire and feeling.[34] This higher faculty relates to the supersensible, and occurs at that point where the faculties (as modes of knowing) surpass themselves and give voice to the unsurpassable itself. This happens paradigmatically in the *Critique of Judgment*, where it is the discordant accord of reason and imagination which pushes the faculties beyond themselves and gives rise to a higher faculty of feeling. "The sublime," Deleuze writes,

> brings the various faculties into play in such a way that they struggle against one another, the one pushing the other toward its maximum or limit, the other reacting by pushing the first towards an inspiration which it would not have had alone. Each pushes the other to the limit, but each makes the one go beyond the limit of the other.[35]

This surpassing of limits by the various faculties in their interrelations is what gives rise to a "higher form" of a faculty of knowledge, desire and feeling. Faculties can be understood both as zones of culture and as modes of knowing. The zones of culture, which Tillich calls dimensions of human spiritual life, cannot be understood as spheres of religion except in their depth (Tillich) or their higher form (Deleuze), that is, at the point or moment when they surpass themselves and (attempt to) give representation to the unrepresentable itself, which is the sublime. The sublime, understood as the formlessness of pure form, or the disorientation induced by the dizzying proliferation of forms, introduces disorientation at the limits of cultural understanding and expression, as well as within the limits of human thinking itself. This very disorientation, however, provides the only real possibility of religious meaning today.

---

[33] Ibid., p. 51. "It can be seen that the imagination-reason accord is not simply assumed: it is genuinely engendered, engendered in the dissension."

[34] Ibid., p. 4.

[35] Ibid., pp. xii.

CHAPTER TWO

RELIGION AND THE PSYCHO-CULTURAL
FORMATION OF IDEALS

James J. DiCenso

It is difficult to attempt far-ranging speculations concerning the nature and function of religion without inviting the disdain of various
specialists. The emphasis on details of history, culture, and tradition
characterizing most contemporary scholarship can have a debilitat-
ing influence on attempts at more encompassing levels of religious
reflection. However, greater awareness of particularity and difference also counteracts the sweeping generalizations, often characterized by a combination of *hubris* and restricted vision, of earlier generations of theorists. Religion, as an umbrella term describing sets of
highly differentiated and multi-faceted phenomena straddling psychology and culture across huge divides of time and space, simply
cannot be embraced by a single interpretive approach, no matter
how complex.

We may grant that no single type of theory can do justice even to
a single religious tradition, let alone to the staggering diversity of the
global and historical variants of religion. Indeed, to speak of "religion" is already to engage in abstraction. Nevertheless, I think that
more has emerged from the confrontations with pluralism, relativism, and subjectivism in the postmodern era than a mere sense
that we need many approaches, many methods, many theories—
and much caution—in approaching something so complex and differentiated as religion. Additionally, the sensibilities of contemporary
thinking, generally indicating a greater cognizance of differentiation,
allow a return to classical theorists in a non-totalizing way. Following Hans-Georg Gadamer, I believe we continue to need the wisdom of traditions in their many forms. This includes the traditions
of religion, but also the traditions of secular rational and critical reflection. I also believe, likewise under the influence of the great
hermeneuticist, that an engagement with these predecessors must be
dialogical, utilizing new perspectives or horizons of understanding.[1]

---

[1] Hans-Georg Gadamer, *Truth and Method*, second, revised edition, translation
revised by Joel Weinsheimer and Donald G. Marshall (New York: Crossroad, 1989).

If we accept these broadly-based conclusions, and eschew totaliz-ing theories of the nature of religion, a number of possibilities pre-sent themselves. I will not attempt to enumerate these options, but will focus on possibilities that arise in re-engaging past attempts at understanding religion. In doing so, I take my lead from another of the great theorists of the present century, who yet appears to be rep-resentative of the narrowness of vision characterizing many "classi-cal" theorists. If I introduce the well-worn name of Sigmund Freud at this juncture, readers might feel able to anticipate the analyses to follow. However, in my view Freud's work is of interest in the pre-sent attempt to reflect on the nature of religion precisely because of its inter-disciplinary and many-layered quality. Hence I emphasize the neglected potential for more differentiated and dynamically ori-ented thinking inherent in his work.

I wish to argue that Freud's confrontations with questions of reli-gion, despite the evident trappings of highly-curtailed reductive ar-guments, remain valuable resources for contemporary reflection. I should point out that the task of substantiating this argument in a detailed way exceeds the scope of the present inquiry. Elsewhere, I have attempted more elaborate exegeses of Freud's writings on reli-gion, and have also developed some of the implications of these crit-ical interpretations.[2] In the present context, I will forego most of the exegetical basis of my arguments, and attempt a more focused artic-ulation of my own interpretations and conclusions.

The first point to emerge in discussing Freud's treatments of re-ligion is that, in the overview, his approach is thoroughly *psycho-cultural*. The more obvious aspect of psycho-cultural analysis ap-pears as a tracing of various aspects of cultural life—symbols, rituals, artworks, literature, and ethical prohibitions—*back* to some posited basis in the mind. One finds this type of explanation in several forms in Freud's work. Of these, the most well-known is the reduction of religion, particularly in its monotheistic forms, to a projected expression of wish fulfilment in *The Future of an Illusion*. In this analysis, religions serve to maintain a regressive psycholog-ical condition. Rather than fostering a rational and empirical ap-proach to reality (as, according to Freud, does psychoanalysis), re-ligions cater to the inner child so as to sustain dependence upon

---

[2] James J. DiCenso, "Religion as Illusion: Reversing the Freudian Hermeneu-tic," *The Journal of Religion*, 71/2 (April, 1991), pp. 167-79; *idem*, "*Totem and Taboo* and the Constitutive Function of Symbolic Forms," *Journal of the American Academy of Religion* LXIV/3 (Fall, 1996), pp. 557-74.

the benevolence of fantasized "father figures." These, of course, can be extended to include any impersonal order of justice, retribution, and consolation seen ultimately to be operative in the order of things. This type of critically reductive analysis is not necessarily *wrong*, but it is clearly too limited, as even Freud seemed to see.

Before pursuing this point, it should be noted that explanation by *tracing back* also occurs in seemingly more positive, but equally closed forms. This is evident in psychological theories such as C. G. Jung's, in which religions are interpreted as projections of archetypal structures in the collective unconscious. Here, religion is seen as *useful* in providing, as it were, maps of the inner world, with specific reference to actualizing the self, or core of the integrated personality. This is a more overtly religious stance: there is an eternal (archetypal) basis to the human condition, so that human self-actualization becomes, in essence, a religious project. This type of view may yield insight into various types of religious phenomena, particularly those of a mystical nature. Nevertheless, there is something static about such models. Above all, they are limited in seeing religion as *reflecting*, but not essentially *affecting* inner reality.

There is, however, a complementary aspect to psycho-cultural analysis that ultimately subverts any form of psychological reduction. As he explored issues related to higher-order personality development, Freud became increasingly (if intermittently) aware that our understanding of human subjectivity cannot be isolated from cultural influences. In other words, cultural structures, and especially those classified as religion, are not simply projections of internal forces or needs. They are equally *formative*, indeed *constitutive* of human subjectivity in many of its key attributes. Of particular importance is that in Freud's model the structuring and re-structuring of the human personality leading to acculturation, especially a capacity for ethical reflection, is predicated on interaction with culturally-formed others.

At the time of writing *Totem and Taboo* (1911-12), the problem of culture was becoming increasingly important to Freud. Cultural influences were not just tangential to a theory rooted in individual psychology, but were seen as intrinsic to psychological formation. Individual development was understood as inseparable from interpersonal and cultural factors, including abstract forms such as language and ethics. These issues were of particular significance to the problem of the ego-ideal, and would take on greater importance as its successor, the super-ego, became more fully formulated. The super-ego is not simply an inner agency, but comes to represent the intersection of psychology and cultural influences in the formation of the personality.[3]

The super-ego takes shape within a series of relations encapsulated into the dynamics of the Oedipus complex. Granting its conditioned and particularized elements, the Oedipus complex provides an overdetermined *symbolic* portrayal of developmental dynamics within culture. This is a point made by Gananath Obeyesekere, who discusses the Oedipus complex as *fictitious*, emphasizing that this is "a way of expressing a truth that cannot be expressed otherwise."[4] In Freud's writings on the Oedipus complex as signifying structural relations in the formation of subjectivity, there is a discernable spectrum of understanding and application. This spectrum of meaning ranges from the highly particular and concrete to the more general and abstract. That is, one end of the spectrum comprises analyses focussing on specific relations to individual parental figures, shaped variously by factors such as the gender of the developing subject, the attitudes of the guardians, and the degree and nature of their presence or absence. This forms the more particularized, interpersonal level of analysis. The other end of the spectrum is partially predicated upon the first level, but examines issues on a less individually variable and particularized scale. Here the analyses still relate to the developing individual, but focus on a broader dynamic of desire and conflict. This dynamic outlines a transformation of desire, from "incestuous" or self-enclosed, to other-directed and culturally-informed. It is along these lines that Freud indicates the status of the Oedipus complex in acculturated personality development. As he states, its resolution allows the individual "to divert his libido from its infantile attachments into the social ones that are ultimately desired."[5]

In these processes, what is *universal* is the necessity of some form of acculturation, involving immersion in a linguistically-shaped world governed by codes of conduct. The specific constructs of language, moral codes, as well as the nature and degree of individual internalization, are open to innumerable variations. The cultural level of oedipal dynamics is also indicated by Freud in the following passage from the *Outline of Psychoanalysis*. Freud is discussing the formation of

---

[3] Sigmund Freud, *Civilization and Its Discontents*, translated by James Strachey (London: The Hogarth Press, 1953-74). Standard Edition (hereafter SE), Vol. XXI, p. 142.

[4] Gananath Obeyesekere, *The Work of Culture* (Chicago: University of Chicago Press, 1990), p. 94.

[5] Sigmund Freud, "A Short Account of Psycho-Analysis," translated by James Strachey, SE XIX, p. 208.

the super-ego ensuing from the "resolution" of the Oedipus complex. "The parental influence," he states, "of course includes in its operation not only the personalities of the actual parents but also the family, racial and national traditions handed on through them, as well as the demands of the immediate social *milieu* which they represent."[6] Here the parental figures are not merely individuals, but bearers of culture. Moreover, the process of acculturation also extends beyond parents or guardians per se to other cultural representatives. Psychological maturation occurs within affective and interpersonal processes characterized by love and hate, attraction and repulsion, identification and differentiation. In these interactive processes, cultural structures embodied in significant others intrude into and inform the psychological make-up of the individual. As Lacan expresses the matter, "the value of the Oedipus complex as a closing off of a psychic cycle results from the fact that it represents the family situation, insofar as by its institution this situation marks the intersection, in the cultural sphere, of the biological and the social."[7] Incorporated into the oedipal dynamic is what Lacan has called the *non/nom de pere*. This plays on the homophony between the French for *no* and *name*, indicating the relationship between the "name-of-the-Father" representing cultural codes and laws and the prohibitions and restrictions that are an essential aspect of the oedipal conflict.[8] The ensuing identification with a parental figure fosters the internalization of cultural codes in the form of the super-ego. Interpersonal and cultural dynamics transform the individual intrapsychically by introducing qualitative structuring acting as a constraint upon desire. As Anthony Wilden states, "constraints are the basis of complexity and the conditions of creativity."[9] This process of internalizing constraint is essential to the formation of subjectivity differentiated from the attachments of the pre-oedipal phase.

Freud tended to see the reliance of personality upon cultural structures as a problem to be resolved, because he focussed on the issue of the *origins* of higher order cultural functions. Interestingly, the rather bleak, anti-idealistic view of the human condition governing much of Freud's thinking pushed him into a form of psycho-cul-

[6] Sigmund Freud, *An Outline of Psycho-Analysis*, translated by James Strachey, SE XXIII, p. 146.

[7] Jacques Lacan, *Speech and Language in Psychoanalysis*, translated by Anthony Wilden (Baltimore: Johns Hopkins University Press, 1981), p. 126.

[8] Jacques Lacan, *Écrits: A Selection*, translated by Alan Sheridan (London: Routledge, 1977), p. 67.

[9] Anthony Wilden, *The Rules Are No Game* (London: Routledge, 1987), p. 77.

tural inquiry yielding several important insights. Freud could not accept that a higher self or soul is implanted in human beings, or that
ethical capacity, and the complex cultural apparatus reflecting and
enabling this, have an innate source. If human beings are primarily
governed by primitive needs, including narcissistic, self-serving ones,
then something *external* is necessary to disrupt this order of being and
lead to some degree of other-directedness. Hence, the pseudo-histor-
ical constructions of both *Totem and Taboo* and *Moses and Monotheism*
are expressly designed to explain a *constitutive break* with an order of
human existence governed by drives and narcissism. This quest for
explanation of origins masks the key insight emerging from these inquiries: human beings are open systems who take shape in relation
to various levels of alterity, including higher-order cultural forms
such as those expressed in religions.

As I have noted, it is advisable to bracket questions of where religions come from, and turn to a functional approach, that is, to ask
what religions *do* in shaping human beings. Within the parameters
set by such an approach, Freud's inquiries indicate that human formation and transformation necessitate the encounter with culturally-
transmitted symbol systems conveying ideals and values. These en-
gender a sense of self and reality that is *qualitatively* informed. How
these cultural forms came to be, whether they reflect structures of
the soul or of reality are questions that can be set aside. In light of
this procedure, the "historical" explanations of religion found in
Totem and Taboo and *Moses and Monotheism* take on unexpected significance.

Totem and Taboo is famous for its construction of a "primal parricide," in which a pre-historic, collective acting out of oedipal desires
creates feelings of guilt that become instituted in religious cultural
formations (totemism). However, the key dimension of Freud's text
lies not in its theory of origins, but rather in insights that depart
from the discursive frameworks of natural science and illuminate our
cultural and psychological self-understanding in more literary, poetic, and mythical ways. That is, the text is split, an uneasy mixture of
science and poetry, fact and fiction.[10] Released from a literal, historical, cause-and-effect interpretation, *Totem and Taboo* remains both
fascinating and instructive. Beyond its surface postulations, Freud's
text symbolically illustrates the way in which cultural religious forms,
in the example of totemism, transform human psychology. This is

---

[10] Tomoko Masuzawa, *In Search of Dreamtime: The Quest for the Origin of Religion*
(Chicago: University of Chicago Press, 1993), p. 83.

described in terms of a transition from "incest," representing a state of self-enclosure governed by unregulated desire, to collective existence structured by law (taboo) and symbols (totems).[11] This shift reduplicates that of the oedipal phase on an individual level, but highlights processes of acculturation related to religion and morality. *Totem and Taboo*'s narrative of the primal parricide elucidates a necessary break with the real (the order of unmodified drives and brute facticity) in the formation of symbolic cultural systems. As Julia Kristeva puts it, "this founding break of the symbolic order is represented by murder... Freud reveals this founding break and generalizes from it when he emphasizes that society is founded on a complicity in the common crime."[12] This transition from the real to the symbolic effects what may be termed a *symbolic distancing*. That is, relations to oneself (for example, to one's drives or desires), and, correspondingly, relations to others become shaped by mediating cultural structures. In effect, Freud seems to be indicating that, whatever their origins, and whatever their particular forms, religions serve an essential psycho-cultural function.

Over two decades later, similar underlying psycho-cultural themes are greatly extended, within the context of a very different cultural scenario, in *Moses and Monotheism*. There are, of course, obvious reductionistic components to Freud's analyses of both the figure of Moses and the monotheistic religion he inaugurates. Most prominent among these are tracing Moses to Egyptian monotheism, and positing a collective trauma ensuing from the murder of Moses (a telling narrative repetition of *Totem and Taboo*'s parricide). However, despite these surface features, Freud's discussions again intersect with a significant inquiry into ideals and values. The text depicts the nature and function of religious dimensions of psycho-cultural existence; that is, its referent is *psychological* rather than *historical*. It tells us about human subjectivity as necessarily interlinked with cultural forms characterized as religious (the Other, that is, Lacan's *Grande Autre* of cultural symbol systems), mediated by specific others.

The crucial section of *Moses and Monotheism* misleadingly translated as "The Advance of Intellectuality" (*Der Fortschritt in der Geistigkeit*), describes far-ranging subjective transformations related to religion. The term *Geistigkeit* seems to describe a developmental process that is at once cognitive, ethical, aesthetic, and emotional. In other words,

---

[11] Sigmund Freud, *Totem and Taboo*, translated by James Strachey, SE XIII.
[12] Julia Kristeva, *Revolution in Poetic Language*, translated by Margaret Waller (New York: Columbia University Press, 1984), p. 70.

it subsumes the various elements of the personality categorized under the psychoanalytic headings of ego, super-ego, and id. Key to this process is distancing from embedment in materially-determined existence through symbolic processes. This distancing is described in various ways, but in each instance deterministic relations of immediacy are offset by the development of cultural symbolic forms. In Freud's discussion, the most prominent vehicle for superseding modes of existence oriented by material immediacy is Mosaic iconoclasm. "Among the precepts of the Moses religion there is one that is of greater importance than it appears to begin with. This is the prohibition against making an image of God—the compulsion to worship a God whom one cannot see."[13] The psycho-cultural implications of this prohibition are profound. "For it meant that a sensory perception was given second place to what may be called an abstract idea—a triumph of intellectuality over sensuality [*einen Triumph der Geistigkeit über die Sinnlichkeit*] or, strictly speaking, an instinctual renunciation [*einen Triebversicht*] with all the necessary psychological consequences."[14] Thus, this is not merely an externally imposed prohibition: it is a simultaneous transformation in worldview and in psychological orientation.

In discussing the advances of iconoclasm in establishing ideas and ideals, Freud makes reference to the constructive dimensions of the psycho-cultural phenomena of religion. "Ideas, memories, inferences became decisive in contrast to the lower psychical activity which had direct perceptions by the sense organs as its content." These symbolically-constituted ideal forms are essential aspects of "the path to hominization (*auf dem Wege zum Menschwerdung*)."[15] To be human is to inhabit a world constituted by cultural symbolic forms, and to internalize these constructs so that they become one's own. That is, they become part of an autonomous reflective capacity to engage self and reality in relation to ideals. Additionally, these forms contain conceptual features resisting reification and hypostatization (i.e., tendencies to reduce them to representations of entities). The iconoclastic prohibition is the paradigmatic figure of this resistance.

The section of *Moses and Monotheism* on "Renunciation of Instinct" (*Triebverzicht*) furthers the insights in Freud's analysis of *Geistigkeit*. This transformative process has as its concomitants what Freud

---

[13] Sigmund Freud, *Moses and Monotheism*, translated by James Strachey, SE XXIII, pp. 112-13.
[14] SE XXIII, p. 113; *Gesammelte Werke* (London: Imago, 1940-48; hereafter GW) XVI, p. 220.
[15] SE XXIII, p. 113; GW XVI, p. 221.

refers to as a "set back to sensuality." This again indicates a *distancing* from the influences of immediate stimuli. Relatedly, this re-orientation leads to an elevation of an individual's or people's self regard. Freud argues that this advance "seems to presuppose the existence of a definite standard of value and of some other person or agency which maintains it."[16] The intrusion of a qualitative dimension into psycho-cultural existence is crucial here. These analyses also disclose co-determinations between creative psychical and cultural processes. The formation of subjectivity, at least partially motivated and informed by ideas and ideals, occurs in the *interplay* between inner and outer. Thus these ideal qualities cannot be collapsed into a fixed source, leading to a psycho-cultural perspective that supersedes the mechanistic, reductionistic, biologistic, and empiricist orientations Freud often seems to avow.

Renunciation involves abiding, far-ranging transformations of personality. Renunciation is enabled by the internalization *and appropriation* of cultural ideals and values in the formation of super-ego functions. Hence the super-ego, as connected with the capacity for drive renunciation, reflects far more than an internalized authority. It indicates an ability to withstand the lure of the tangible and immediate by virtue of *meaningful abstractions*. There is also more at issue here than a demarcation of mental and physical. The lure of immediacy includes not only material objects but narcissistically gratifying orientations. Thus, renunciation involves a transformation in the personality such that a mode of being centered on oneself—i.e., narcissism—is relinquished in favour of a more other-directed orientation. Renunciation, while inextricable from cultural developments and attitudes toward existence, engenders and is sustained by "psychological consequences," that is, essential alterations in the very structure of the personality.

Throughout *Moses and Monotheism*, Freud uses the language of transcendence, spirituality, ideals, and even the soul to characterize the psychological effects of religion. He seems to be struggling to articulate a psycho-cultural dimension that cannot fit smoothly into either of the oppositional categories of spirit or matter, superficially defined. The tension in Freud's articulation ultimately indicates a formative interplay of forces in the emergence and function of cultural and psychological ideals. It is somewhat ironic that Freud's text appropriates some of the language of religion and metaphysics, in a

---

[16] SE XXIII, p. 116; GW XVI, p. 223.

de-literalized form, to convey the dynamic, constitutive relations. In so doing, Freud offers insight into aspects of religion, as a set of psycho-cultural formations, differing significantly from the critical orientation at the surface of his analyses.

I have merely attempted to sketch out and elaborate certain lines of thought in Freud's writings on religion and culture. However, I hope that enough has been said to indicate the main elements of a psycho-cultural approach to religion, one that ultimately should not be confined either to the particulars of psychoanalytic theory, nor to the particular religious traditions Freud explored. *Mutatis mutandis,* all religious traditions operate psycho-culturally, in that they provide cultural symbol systems that effect transformations of the personality. These transformations involve some capacity to reflect, judge, and act in relation to ideals such as justice, goodness, and truth (although, quite importantly, the specific features of these ideals vary significantly). In this respect, psychoanalysis adds detail to the Gadamerian argument that reflection, and understanding, and indeed subjective existence itself, are predicated upon and informed by the cultural resources of tradition. Just as it offers a differentiated model of the personality, so too Freud's work indicates that religion is essentially multi-faceted. It incorporates worldview, ethics, and symbolic and ritual forms that convey and instil these. Thus, religion is both *inner* and *outer*: it exists as particular cultural forms, and it occurs as the effects of those forms upon human existence. It is not surprising, then, that Freud should have chosen the overloaded term *Geistigkeit,* spirituality, to indicate the nature of these transformations.

Besides indicating the necessary interdependency of culture and psychology, the approach to religion I have derived from Freud has another important feature. Because this is not a static view, it raises *critical* questions. These are not the more simplistic critical questions sometimes associated with psychoanalysis concerning, for example, whether the tenets of specific religions are empirically verifiable. Rather, the potential for critique is more constructive. It concerns the efficacity of religious forms in fostering psycho-cultural development that is mature and ethically-oriented. Of course, any attempt to define these qualities must be tentative; suffice to say that they involve a capacity for self-reflection and for other-directed behaviour based upon values rather than immediate ends. Here, psychoanalysis presses us to examine the overlapping of constructive, transformative aspects of cultural symbols with indoctrinating or ideological aspects. The latter characterize tendencies to reify symbol systems and, relatedly, to suppress their ability to foster reflection.

Freud's inquiries also provide tools for addressing broader issues of cultural change, especially where religions no longer play their traditional role for many people. To be sure, other cultural resources appropriate functions historically associated with religion: the juridical, the ethical, the aesthetic, and the philosophical being primary among these. However, the fragmentation of these functions into discrete and sometimes conflicting forms, and the frequent disconnection of powerful cultural vehicles (e.g. media) from ethical and qualitative considerations, raise issues for personality formation. Because psycho-cultural inquiry indicates the enormous reliance of higher development of the personality upon cultural symbol systems, this approach adds weight to the question: what cultural vehicles can fulfill the functions of religion in providing ideals that shape human subjectivity as ethical and, indeed, as spiritual?

CHAPTER THREE

THE DIFFICULTIES OF UNDERSTANDING RELIGION

Thomas A. Idinopulos

> Religion...means the voluntary subjection of oneself to God.
> —*The Catholic Encyclopedia.*[1]

> We have learned more about 'the religions,' but this has made us perhaps less...aware of what it is that we...mean by 'religion.'
> —Wilfred Cantwell Smith.[2]

I begin with two epigrams. The first, which speaks for itself, is useful in pointing to the transcendent dimension of religion. Today increasingly, we who are students and teachers of religion, are in danger of ignoring this dimension. The second epigram is drawn from Wilfred Cantwell Smith's excellent study of the dilemma facing any serious study of religion. In my own words I should express the dilemma this way: our rationally-based academic study of religion, must be the study of what is observable. And the observable includes historical knowledge of the rituals, mythologies, religious communities, ideas, teachings, institutions, arts, architecture. But religion is not exhausted by the observable. There is another dimension called the non-observable, which is the source of religion's purpose and meaning. It is the failure to recognize the difference between the observable and the non-observable, confusing one with the other or by denying one in behalf of the other, that confounds our understanding of religion. I want to come back to this point later in the essay.

I

What are the difficulties in understanding religion? Begin with the multiplicity of religions. History shows a bewildering variety of religions, cults, sects, denominational developments and spiritual movements of every sort. Taken together the world's religions reflect the

---

[1] Charles G. Herbermann et al. (eds.), *The Catholic Encyclopedia*, Volume XII (New York: The Encyclopedia Press, 1913), p. 739.
[2] Wilfred Cantwell Smith, *The Meaning and End of Religion* (New York, Mentor Books, l962), p. 74

geographic, social, and linguistic diversity of the planet itself. While
no scholar can be expected to know about all these religions, anyone
seriously studying any of them will hunt for some principle, definition or criterion of meaning that identifies the "one in the many."
What should we understand by "religion" amid the study of religions?

The question inevitably leads to comparison. Comparison is a rational act of seeking the intelligible, common element or pattern of
meaning in a group of otherwise diverse entities. Comparison
among religions assumes some sort of commonality among religions.
And that, one must say, is a very big and perhaps faulty assumption.
For most comparisons of religion seem to consist less in the discernment of commonality than in the imposition of it. Whenever, for example, different religions are compared according to such notions as
deity, eternity, grace, judgment, salvation, and so on, we have the
use of selected criteria of meaning that are used to organize data
rather than to discern a pattern within them.

If there is something common to religions that makes useful comparison possible, it is not obvious to everyone. This should not sur-
prise us if we recognize what Smith called "the inebriating variety of
man's religious life."[3] Today, increasingly, religion scholars are mov-
ing away from comparison towards area studies, which eschew comparison in favor of concentrating on what is distinct or unique in
any ethno-cultural configuration called religion.

The more we learn about religions, the more we appreciate not
their similarities but rather their differences. Here are some examples of the importance of differences. The religion of ancient Israel
was shaped by the pre-existing religious culture of the ancient Near
East; but Israelite religion is not finally understood without grasping
how and why the Israelites distinguished their deity, Yahweh, from
the deities of Canaan. Another example: Christianity was mothered
by first-century apocalyptic Judaism, but (as the present-day Jesus-
studies industry demonstrates) the uniqueness of the Christian religion is wrapped in the mystery of how and why the person of Jesus
inspired (if not actually caused) a religion separate and distinct from
first-century Judaism to come into being.

To take a more extreme example of how differences more than
similarities are crucial in shaping and understanding a religion, take
the case of Theravada Buddhism. Here is a something called "religion" which is not a religion. Customarily Theravada Buddhism is

---

[3] Ibid., p. 135.

included in any book on the world's religions. Yet Theravada Buddhism is not theistic, recognizes no sacred being or beings, does not officially encourage worship of Buddha or any "higher being" (despite popular veneration of the Buddha-ideal). Theravada Buddhism appears to be a technique or program for human self-purification or self-fulfillment or self-negation. So if the word religion is attached to Theravada Buddhism, it must be done so loosely, as to allow the differences from other religions to prevail.

What then are we to do about with the books that stress the similarities of religion? I am thinking of books like those of the late Alan Watts, Aldous Huxley, Gerald Hurd, and more recently by Huston Smith. Such books will always be interesting and always in demand because human beings will want to believe that there is an inner core of common religious meaning, one ultimate truth, that provides the intelligible unifying structure of meaning amid the bewildering multiplicity of world religions. Perhaps there is a universal religious truth and perhaps there is not. If there is such truth, then I believe we should look for it not in what a religion asserts as truth but in how it asserts its truth. As I will show later in discussing W. C. Smith's ideas, it is form not content that religions have in common.

In any event, no matter how much we stress the difference between religions, the public desire for assurance about religious unity will inspire authors to continue to invent overarching pseudo-philosophical categories like "Eternal Wisdom," "Universal Spirit," "Cosmic Soul," or "The Divine," and promote them as the "truth" to which the various religions point.

There are other problems in comparing religions. Comparison proceeds through an act of abstraction by detaching a religion from its cultural matrix and viewing it as a discrete set of symbols, myths, ritual ceremonies, and verbally stated beliefs or teachings. This practice reduces religion to a set of meanings, principles, or truths. The result is a kind of intellectualized scholars' religion, which can be discussed, taught, and written about. The only question is whether or not this scholar's religion bears any relationship to the religion which human beings live by on a daily basis.

I can illustrate scholar's religion by my own experience as a graduate student at the University of Chicago Divinity School more than thirty years ago. My professors, with a few notable exceptions, approached the teaching of Christianity on the basis of what Christians believe or have believed. Thus the study and teaching of Christianity, hence the understanding of it, was based almost exclusively on formal doctrines or the belief-content of the religion. What interested my professors at that time was the Christian religion taken as a set of formal confessional and theological meanings, together with the theoretical methods or philosophical ideas which could illuminate and extend those truths.

I cannot say that my professors showed much interest in the thoughts, feelings, and practices of Christian believers. They did not pay much attention to Christianity as a practiced religion. Virtually no attention was paid to the diversity of Christian expression in different cultures. In fact religion per se, was hardly studied at Chicago in my day. What little religion was studied was done so in the History of Religions field, which, for all the attention paid to myth, ritual, and symbol, was top-heavy with methodology and theory.

It is remarkable how the trends of study in our profession have changed in the thirty years since I left Chicago. Today, I would say that not Christian theology but the Christian religion in its cultural context is what scholars want to know about and what students want to learn about. This does not mean that confessional beliefs, doctrines, theological ideas are not relevant, but they are now put on the same footing as church festivals, ritual practices, and the ordinary day-to-day habits of faith that distinguish one Christian from another.

I think this is a healthy development. For when emphasis shifts away from what a Christian believes or does not believe (the ultimate question which mattered at Chicago in the late '50s and early '60s), we can begin to understand the power and meaning of the Christian religion in human life in a given culture, at a certain time. Stated differently, I should say that a better way to ascertain Christian belief is to focus on how Christians actually live their lives. I say this on the basis of years spent with Greek villagers, who when asked what do you believe, can hardly tell you in any precise way what they believe. But ask them how they would identify themselves as Greek Orthodox and you will hear a recital of ritual observances and traditional acts of faith that leave no doubt that faith to Greek villagers is not a matter of what is believed or thought about, but rather what is done or felt or imagined. For such villagers the daily life of faith is not reducible to or equatable with a set of formal beliefs. The academic or pedagogical implications here are enormous. For when professors teach Christianity as a matter of beliefs, ideas, and institutions, they may be teaching something not at all equivalent to the religion practiced by the people who claim the Christian religion as their own. But if they were to teach Christianity as practiced, they would have to pay attention to that which is not so easily categorized as doctrine, namely the unspoken, often emotional undertones of faith on the part of ordinary believers.

II

A big part of the difficulty in understanding religion is that of definition. We don't exactly know what we mean by the word, religion. We don't know how to use the word and what is a misuse of the word. It would be convenient to assume that by "religion" we mean the fetishisms, animisms, polytheisms, and monotheisms of the known historic religions. It would also be convenient to assume that all the religions were like branches of one large tree, with a visible trunk. And that if we looked hard enough at the tree trunk, we could discover a common structure of meaning that would lead to an accurate, comprehensive, and convincing definition of religion.

But, if what was already said about the diversity of religions is taken seriously, then we should not think that religions are branches of a single tree. Therefore no single definition of religion seems possible. Efforts to define religion according to conceptions such as "the supernatural," the dichotomy of "sacred and profane," and "ultimate concern," may or may not clarify aspects of religious expression; but they are hardly adequate to the meaning of religion itself. Buddhism does not easily accommodate references to the "supernatural." Nor does the sacred/profane dichotomy do justice to the complexity of religious feeling, which is often a mixture of the two. And the phrase "ultimate concern" suffers from such an excess of vagueness that it hardly qualifies as a general definition of religion.[4]

Examination of writings on theories of religion shows that most definitions of religion are achieved not by exhaustive empirical study but rather by singling out one or other attractive or compelling feature of religious practice, and then elevating that feature normatively as a criterion of meaning. Certainly this is true of John Dewey's definition of religion as "the active relation between the ideal and the actual," and A. N. Whitehead's, "what a man does with his solitariness," or Westermarck's more wordy rendering, "a regardful attitude towards a supernatural being, on whom man feels himself dependent and to whom he makes an appeal in his worship."[5] In one way or another these and similar definitions suffer from the old

---

[4] See W. Richard Comstock, *The Study of Religion and Primitive Religions* (New York: Harper & Row, 1972). See also Comstock's probing article, "Toward Open Definitions of Religion," *Journal of the American Academy of Religion*, LII/3 (1986), pp. 499-517.

[5] Cited in Bernard Meland's *Faith and Culture* (Carbondale: Southern Illinois University Press, 1953, 1972), p. 107 and Gordon W. Allport, *The Individual and His Religion* (New York: Macmillan Paperbacks, 1960), p. 65.

Greek philosophical practice of hunting for essences among a welter
of related particulars. Once the essence of the religion is defined,
then one can claim to possess the intelligible, normative, and unal-
terable structure of Christian meaning. The problem is that any exception from the norm is simply called that, an exception; the norm
remains unaffected. Another very large problem is that so much of
actively practiced religion is on the level of feeling, remains mysterious, and is mystical or ineffable. Words like "ideal," "actual," "solitariness," "supernatural," can hardly do justice to religion as experience of and response to mystery.

Exceptions to norms is no small matter in religion. People are
willing to die to prevent exceptions and other people to fight to the
death to prevent being seen merely as an exception. Historic
Christianity has had its own struggles with exceptions. Having gone
through the agony of the Reformation, the Catholic church eventually recognized, if it did not approve, the existence of exceptions to
itself. Judaism has never been so tolerant. When Halachically-cor-
rect Orthodoxy firmly established itself as the essential norm of
Judaism, Orthodoxy rejected both Conservative and Reform
Judaism. They would not be seen even as exceptions to the essentialist norm of Orthodox Judaism.

That essentialist norm of Orthodoxy proved so powerful that it
prevailed for all three branches of Judaism. For none of the three
traditions of Judaism were tolerant of real deviations from the norm.
Thus none will accept the authenticity of a new movement called
"Jews for Jesus." Members of the movement champion the messi-
ahship of Jesus. They go to great lengths to deny that they belong to
the Christian church and do not want to be called Christians. They
consider themselves Jews, "Jews for Jesus," they say, and want to be
so recognized by all other Jews.

Here then is the interesting problem about defining religion. If we
accept the Orthodox definition of Judaism, then the "Jews for Jesus"
movement is not Judaism. What then is it? Is it an exception to
Judaism, a sect, a thing all its own? Or is it like one of the Protestant
sects of the sixteenth and seventeenth century, which was detested
and rejected by the established Catholic church—only to find themselves several hundred years later fully recognized and respected as
the Baptist and Methodist churches. Whether or not the "Jews for
Jesus" movement is a religion or a sect will not matter to established
Judaism today. Committed, as they are, to an essentialist, unchang-
ing, and non-fluid conception of Judaism, none of the three branches of Judaism will accept the credentials of the Jews-for-Jesus movement.

III

A further difficulty in understanding religion arises over the issue of values. As scholars and teachers of religion, we would like to believe that there is a specific beneficial religious value, not in conflict with other values. I doubt there are very many professors of religion who in their teaching are not in some way recommending positive religious meanings or values to their students. The constant reliance in our teaching on terms like "sacred," "spiritual," "ultimacy," suggests that, try as we might, our teaching of religion is not value-free. Each of us has some working notion of what constitutes good religion and what is bad religion—and that notion figures in our teaching.

The social scientists would scold us for this. If we listen to them we should be able to study and teach religion according to its multiple functions and its social dynamics. Richard Comstock is a scholar and teacher who admires the social scientific approach to religion. In his informative primer on religion he has this to say:

> The normative problem of what a good religion ought to be is a problem for philosophers, theologians, religious thinkers; however the scholarly study of religion is rather concerned with an understanding of how religions have actually operated in human history, not with how they ought to operate according to the particular value scheme of the critics.[6]

I wish it were possible to make a neat distinction between critics and scholars of religion, as Comstock does. But for me the difficulty of understanding religion increases in confronting religious practices that are wrong, evil, degraded, demonic, and don't appear any the less religious for being so. Consider the Hebrew Bible. One recalls Lucretius' remark: "To how many evil deeds has religion persuaded men." Has anyone satisfactorily explained why Yahweh, the author of the Covenant law prohibiting murder, orders Abraham to sacrifice his son, Isaac, and also commands Saul to massacre the Amalekites, down to the infants? Consider the immolation of infants on ancient altars; the blood sacrifices of the Aztecs; the Hebrew *herem*, which gave rise to the Muslim *jihad* and to the Christian crusade. I would not hesitate to bring moral judgment down on these practices. Nor would I hesitate to condemn the American church community called "Faith Tabernacle," which finds in *The Letter of James* warrant to prohibit the use of modern medicine and allow their own children to die from sickness rather than resort to doctors.

---

[6] Comstock, *The Study of Religion and Primitive Religions*, p. 20.

Professor Comstock, it seems, would caution scholars not to judge religious practices that are different from our own. But is this not asking us to suspend our moral intelligence? Most people would distinguish between faith and fanaticism. Whether we rush quickly or slowly to judgement, we who are professors of religion know that the line between faith and fanaticism is very thin indeed. And that thinness only in turn thickens the difficulty of understanding religion. For if religion is one of the forces within the complex psychic energy of human beings, that force is both creative and destructive.

Faced, then, with the powerful and morally complex character of religion, some scholars will want to emphasize the right and good in religion and forget the rest. Such is the case with Gordon Allport in his classic study of religious psychology, *The Individual and His Religion*. Allport has much to talk about. For none can doubt that religion is a source of psychic strength, providing support, solace, warmth in a world experienced as cold and cruel.

Allport says that he writes "as a scientist" and that his approach is "naturalistic." Further he wishes to dissociate his analysis from any sort of psychopathology of religion, which is an approach favored by skeptics. His explanation is worth quoting:

> My reason for not dwelling more fully than I do upon the function religion plays in infantile and neurotic personalities is that I am seeking to trace the full course of religious development in the normally mature and productive personality. I am dealing with the psychology, not with the psychopathology, of religion. The neurotic function of religious belief, its aid as an "escape from freedom," is indeed commonly encountered, so commonly that opponents of religion see only this function and declare it to dominate any life that harbors a religious sentiment. With this view I disagree. Many personalities attain a religious view of life without suffering development and without self-deception. [7]

I couldn't agree more with Allport's last sentence. Indeed, we know of countless human beings who are well-adjusted religiously and who are mentally healthy because of their religious convictions and associations. But we also know, as Allport certainly knows, of numerous individuals who suffer their "dark nights of the soul," and never truly experience the dawn of psychic health. Many of those individuals are famous as spiritual heroes and pioneers, such as St. John of the Cross, Martin Luther, and Soren Kierkegaard. We also know that Moses, Gautama, Jesus, and Muhammad suffered their Gethsemanes as prelude to a greater vision of the ideal, for which they strove.

---

[7] Allport, *The Individual and His Religion*, pp. xii-xiii.

But the "dark night of the soul" is not always creative. It can also be an invitation to madness. Is not madness often intertwined with spirituality? Molesters, murderers, mass murderers, demagogues, terrorists—do they not all invoke some sacred being or meaning as cause or justification for their actions? Why should we doubt their sincerity? Their religious sincerity? For is it not true that the religion which condemns murder also legitimizes it?

I have had my own experience of the connection between religion, madness, and murder. I once tried marijuana. Quite a lot in one evening. Three joints in ten or fifteen minutes, washed down with glasses of Southern Comfort. Whereupon my brain cracked. Call it madness. I was suddenly seized by anxieties of great intensity. I imagined myself under a judgment so severe I thought myself doomed. I remember telling my wife that I feared throwing myself off the balcony of the house down into the ravine below. I also felt this terrible fear that I would harm the children who were sleeping nearby. Don't ask me why I had this fear. I was seized by it. As my fears mounted I urged my wife to call the police to come and get me. Fortunately she didn't. She had drunk nothing and had taken only a puff or two off one joint. More sober and sane than me, she ignored my request and called a friend, who was experienced in drug counseling.

Upon arriving the friend sat me down and began what became a two hour conversation. Her intention was to coax me away from anxiety until the liquor and drugs wore off. In the middle of the ordeal, suddenly, unexpectedly, I experienced a moment of total lucidity. I announced that I knew who God was. Yes, I knew all about God. I remember it as a very good feeling. I believed I had solved an immense theological problem. I was ahead of my colleagues. I would be recognized for my achievement. Then I was asked to explain God. I wanted to but couldn't. I said nothing. There was silence. I had nothing to say. I was sure I knew all about God but I couldn't say anything about God.

I recalled this experience in recently re-reading Allport's book about the positive effects of religion on the human psyche. But just as there is religion which can help to socially organize a human being, bringing about a more mature outlook on life, so there must also be another kind of religion which is unpredictable, chaotic, and potentially destructive.

My one experience with marijuana and booze convinces me that just below the surface of the mind lies a pool of chaotic psychic energy that finds expression in forms we call religion. Could this be the source of the so-called "innateness" of religious feeling in human beings? Just how we are to understand this energy, what meaning we are to give it, I cannot be sure. What is most difficult to understand about religion is that the angels which Allport describes so well and the demons I have tried to describe from my own experience, seem to lie so close together that it may be difficult to tell them apart.

IV

Another difficulty in understanding religion focuses on our ignorance of the originative sources of religion. If we knew with any certainty how and why religion came into being, we might then know what religion is. The quest for knowledge about religion's origins was the intellectual motive behind the pioneering anthropological research on religion carried out by such major scholars as Muller, Tylor, Frazer, Spencer, Marett, Durkheim, and others. This effort to uncover religion's origins cannot be dismissed as "speculative" or disregarded merely because there is considerable disagreement among the scholars about those origins. The anthropological data itself does not allow one to conclude that the human is essentially *homo religiosus.* But it is equally true that we know of no period of history in which the human has not expressed itself religiously. Religion may or may not be innate in human beings, but the evidence for its inevitability is overwhelming.[8] For us the outstanding question should not be when did religion emerge but rather how to understand the dynamics of religion's inevitableness. This means trying to understand the function of religion in human experience.

Richard Comstock would have us eschew questions of religion's origins. He would do so in favor of what he calls the "function" of religion. As he writes:

> The quest for origins has been superseded by a quest for more adequate description. A different question is now being asked. Instead of asking, "What is the origin of religion? scholars now tend to ask, 'How does religion function?' 'What is it like?' 'What does it do for the individual or for his society?' [9]

What is a functional analysis of religion? The answer seems to be that religion has a host of observable functions: psychological, social, aesthetic, moral. A functional analysis of religion would avoid questions of origins and concentrate on observable functions. Presumably in a functional analysis, myths, dogmas, creeds, confes-

---

[8] See John Herman Randall, Jr., *The Meaning of Religion for Man* (New York, Harper Torchbooks, 1968), pp. 27-28.
[9] Comstock, *The Study of Religion and Primitive Religions,* p. 10.

sions, and theological teachings would be conveniently categorized as the "belief system," and placed alongside the more practical system of priestly functionaries, rituals, ceremonies, etc. These "systems" would then be listed together with another "system," the institutional or social organization of the religious community. Any number of sub-systems could also be described.

Just what we are finally to understand by such "systems," what meanings are to be discerned in them, we cannot be sure. One thing seems clear. The functionalist method is championed as a truly empirical way to study religion. For consider what Comstock next tells us:

> ...a more empirical approach to religion is now being adopted. The question as to how religion originated is a speculative question, difficult to answer in a scientific way. But the fact remains that religion does exist as a very concrete factor in human experience and behavior. May it not be more fruitful to accept it as a "given" which it is our task to examine according to the best analytical tools and methods of accurate description that can be devised.[10]

Certainly we can accept religion as a "given." But that hardly settles the issue of how to study religion. It is significant that Comstock urges his readers to use the "best analytical tools and methods of accurate description," without telling his readers what those tools and methods are. Just how are we to practice the "empirical approach?" One would have thought that if one really took an "empirical approach" and made an effort to describe religion, the first thing one would do would be to take a long, careful look at the lives of religious people. And if one did that one would soon discover that a religious life, filled with energy and faith, providing a vision for living and will-to-live is a whole life that cannot be reduced to functions. To put the matter differently: the authentic religious life is so filled with "non-observables" as to defeat any application of the so-called "empirical method."

It is one thing to preach empiricism and another thing to practice it. Here we should ask how one actually practices the empirical investigation of religion? What can we learn of American Catholics by describing the functions of American Catholics? We can count their numbers. Place of residence. How much money they make. How they vote. How they view the Pope. How they stand on political issues. What they believe or don't believe. Certainly the answers to our questions yield information. Is information the goal of an empir-

---

[10] Ibid., p. 11.

ical study of religion? Or is something more than information needed?

Is there a point after a great quantity of information has been
recorded, after the descriptive task has been done, when one wants
to sit back and ask thoughtfully, What makes an American Catholic
just that? What keeps him or her Catholic? Why does someone stop
being Catholic? What meaning does Catholicism hold for the
Catholic? Is there such a thing called Catholicism over and above
what Catholics feel and think? These questions can arise from information, but the questions are not answered by the search for more
information. Ultimately they are questions of meaning, of aim or
purpose, of self-identity. Such questions do not require further observation and are not answerable by observation. They are questions
that require intuition, insight, discernment. Questions of religious
self-identity are not Comstock's kind of functional questions. They
are old-fashioned humanistic or ontological questions that drive us
back to speculative, philosophical or theological probings about religious being and meaning.

V

I spoke a moment ago of religion as energy, faith, a vision of transcendence and the will to live in relation to it. When religion is
thought of in this way, then religion ceases to be merely *a religion*. To
illustrate the point, allow me to speak of my mother.

My mother would be amused to learn that her son discussed her
in this essay. She would question the need of it. She is a conventionally Greek Orthodox woman, who has never felt the need to pon-
der, much less question, her religion. To her being religious is as
natural as breathing. She recites a few simple prayers before going
to bed and lights candles in church on Sunday. She has no sophisticated beliefs about God and God's relation to the world. Hers is a
simple, strong, direct faith that sustains her life. When she reads the
Bible she does so to learn how to lead her life and to gain the inspi-
ration to do so. In every way she conforms to Allport's account of a
person strengthened in life by religious faith.

When religion and life blend as they do with my mother, religion
ceases to be anything distinctive, objective, something external, a
mere practice. It is well-known that religious people do not think of
themselves as religious because they cannot imagine themselves as
other than religious. One could think of an authentically religious
person as growing a kind of skin which covers their whole body,
gives them their appearance, holds them together, contains the

pores through which they breathe; and when breathing stops, they are buried with this one skin and no other. For that reason religion to a religious person is not something "practiced," a "something" that could be listed on a resume of personality traits and career achievements.

When one is religious as my mother is religious, then the word, religion, loses its meaning or becomes irrelevant. No scholar has made us more aware of the inadequacies of the word, religion, than Wilfred Cantwell Smith.[11] Smith urges us to abandon the word altogether in favor of another word, faith, which he contends more accurately expresses the meaning of religion.

Smith defines faith so: "...an inner religious experience or involvement of a particular person; the impingement on him of the transcendent, putative or real."[12] It is the experience of the transcendent, including the human response to it, that creates faith, or more precisely the life of faith. Smith also seems to regard human beings as having a propensity for faith, so that one speaks of their faith as "innate."[13]

On Smith's analysis, both faith and transcendence are more accurate descriptions of the lives of religious human beings than conventional uses of the word, religion. The reason for that has to do with the distinction between participant and observer. This is a fundamental distinction for Smith which separates religious people (the participants) from those who are the detached, so-called objective students of religious people (the observers). Smith's argument is that religious persons do not ordinarily have "a religion." The word, religion, comes into usage not as the participant's word but as the observer's word, a word which focuses on observable doctrines, institutions, ceremonies, and other practices. By contrast, faith is about the non-observable, that life-shaping vision of transcendence held by a participant.

To illustrate the difference between participant and observer, Smith speaks of heaven and hell. "Heaven and Hell, to a believer, are stupendous places into one or another of which irretrievably he is about to step. To an observer they are items in the believer's mind. To the believer, they are parts of the universe; to the observer, they are parts of a religion."[14]

---

[11] Smith, *The Meaning and End of Religion.*
[12] Ibid., p. 141.
[13] Ibid., p. 37.
[14] Ibid., p. 119.

Transcendence is taken to be the one dimension common to all peoples of religious faith. Here is how Smith speaks of transcendence:

> I certainly do not deny...that Christians in their religious life have something in common—or Muslims, or any group, or indeed all men together. What rather I am asserting...is that what they have in common lies not in the tradition that introduces them to transcendence, not in their faith by which they personally respond, but in that to which they respond, the transcendent itself.[15]

If both faith and transcendence lie beyond observer's knowledge, what then is possible within the limit of observation? The answer, it seems, begins with the frank admission that the academic study of religion is about religion, a historical object, not about the living faith of countless human beings. In grasping this point we are in a position to see that all academic study of religion is actually study about (what Smith calls) "the cumulative tradition," which is

> the entire mass of overt objective data that constitute the historical deposit...of the past religious life of the community in question: temples, scriptures, theological systems, dance patterns, legal and other social institution, conventions, moral codes, myths, and so on; anything that can be and is transmitted from one person, one generation, to another, and that an historian can observe.[16]

It would seem that the "cumulative tradition," in Smith's view, gives the religion scholar ample data for study. And the recognition that the "cumulative tradition" is the observable facts of religion, not the non-observable reality of faith, should keep the scholar from presuming that through study alone the essential meaning of religion can be understood. It is equally true that no academic study of religion is worth its salt that ignores or dismisses the dimensions of faith and transcendence that are an inherent part of the religious life. It is not necessary for the scholar to define transcendence, to name the gods, so to speak. There are as many envisagements of transcendence or names of the gods, as there are types of faith; and there are as many nuanced conceptions of transcendence, with or without gods, as there are persons of faith. What matters is that human faith be understood to have an ultimate reference, whose meaning, it seems, must remain mysterious.

At the conclusion of his book Smith writes: "There would seem little doubt but that the conscious application of a tradition-faith

---

[15] Ibid., p. 173.
[16] Ibid., p. 141.

analysis to an understanding of outside cultures would prove quickly and richly effective."[17] Unfortunately, Smith gives us no direction as to how make the "application of a tradition-faith analysis." And we put down his book with a sense that we have been introduced to a powerful critique of what is wrong with the study of religion without being told just how to correct that study.

Part of the problem is that Smith draws sharp lines between faith and religion, participant and observer, the non-observable and the observable. This tends to suggest that he views tradition, faith, and transcendence as three discrete, even disjunctive elements of experience. This is unfortunate because this is not, I think, what he intends. Smith is no Barthian setting faith against culture, God against religion. Yet, lacking any concept of relationship, we are left in his analysis with three elements, whose organic connection, one to the other, remains unexplained.

The absence of explicit connections is no small omission in Smith's thought. It betrays a reluctance to extend his thinking beyond the historical and the personal to the nature of experience itself. Had he done so he would have found that there is considerably more continuity to human experience, including the experience of faith, than his analysis allows for.

My own understanding of the continuity of experience and of faith was deepened by the late Bernard Eugene Meland, my theology professor at Chicago many years ago. According to Meland, faith is not only personal (as Smith states) but also social.[18] The social aspect of faith is an inheritance, which can include the "cumulative tradition," but which goes deeper into qualities of feeling that pass from one generation to another, from older family members to younger.[19] Thus faith cannot be just "an experience"; it is also a quality of experience itself, mediated through the structure of experience that links the past to the present in human life.

I can illustrate this social and inherited aspect of faith by again referring to my mother. To use Smith's analysis my mother's faith is expressed or made observable through the "cumulative tradition." I do not share much of my mother's appreciation of the "cumulative tradition"; but I can say that her faith has entered my feelings and shaped my life in creative, transforming, even redemptive ways. In that respect her faith has shaped my own faith. If I were to use

---

[17] Ibid., p. 176.
[18] Meland, *Faith and Culture*, pp. 98-116.
[19] Randall, *The Meaning of Religion for Man*, p. 56.

Meland's analysis I would have to say that what made this possible was the structure of experience, a "context of feeling," which mediates faith. Thus faith is not only personal, "an experience," but also a social energy, which links past to present by giving new forms to old valuations.

The structure of experience also means that transcendence cannot be wholly non-observable and utterly mysterious, as Smith would have it. For if faith is experienced within a structure of experience, then transcendence is not only "an experience," but also a relationship of depth or ultimacy mediated through human feeling. Apart from how transcendence is identified or named, transcendence is experienced as a creative advance, linking past to present, one generation to another, offering a vision of the creative and redemptive good that gives hope and a sense that life is worth living.

It is only left to say that the scholar of religion need not feel limited to the observable, to the "cumulative tradition," as Smith would have it. The structural connections between the "cumulative tradition," faith, and transcendence make it possible for the academic study of the religious dimension of human life to be not merely descriptive of data but also insightful as to meaning. Acknowledging the structure of experience makes it possible for our study to avoid both historicism and social scientific reductionism. Acknowledging that structure restores to the study of the religious a sense that this study is about something more than mere data, just as religion is about something more than itself.[20]

[20] I gratefully acknowledge the critical attention given to earlier drafts of this paper by my colleagues, Wayne Elzey and Alan Miller, who do not necessarily share my views of all the issues discussed in this paper.

CHAPTER FOUR

DEFINING RELIGION...
GOING THE THEORETICAL WAY

E. Thomas Lawson

> Saint Thomas Aquinas was careless enough to die in a monastery.
> The 'Angelic Doctor' was promptly decapitated by awestruck
> monks, his body boiled and the bones preserved as holy relics.
>
> When the widely admired Saint Elizabeth of Hungary was lying
> in state in 1231, fervent fans took cuttings of her nails, her hair,
> and her nipples.
> —Brian Silver, *The Ascent of Science.*[1]

Knowing what counts as an example of something is crucial for understanding something. For example, in *The Ascent of Science,* Brian
Silver reports on what purportedly happened to the bodies of St.
Thomas Aquinas and St. Elizabeth of Hungary after their deaths.
Do the actions described in Silver's reports of these two groups'
treatment of Aquinas and Elizabeth count as religious behavior? Do
they fit a definition of religion? How do we decide? Does it all depend on how we define "religion"? But then how do we decide what
counts as a definition? Does it all depend on how we define "definition"? And so on *ad infinitum*? There has to be a better way than
playing the game of the infinite regress, unless it is preferable to engage in endless philosophizing.

Rather than falling prey to interminable and fruitless arguments
about the nature of definition, it might be worth it simply to try to
get a handle on why definitions are important in investigations of
the world. From such a perspective it is not definitions that are
worth arguing over but theories because, at least in scientific inquiry, definitions are nothing but very short versions of much longer
theories. So rather than disputing about definitions let us contend
about theories—at least those theories that are explanatory in intent.
(I am willing to acknowledge that theory is used quite differently in
the humanities and the social and natural sciences.) In the context of

[1] Brian L. Silver, *The Ascent of Science* (New York: Oxford University Press, 1998),
p. 35.

inquiries in the humanities, a theory can be any suggestion, speculation or "reading" about some content. Essentially here "theory" simply means interpretation. For example, in Shakespeare's *Hamlet* the
question arises for the reader about whether Ophelia was mad or
not. The answers given to such questions are not arbitrary in the
hands of a good literary critic or an attentive reader. Passages in the
text under consideration can be shown to be more or less relevant to
providing an answer. But in such interpretive pursuits one never es-
capes from the hermeneutic circle. One begins and ends with interpretation. There are no independent tests which can ensure that one
interpretation is clearly truer than another, although some are certainly more appealing because all the information necessary is in
and only in the text. In such pursuits we learn to trust those who
have experience with drama and demonstrate good judgment by a
close reading of the text, remembering that what comes later may
very well clarify what has gone on earlier.

When one moves from interpretation to explanation, however,
the picture changes. Take, for example, the question: Why does
water boil? Certainly an answer to such a question can lead the
questioner to engage in "interpretation": one can say that water
boils because there are little homunculi with simple minds which
speak to each other in a whisper and say "let us make us some
steam!" But most of us have learned enough science to prefer the ki-
netic theory of gases which can be corroborated by independent
tests and is revisable on the basis of new evidence. In fact, if you
want a fine account of why water boils then read Richard P.
Feynman's first lecture in *Six Easy Pieces* entitled "Atoms in Motion."
There, Feynman defines atoms as "little particles that move around
in perpetual motion, attracting each other when they are a little distance apart, but repelling upon being squeezed together."[2] While
the language is, in fact, metaphorical, Feynman here is actually presenting us with a definition of an atom without employing any equa-
tions. But this definition is nothing but a very short version of a very
long story involving highly abstract ideas and requiring mathemati-
cal formulae for their adequate elaboration.

How does any of this apply to religion? It is applicable by approaching religion as a theoretical problem. When we do so we discover that there are two types of theories about religion. The first set
of theories I shall call inflationary and the second deflationary. An

---

[2] Richard P. Feynman, *Six Easy Pieces* (Reading, Mass: Addison-Wesley Publishing Company, 1994), p. 4.

inflationary type of theory of religion assumes that there is an entity of some kind called religion that can clearly be distinguished from all other things in the world and that should not be confused with anything else in the world. From this theoretical perspective, religion is a unified system of ideas and practices with particular instances known as actual religions such as Islam, Buddhism, Hinduism, Christianity and so on. Because of the great difficulty of identifying properties which can clearly and decisively distinguish one cultural form from another (e.g. "religion" from "politics") most scholars have grown very cautious about proposing inflationary theories of religion. If anything they have often been only too willing to thoroughly conflate putatively different cultural forms. Only a few scholars have held out for the inflationary view. I have in mind for example the work of Mircea Eliade which unabashedly not only argues for religion as a distinct category but argues that it requires special treatment. Eliade and his followers argue not only for the autonomy of religion as an object of consideration, but also for the autonomy of the method by means of which the object should be studied. Given such a view problems such as how a religious tradition is transmitted from generation to generation are rather easy to explain. We are all born with minds which are blank slates and by some rather complex process this entity called religion imposes itself on our minds. The fortunate or unfortunate few who escape this imposition end up not being religious. They presumably are born with some kind of resistance mechanism which has created corrugations on the blank slate which serve as a deflector, diverting the imposed system from taking hold in some minds. Ironically such views smack of empiricism in disguise because only divine revelation or "hierophanies" are capable of showing us the significance and meaning of "the sacred."

This whole approach is, of course, part of a larger theoretical context which regards culture as an autonomous entity which requires an autonomous method of study and which likewise makes human beings prisoners of cultural transmission. Much of social science makes similar autonomous claims.

Both the theory of the autonomy of religion and the theory of the autonomy of culture have been severely shaken in the latter part of the twentieth century by the cognitive science revolution, exemplified, for example, in the science of psychology, particularly cognitive and developmental psychology. Briefly, what we have learned through a wide variety of experimental work is that children do not come into the world with minds which are blank slates. Rather they come predisposed or equipped to acquire various forms of knowledge. Many of the mechanisms for the acquisition of domain-specific types of knowledge are in place at birth as part of our evolutionary heritage. Language, for example, is acquired far too rapidly to have been imposed on the minds of children by cultural instruction. While there are some deep arguments about why it is that children acquire language so rapidly (an argument that has divided classical from the connectionist approaches), the competing theories about language acquisition both agree that the answer lies not in culture but in psychological structure. Culture provides the occasion for the acquisition of the various forms of knowledge, but our biological and psychological heritage plays a fundamental role in interaction with the environment.[3]

But let me take another example which is much closer to theorizing about religion, the notion of agency. Very young children, infants in fact, know almost immediately the difference between agents and everything else in the world. They are not only good motion detectors from the moment of birth (which is interesting in its own right), but they are also capable of recognizing the difference between things that move only when other things cause them to move and things that can move themselves—an important aspect of the notion of agency. There are very clever tests which psychologists have designed to demonstrate such capabilities.[4]

My interest in agency, however, arises because of the crucial role that agents play not only in the *representation of action*, but the way in which religious systems employ the notion of *agents with special qualities engaged in action*.[5] And this is where my deflationary view of religion comes in. Rather than viewing religion as a unified, autonomous system of ideas and practices, radically different in tone and quality from all other systems, I view religion (at least as this is represented in religious ritual contexts) as *a system which employs all of our normal cognitive resources for the representation of action, and it does so by adding only the notion of special qualities*. What makes these agents' qualities special is their counter-intuitiveness. They go against our normal expectations of what the world is like and especially what agents in the world are like.

---

[3] See Jeffrey Elman et al., *Rethinking Innateness: A Connectionist Perspective on Development* (Cambridge, MA: The MIT Press, 1996) and Jerry A. Fodor, *The Modularity of Mind: An Essay on Faculty Psychology* (Cambridge, MA: The MIT Press, 1983) for different approaches to the notion of predisposition.

[4] See Elman et al., *Rethinking Innateness* for a discussion.

[5] Lawson E. Thomas and Robert N. McCauley, *Rethinking Religion: Connecting Cognition and Culture* (Cambridge: Cambridge University Press, 1990).

In order to explicate this notion of counter-intuitiveness, I shall appropriate an idea from Pascal Boyer, who, in an unpublished paper which nevertheless has been very widely read and quoted, shows that in order to come up with a religious idea about the kinds of things that there are in the world, one only has to recognize that basic ontological categories such as "person," "animal," "plant," "artifact," or "physical thing" need only have one of their properties violated.[6] For example, take the ontological category of "person." Persons have the properties of intentionality, life, and physicality. These properties are the default assumptions of the category of person. "Persons" have minds, are capable of birth, growth, and death, and are material beings. In our everyday intercourse we consistently employ the concept of "person" in this manner. Notice however that one only has to violate one of the default assumptions of "person" such as "will die in due course" and you have the religious notion of a person who lives forever. This is a violation of the biological properties normally associated with human beings. Or to take another example: Violate the property of mind, and you have something that is alive and physical but cannot think; in other words, you have the notion of a zombie.

Boyer also talks about another process, that of transfer. One can transfer properties from one ontological category to another. So for example, if you were to transfer the property of intentionaltiy to a statue (an artifact), you would have a statue that can read minds, absorb and even dispense information. Who can deny that artifacts in many religious systems play precisely such a role?

Now with ideas such as these easily available, and made available by our common sense, intuitive ontologies, it follows rather directly that such ideas fit very well with systems for the representation of action in religious contexts. I have in mind, specifically, religious rituals. Religious rituals have a rather simple action structure: Agents acting upon patients (or logical objects, if you prefer) by means of some instrument or other (e.g., the priest baptizing the person with water). From a deflationary point of view, the reason why people have the religious ideas they have and perform the religious practices that they do, is 1) because they have a basic ontology which provides the concept of agency for them to do so, and 2) because the violations and transfers involved in the special qualities that such agents possess make them sufficiently interesting, because they are

---

[6] Pascal Boyer, "Religion and the Bounds of Sense: A Cognitive Catalogue of the Supernatural" (Forthcoming). See also Pascal Boyer, *The Naturalness of Religious Ideas: A Cognitive Theory of Religion* (Berkeley: University of California Press, 1994).

sufficiently counter-intuitive. We hardly notice things which match our intuitions completely. And why are these special qualities interesting? Because in the competition for ideas characteristic of any situation, it is the ideas that contain the right balance of counter-intuitiveness and intuitiveness to make them memorable. And that which is memorable is more easily transmitted. Human beings are fascinated with concepts that go against their expectations. But they are also conservative enough to be capable of ignoring or forgetting things that are simply too bizarre to be taken seriously. So if there are too many violations and too many transfers people can quite easily ignore them. They just end up being silly.

Can such an explanatory theory be tested? Not only can it be, but it has been. Boyer has tested his ideas in both England, France, and Nepal and will soon be testing them in Gabon. He has been able to show that ideas that violate basic assumptions, or that transfer basic assumptions from one category to another, are more memorable than ideas which do not engage in such processes.

Now, if by this time, you are becoming just a little bit irritated and are ready to shout, but what about all those marvelous sophisticated theologies which talk about being-itself, or the god beyond the god of theism, or are ready to call upon the aid of Whitehead, Hegel or Habermas, and are willing, further, to argue that true religion is not such childish notions built upon simple-minded intuitive ontologies, but, instead, consists of profound notions which transcend not only agency but everything in the world, then I should warn you that psychologists such as Justin Barrett have performed experiments showing that while some people in particular societies certainly possess very sophisticated theological notions they, nevertheless, employ these same simple notions rather than their theological concepts in their on-line religious reasoning.[7] They may entertain ideas about God's omnipotence, omniscience and omnipresence, for example, but when called upon to make judgements about real life situations, they abandon such highly abstract notions for the notion of superhuman agents with limited powers and properties very much like the agents we recognize all around us. Human beings seem to be built to think about even the gods anthropomorphically, i.e., as intentional agents with the built-in limitations of ordinary agents.

So now we need to make a decision. When we study the religions of humankind what do we take as paradigmatic of religious ideas

---

[7] Justin L. Barrett and Frank C. Keil, "Conceptualizing a Non-natural Entity: Anthropomorphism in God Concepts," *Cognitive Psychology* 31/3 (1996), pp. 219-47.

and practices? Do we take the great theological texts, doctrinal treatises, deep mystical insights, or do we try to get inside the heads of ordinary religious people and try to identify and explain their cognitive processes? As Peter Brown has shown in his *The Cult of the Saints*, even the sophisticated theologians, when the chips were down, were not all that different in their thought processes from the common folk.[8]

What all of this boils down to is that we need to make a decision in the study of religion about whether we will focus on the epistemic or the cognitive. Epistemology (and its distant cousin theology) tells how we ought to think. This is the underlying motivation of orthodoxy. Proper religious thoughts, and the proper religious actions that are supposed to follow from them should conform to the abstractions of the theologians and the institutional powers which preserve them. But paying attention to cognition changes the picture. Here we learn how to focus upon actual religious behavior and the concepts that inform it. And the study of cognition has a name: Cognitive Science. Cognitive Science develops explanatory theories of how we actually think, or at least identifies the constraints on such thinking. A new world of investigation lies waiting to be recognized by scholars of religion, but whether they recognize it or not, psychologists are already invading their territory and are beginning to move beyond the interpretation of religious texts to the explanation of religious ideas and practices.

Now let us return to the beginning. Were the monks who took such drastic means to preserve St. Thomas Aquinas' bones as relics engaged in religious behavior or not? Of course! They understood Thomas to be an agent with such special qualities that his bones would be capable, for example, of transmitting their power to the faithful. That is why he is revered as a saint. The saints are still with us.

---

[8] Peter Brown, *The Cult of Saints: Its Rise and Function in Latin Christianity* (Chicago: Chicago University Press, 1981).

CHAPTER FIVE

REDESCRIBING "RELIGION" AS SOCIAL FORMATION: TOWARD A SOCIAL THEORY OF RELIGION[1]

Russell T. McCutcheon

> A society can neither create nor recreate itself without creating some kind of ideal by the same stroke. This creation is not a sort of optional extra step by which society, being already made, merely adds finishing touches; it is the act by which society makes itself, and remakes itself, periodically....A society is not constituted simply by the mass of individuals who comprise it, the ground they occupy, the things they use, or the movements they make, but above all by the idea it has of itself.
> —Émile Durkheim.[2]

> Religion as mythmaking reflects thoughtful, though ordinary, modes of ingenuity and labor... [B]oth religion and the study of religion are concerned with the human quest for intelligibility, with taking interest in the world and making social sense, without recourse to mystification or special pleading.
> —Ronald Cameron.[3]

Introduction

Recently, some scholars in our field have been more open to scrutinizing the history of our categories, the theories that ground them, and the social contexts in which scholarship takes place—they have rediscovered the need to engage issues of definition and category formation. Increased interest in the category "religion" itself suggests

---

[1] An earlier version of this paper was presented to a session of the North American Association for the Study of Religion (NAASR) in San Francisco, November 23, 1997. My thanks go not only to Willi Braun, Gary Lease, and Tim Murphy for their helpful comments on an earlier draft, but also to Willi and Burton Mack for prompting me to think more seriously about a thoroughly social theory of religion.
[2] Emile Durkheim, *The Elementary Forms of Religious Life*, translated by Karen E. Fields (New York: Free Press, 1995), p. 425.
[3] Ron Cameron, "Mythmaking and Intertextuality in Early Christianity," in Elizabeth A. Castelli and Hal Taussig (eds.), *Reimagining Christian Origins: A Colloquium Honoring Burton L. Mack* (Valley Forge, PA: Trinity Press International, 1996), pp. 37-50, p. 39.

as much.[4] In fact, even at the 1997 meeting of the American Academy of Religion there was a panel on "The Emergence of 'Religion' in the Enlightenment and Post-Enlightenment." Such a change in attitude is important for it signals that what a previous generation of scholars took for transparent self-evidencies are now recognized as tools developed over time, tools with a history that come with theoretical, even political, baggage, tools that are used to classify, sort, and analyze human behavior.

Once, the vast majority of scholars followed such influential writers as Max Weber when, in a suitably inductivist vein, the first sentence of his influential *The Sociology of Religion* (1922) stated: "To define 'religion,' to say what it *is*, is not possible at the start of a presentation such as this. Definition can be attempted, if at all, only at the conclusion of the study."[5] Contrary to Weber, take Brian K. Smith's opening to his study of Vedic ritual where, after noting Weber's view, he suggests just the opposite:

---

[4] See, among others, Talal Asad, *Genealogies of Religion: Discipline and Reasons of Power in Christianity and Islam* (Baltimore: Johns Hopkins University Press, 1993); Robert D. Baird, *Category Formation and the History of Religions* (The Hague: Mouton, 1971); Catherine Bell, "Modernism and Postmodernism in the Study of Religion," *Religious Studies Review* 22, pp. 179-190; Ugo Bianchi, *The Notion of "Religion" in Comparative Research: Selected Proceedings of the XVI IAHR Congress* (Rome: L'Erma di Bretschneider, 1994); Peter Byrne, *Natural Religion and the Nature of Religion: The Legacy of Deism* (London: Routledge, 1989); David Chidester, *Savage Systems: Colonialism and Comparative Religion in Southern Africa* (Charlottesville: University Press of Virginia, 1996); Timothy Fitzgerald, "A Critique of the Concept of Religion," *Method & Theory in the Study of Religion* 9/2 (1997), pp. 91-110; Stewart Guthrie, "Religion: What is it?" *Journal for the Scientific Study of Religion* 35/4 (1996), pp. 412-19; Peter Harrison, *"Religion" and the Religions in the English Enlightenment* (Cambridge: Cambridge University Press, 1990); Gary Lease, "The History of 'Religious' Consciousness and the Diffusion of Culture: Strategies for Surviving Dissolution," *Historical Reflections/Reflexions Historiques* 20/3(1994), pp. 453-79; Russell T. McCutcheon, "The Category 'Religion' in Recent Publications: A Critical Survey," *Numen* 42/3 (1995), pp. 284-309; Russell T. McCutcheon, *Manufacturing Religion: The Discourse on Sui Generis Religion and the Politics of Nostalgia* (Oxford: Oxford University Press, 1997); Benson Saler, *Conceptualizing Religion: Immanent Anthropologists, Transcendent Natives, and Unbounded Categories* (Leiden: E. J. Brill, 1993); Jonathan Z. Smith, "'Religion' and 'Religious Studies': No Difference At All," *Soundings* 71/2-3 (1988). pp. 231-44; Donald Wiebe, "From Religious to Social Reality: The Transformation of 'Religion' in the Academy," in Ugo Bianchi (ed.) *The Notion of "Religion" in Comparative Research*, pp. 837-845.

[5] Max Weber, *The Sociology of Religion*, translated by Ephraim Fischoff (Boston: Beacon Press, 1993/1922), p. 1. Note that Weber does not return to the topic of definition at the close of his study. The same stand can be found in the opening to chapter two of Weber's *The Protestant Ethic and the Spirit of Capitalism*, introduced by Randall Collins (Los Angeles: Roxbury Publishing Co., 1996/1930), p. 47: "Thus the final and definitive concept cannot stand at the beginning of the investigation, but must come at the end."

> To define is not to finish, but to start. To define is not to confine but
> to create something and eventually redefine. To define, finally, is not
> to destroy but to construct for the purpose of useful reflection...In
> fact, we have definitions, hazy and inarticulate as they might be, for
> every object about which we know something...Let us, then, define
> our concept of definition as a tentative classification of a phenomenon
> which allows us to begin an analysis of the phenomenon so defined.[6]

Unfortunately, not all of our colleagues agree, for a number of them
continue to employ categories that have questionable analytic use.
For instance, we still find courses and monographs on "primitive religion," "cult" experts populate daytime TV and news telecasts
whenever marginalized social movements get into the newspapers,
and the world's religions are continually portrayed as socially autonomous (i.e., *sui generis*) systems of "salvation." What fuels the continued use of such terms is the general confusion of phenomenological *description* with social scientific *analysis*; for the descriptive value
that most of our traditional, scholarly categories possess is largely the
result of their being derived from, and fully inscribed within, the vocabularies and belief systems of the groups we study *rather than* the
analytic vocabularies of scholarship. The long history of conflating
these two distinct domains of inquiry—or, worse, failing to see any
role for second order analysis whatsoever—is sufficient evidence of
the theoretical bankruptcy of the modern study of religion.

When seen as an end in itself, phenomenologically-based description of religious claims and behavior confuses data with colleagues,
such as when the writings of a Rudolf Otto or a Paul Tillich are
treated not as data in need of analysis and contextualization but as
contributions to the academic study of religion. In fact, this confla-
tion of data with colleagues is one reason why, in my own work, I
find it so attractive to make this sort of confused scholarship my own
datum.[7] So-called scholarship on religion ought to be our subject of

---

[6] Brian K. Smith, *Reflections on Resemblance, Ritual, and Religion* (Oxford: Oxford University Press, 1989), pp. 4-5.

[7] For example, see two recent essays where I offer critiques of modern scholarship on religion that fails to move beyond description: "'My Theory of the
Brontosaurus': Postmodernism and 'Theory' of Religion," *Studies in Religion* 26/1
(1997), pp. 3-23 and "The Economics of Spiritual Luxury: The Glittering Lobby
and the Parliament of Religions," *Journal of Contemporary Religion* 13/1 (1998), pp. 51-
64. Part of my thesis in these critiques is that failures to redescribe and analyze indigenous claims and behaviors come with a usually undetected socio-political price;
for an elaboration on this thesis, see my own article, "A Default of Critical
Intelligence? The Scholar of Religion as Public Intellectual," *Journal of the American
Academy of Religion* 65/2 (1997), pp. 443-468. For the sometimes spirited replies of a
theologian and a humanist to this article, plus my own rejoinder, see *Journal of the*

study when it fails to posit emic claims and behaviors as data, data that becomes meaningful to a scholarly discourse once it has been redescribed by means of theoretically-driven etic categories.[8] To appeal to Marvin Harris, writing nearly twenty years ago, "[r]ather than employ concepts that are necessarily real, meaningful, and appropriate from the native point of view, the observer is free to use alien categories and rules derived from the data language of science."[9]

That this point is not widely accepted by scholars of religion is troubling indeed; reacting against what certainly was imperializing scholarship of previous generations, there is today an unfortunate tendency among those who call themselves post-colonial or reflexive theorists to think that scholars not only can but ought to let indigenous people simply "speak for themselves." However, such scholars fail to see that the people we study often do not seem to be particularly interested in speaking to the academic community for themselves; instead, they, like human beings in general, are deeply interested simply in living their lives and it is the scholar who selects them from out of their complex social worlds and represents them (for whatever reason) to their colleagues and the wider reading public. For example, the moment one refers to certain repetitive, seemingly symbolic practices as "rituals," one has classified, organized, and compared these local behaviors to a host of diverse human behaviors by means of a higher order category which is likely foreign to the person under study. I therefore find it troubling that so many colleagues seem to presume that their pre-observational commitments, values, and theories are so transparent and in a one-to-one fit with reality that their reports allow their subjects to speak for themselves.[10] So, right off the bat, let me say that future scholarship in our field needs to address two related issues: the problem of articulating explicit working definitions and the problem of theoretically based analysis of the data created by our acts of definition and clas-

---

American Academy of Religion 66/4 (1998): forthcoming. For another reply, see Linell E. Cady, "The Public Intellectual and Effective Critique," *Bulletin of the Council of Societies for the Study of Religion* 27/2 (1998), pp. 12-14.

   [8] On the logical distinctions between description and explanation see Jeffrey R. Carter, "Explanation is Not Description: A Methodology of Comparison," *Method & Theory in the Study of Religion* 10/2 (1998): forthcoming.

   [9] Marvin Harris, *Cultural Materialism: The Struggle for a Science of Culture* (New York: Random House, 1979), p. 32.

   [10] In a forthcoming essay I have explored the neo-colonial nature of some post-colonial scholarship: "The Imperial Dynamic in the Study of Religion: Neo-colonial Practices in an American Discipline," in C. Richard King (ed.), *Postcolonial America* (Urbana: University of Illinois Press).

sification. In a word, future scholarship on religion must be re-descriptive.[11]

I have borrowed the term "redescription" from Jonathan Z. Smith, in particular his essay, "Sacred Persistence: Toward A Redescription of Canon."[12] Referring to the work of Max Black and Mary Hesse, Smith understands scholarship as the activity of building models by means of which "we may see things in a new and frequently unexpected light. A model, in short, is a 'redescription'."[13] Applied to the study of religion, redescription nicely sums up the complicated work of scholarship, work that a former generation of phenomenologists thought simply involved accurate or nuanced descriptions of what was simply given or that which presented itself. Redescriptive scholarship, as consistently demonstrated throughout Smith's body of work, avoids presuming a perfect fit between the concepts we use and the world we encounter through those concepts. As argued in his essay, "The Bare Facts of Ritual,"[14] there is an incongruity not only between words and deeds of the groups we study, but also between human expectations of events and the events that actually transpire. Even someone as removed from Smith as Max Weber understood the role religious systems played in mediating the inevitable incongruities of sensory experience. He writes:

> The conflict between empirical reality and this conception of the world as a meaningful totality, which is based on the religious postulate, produces the strongest tensions in man's inner life as well as his external relationship with the world.[15]

In the words of Gay Becker, a medical anthropologist writing on personal responses to health issues, human life is best characterized as a series of disruptions against which we construct coherent plots and narratives of what is in fact an ever-changing past and an anticipated yet inevitably frustrated future.[16] With such incongruity or disruptions in mind, redescriptive scholars are aware that, to quote

---

[11] Although I have taken a rather bold stand on the old insider/outsider problem, in a forthcoming class anthology I have attempted to describe fairly and accurately the various solutions to this problem offered by scholars of religion over the years. See *The Insider/Outsider Problem in the Study of Religion: A Reader* (London: Cassell Academic Publishers, 1998).

[12] Jonathan Z. Smith, *Imagining Religion: From Babylon to Jonestown* (Chicago: University of Chicago Press, 1982), pp. 36-52.

[13] Ibid., p. 36.

[14] Ibid., pp. 53-65.

[15] Weber, *The Sociology of Religion*, p. 59.

[16] Gay Becker, *Disrupted Lives: How People Create Meaning in a Chaotic World* (Berkeley: University of California Press, 1997).

Harris once again, the "road to etic knowledge ... is full of pitfalls and impasses."[17]

The first step toward such etic knowledge is the redescription, or as Smith might say, the rectification, of a number of our key categories so that, as Harris suggested, their usefulness is based in the vocabularies of scholarship rather than the vocabularies of the communities we study. The first candidate for such redescription is "religion" itself. Because many of our colleagues invest this term with an ontology of its own they are able to gloss over the fact that most of the people they study by means of this category actually have no functional equivalent to the term whatsoever. By means of this gloss, they effectively avoid confronting the hazards of the insider/outsider problem, for they perpetrate the supreme, imperial act of reduction: they declare that, regardless of what those under study may think, everyone is religious in just this or that way. Precisely because some of our colleagues presume religion, or, more properly, religious experience, to be a universal human impulse of fundamental, deep, real, and therefore self-evident value, they lack the ability to see that their comments on, for example, Chinese religions or the religion of Islam are already highly abstract redescriptions of indigenous social systems and categories. Accordingly, the very ones yelling loudest about the need to "take religion seriously" have, so far, been the least serious in how they treat the most fundamental category in our scholarly vocabulary.

Despite "religion" possessing some descriptive value—for even to me it makes eminent sense, at least on an initial, descriptive level, to distinguish talk of such non-obvious beings as gods or demons from talk of the family or talk of the nation state—we must confront the fact that the category "religion" has no analytic value whatsoever. Taking religion to be a self-evident, eternally existing phenomenon of deep importance, most of our colleagues have failed to recognize just how intriguing so-called religious behaviors are; they fail to inquire as to just why it is that human beings sometimes expend such great amounts of energy in activities that engage invisible agents and immaterial states of existence. What on one level is a useful set of descriptive markers turns out, on another, to be the very problem in need of explanation. If our scholarship amounts to more than a mere collection of descriptions (I think here of the old phenomenological handbooks), then "religion" will surely have to be redescribed for despite its apparent usefulness as a descriptive marker that desig-

---

[17] Harris, *Cultural Materialism*, p. 39.

nates a loosely (even arbitrarily) collected grouping of observable behaviors and institutions, it fails to offer any assistance in analyzing or
explaining these behaviors.[18]

As is probably clear by now, I favor redescribing religion by
means of a thoroughly social theory of religion. Despite the promise
of other equally interesting theoretical frameworks, it is on the level
of constructing, legitimizing, and contesting social authority and
privilege that I find so-called religious systems to be of most interest.
(To the obvious influence of Jonathan Z. Smith, I now add the influence of Bruce Lincoln on my thinking.[19]) Therefore, for me, on
the redescriptive level what we usually term religion turns out to be
but one sub-species of larger socio-historical, ideological systems.
The challenge, then, is to develop a coherent, theoretically-based
vocabulary capable of placing what we generally term religion firmly within the social world, with no leftover residue that prompts su-
pernaturalistic speculations.

Although the category "society," at least as it is used to denote a
supposedly uniform collectivity, may deserve a place in what Willi
Braun has aptly called the museum of scholarly categories, unlike
some of its fellow exhibits, it can be effectively rehabilitated for future use in a social theory religion. Instead of the naively monolithic
connotations of "society,"[20] the category "social formation" provides
us with a more useful tool for classifying and organizing for the sake

---

[18] See Fitzgerald, "A Critique of the Concept of Religion," pp. 92-93.

[19] Specifically, I have in mind Lincoln's more recent works: *Discourse and the
Construction of Society* (New York: Oxford University Press, 1989); *Authority: Construction
and Corrosion* (Chicago: University of Chicago Press, 1994); and his brief but significant "Theses on Method," *Method & Theory in the Study of Religion* 8/3 (1996), pp.
225-27. See also his essay "Culture," in the forthcoming *Guide to the Study of Religion*,
edited by Willi Braun and Russell T. McCutcheon (London: Cassell Academic
Publishers).

[20] Ronald Inden outlines a variety of reasons why we should be weary of using
"society" uncritically. As he puts it: "Social scientists…have relied heavily on the
term 'society,' to talk about the human world. It has become the term used in social
scientific discourse to talk about virtually any complex agent—tribe, village, clan,
nation-state, linguistic or ethnic group that occupies, or is seen wishing to occupy,
its own territory. These are the entities likened to the machine or organism of the
physical and biological sciences. This usage masks the empirical complexity of these
agents by treating them (or ideal types of them) as if they were unitary, determinate
objects, the manifestations of some underlying essence of product of some substan-
tialized agent, a pure class of persons who share some permanent something despite
their actual (dis)organization at any one time. Another voluntarist usage of the term
'society,' evoked in the same breath as this mechanistic one, gives the almost opposite impression—that these compound agents are purely purposive organizations,
all of whose members have consciously and freely joined their wills to its. Both are
also implicit in the metaphor of the body politic as a machine" (Ronald Inden,
Imagining India [Oxford: Blackwell, 1990], p. 27).

of study those ways in which human communities construct, maintain, and contest issues of social identity, power, and privilege
through what, for the sake of initial description, we can term religious discourses. In this exploratory paper, I would like to pull together a number of writers who are making significant contributions
toward just such a social theory of religion. The originality of this
essay is therefore limited to being among the first to repeat (with appropriate citations, of course) the good ideas of other people, but re-
peating them in proximity to other equally good ideas, hopefully
working toward a coherent theory of religion as social formation.

Religion as Social Formation

Jonathan Z. Smith anticipated the current use of "social formation"
in his programmatic essay, "The Social Description of Early
Christianity."[21] Smith identifies the need for a sociological model to
help overcome the excessive focus on literary-historical and theological approaches in the study of Christian materials: "We have been
seduced into a description of a *Sitz im Leben* that lacks a concrete
(i.e., non-theological) 'seat' and offers only the most abstract understanding of 'life'."[22] He rightly castigates scholars for producing studies that "have been written in a theoretical vacuum in which outdat-
ed 'laws' are appealed to and applied,"[23] studies that "have been
clouded in the majority of cases by unquestioned apologetic presuppositions and naive theories."[24] Of the four possible directions Smith
outlines for such a social description (or what we would now term a
*re*description), the third entails investigating "the *social organization* of
early Christianity in terms of both the *social forces* which led to the
rise of Christianity and the *social institutions* of early Christianity."[25]

---

[21] Jonathan Z. Smith, "The Social Description of Early Christianity," *Religious
Studies Review* 1/1 (1975), pp. 19-25.

[22] Ibid., p. 19.

[23] Ibid., p. 19.

[24] Compare Smith's comments to those of the sociologist Rodney Stark from two
decades later: "for too many sociologists, 'work' is a form of ancestor worship. That
is, theory is believed to consist of the opinions, prejudices, insights, analyses, and
metaphors about social life contained in the works of dead founders" (Rodney
Stark, "Bringing Theory Back In," *Rational Choice Theory and Religion: Summary and
Assessment* [London: Routledge, 1997]: 3-23, pp. 20-21).

[25] Smith, "The Social Description of Early Christianity," p. 20. The other three
consisted of describing the social facts or *realia*, the social history, and the social
world. Smith finds in Peter Berger's work an example of the last, a description of
"the creation of world of meaning which provided a plausibility structure for those
who chose to inhabit it." More recently, the work of William Paden provides an excellent example of the ways in which religious systems build worlds inhabited by

Simply put, Smith recommends treating religion as a social formation.

Although "social formation" is a category that can be traced directly back to the French Marxist Louis Althusser, and even though it can easily be found in the work of a number of contemporary scholars of religion, popularizing the category seems to have been the doing of Burton Mack.[26] It is a complex category and one which we unnecessarily limit if we mean by it only the factors that initially form or bring a social movement into existence. "Social formation" is of use not only in the study of how new social organizations develop but also when studying how they are institutionalized, maintained over time and place, how they are contested and, eventually, how they come to an end. If we see society as a continually re-emerging, shared construct, then social formation nicely represents not only the ongoing work of bringing an imagined social group into existence but also the sleight of hand in making it appear always to have existed.[27]

When used to redescribe religion, social formation refers to a specific and coordinated system of beliefs, acts, and institutions that construct the necessary conditions for shared identities. By coordinating discourses on such things as nonobvious beings, absolute origins (as opposed to historic beginnings), and ultimate endtimes within highly rule-driven systems of practice we create a system of socio-rhetorical strategies that facilitate the development of enduring social and self identities. However, I must be clear on one important

---

their participants. See William Paden, *Interpreting the Sacred: Ways of Viewing Religion* (Boston: Beacon Press, 1992); *Religious Worlds: The Comparative Study of Religion* (Boston: Beacon Press, 1994); and "Elements of a New Comparativism," *Method & Theory in the Study of Religion* 8/1(1996), pp. 5-14.

[26] Interested readers are referred to Mack's extremely useful essay "Social Formation" in the forthcoming *Guide to the Study of Religion* mentioned earlier. For a useful commentary on Mack see Karen L. King, "Mackinations on Myth and Origin," in Castelli and Taussig (eds.), *Reimagining Christian Origins*, pp. 157-172; for Althusser's thoughts on social formation, see Robert Paul Resch, *Althusser and the Renewal of Marxist Social Theory* (Berkeley: University of California Press, 1992); Louis Althusser and Etienne Balibar, *Reading Capital* (London: New Left, 1970); and Louis Althusser, "Ideology and Ideological State Apparatuses (Notes Toward an Investigation)" in his *Lenin and Philosophy and Other Essays* (New York: Monthly Review Press, 1971), pp. 127-86.

[27] Fearing that, for many scholars, "social" connotes an intentional, homogenous reality, Inden (see n. 20 above) opts, instead, for the category "imperial formation." As useful as this might be, especially if one takes into consideration how David Chidester divides the history of our field in Southern Africa by means of such categories as frontier or colonial comparative religion, a sufficiently complex understanding of the role contestation, persuasion, and brute force play in all social groups lessens the need for this category.

point: there is no such thing as a specifically *religious* social formation; it is just that among the host of mechanisms available to social groups in their ongoing efforts to define and reproduce the conditions (both intellectual and material) that have allowed them to be a them in the first place, discourses on nonobvious beings, origins, endtimes, and control are sometimes used and are often found together in interrelated systems of belief, behavior, and institution. For purely descriptive, taxonomic reasons, such social formations are often considered to be distinguishable "religions" but this only serves to confuse a collection of social behaviors or strategies (what we as scholars classify as myths, rituals, institutions) with their effect (social formation).

Therefore, unlike Catherine Albanese who has recently employed the category "religious formation" in her discussion of the relations between religion and popular culture,[28] our category "social formation" suggests that there is nothing specifically religious, moralistic, spiritual, or mystical about the social groupings we describe as religions or world religions. Where "religion," "world religion," "mysticism," and "spirituality" all operate on the phenomenological or descriptive level of analysis, "social formation" is openly redescriptive and operates on a higher logical level of analysis. It is for this reason that Albanese's discussion of "spiritual structures" not only holds little promise for future analytic research but actually threatens the advances we have already made.[29] In fact, by invoking the Tillichian juxtaposition of "culture/religion," Albanese perpetuates a long-standing confusion noted earlier: for the redescriptive scholar, religion is an aspect of human social organization and not an uncaused force that operates over against culture; so-called religious beliefs, behaviors, and institutions are merely a few of the many sites where social formations develop and are contested. To maintain otherwise, to suggest that religion is somehow separate or free from social and historical causation, is to rely upon the intellectually and politically suspect notion of *sui generis* religion.[30] Therefore, because it is a

---

[28] Catherine L. Albanese, "Religion and American Popular Culture: An Introductory Essay," *Journal of the American Academy of Religion* 64/4 (1996), pp. 733-42, p. 734.

[29] Ibid., p. 735.

[30] For a convincing critique of the way in which some current social scientific research on religion implicitly relies on the undefended claim that religion, religious beliefs and institutions constitute socially independent variables (e.g., studies on how prayer or church membership affects mental health, physical health, or attitudes to abortion), see Dan Krymkowski and Luther Martin, "Religion as an Independent Variable: Revisiting the Weberian Hypothesis," *Method & Theory in the Study of Religion* 10/2 (1998): forthcoming.

merely descriptive category that is itself in need of further analysis, there is little analytic value to the category "religious formation." In the words of Gary Lease, there can in fact be no such thing as a religious formation or even the history of a religion strictly speaking "for the simple reason that there is no religion: rather such a history can only trace how and why a culture or epoch allows certain experiences to count as "religion" while excluding others."[31] To investigate the how and why Lease mentions will require us to lay bare the strategies that enable the conditions of social formation. It should be clear, then, that "religion" is not a clean theoretical construct and, accordingly, provides the field with a questionable basis.

Social formations, then, are active processes that never arrive and are never completed. In one sense, the process implied by social formation simply suggests the active constitution and reconstitution of a social group. In this sense "social" qualifies the process of "formation." But in another sense, *a* social formation denotes the continually changing results of these active processes and the context in which these processes take place—in this case social formations are more *things* than *processes*. What is crucial is to recognize that both senses are necessarily related; despite the ever-present danger that Marx and Engels warned us about long ago—of mistaking our abstract concepts for real things—the utility of "social formation" is precisely its ability to avoid the traps of reification, all of which comes from its status as a gerund.[32] In other words, social formation is not a thing or an it.

Therefore, when we examine social formations we are not studying stable, self-evident things so much as analyzing system-wide strategies whose end result is to portray the many as one and heterogeneity as homogeneity. The social formations we are able to study are therefore always analytic constructs and therefore mere shadows of their former selves; they are abstractions of what are in reality constantly changing processes. So, when we study social formation we are not studying something that has an absolute origin nor an absolute end. When we study social formation we are also not studying a unified, intentional process with a *telos*. Taking seriously that

---

[31] Lease, "The History of 'Religious' Consciousness and the Diffusion of Culture," p. 472.

[32] My understanding of "social formation" as a gerund has benefited tremendously from my correspondence with Burton Mack. Interested readers can consult Burton L. Mack, "After *Drudgery Divine*," *Numen* 39/2 (1992), pp. 225-33; *The Lost Gospel: The Book of Q* (San Francisco: Harper & Row, 1993); *Who Wrote the New Testament? The Making of the Christian Myth* (San Francisco: HarperCollins, 1995); "On Redescribing Christian Origins," *Method & Theory in the Study of Religion* 8/3 (1996), pp. 247-69.

human social formation actually makes possible the conditions necessary for such things as linear narratives of distinction (then, now,
and later), or value (bad, better, best), we will instead study the
means by which human groups respond to the inevitable disruptions
and plain old accidents of historical existence. Taking these accidents and disruptions seriously, we will avoid positing a smooth, linear development to social formations, as if they were the outcome of
individual actors' intentions, careful planning, and coherent organization.

We will avoid all this because a thoroughly social theory of religion posits individual actors' intentions, plans, and organizations not
as *causes* of, but as *artifacts* that result from social formation, as the
evidence of pre-existent, communally shared intellectual and material conditions beyond the scope or control of the individual.
Contrary to Weber's tradition of individualistic sociology (something
we today find in rational choice theorizing), it is only in light of such
pre-existent conditions that one gets to count as an individual in the
first place (think no further of the ongoing U.S. abortion debate and
whether a fetus is to be considered a person under the law). As
Smith has stated so succinctly when commenting on early Christian
social formation, "[t]here is no post-Easter experience which then is
'given voice' in Christian discourse; the experience is contained in
and by that discourse."[33] In saying this, we must not lose sight of the
fact that the pre-existent intellectual and material conditions determinative of our current social existence and identity are certainly the
result, to whatever degree, of individual decisions and actions carried out by our predecessors. However, as already suggested, we
must not fail to recognize that our predecessors were themselves operating, as we are, in complex, inherited social worlds not of their
making. We might say, then, that because of, as well as despite, our
best intentions, we not only are involved in making social formations
but social formation in fact happens to us. Social formations are
therefore complex, interactive, partially intentional yet completely
blind processes. We should therefore not approach their study lightly, for they simultaneously make us and are made by us. Agency and
structural constraints come together in a complex process in all social formation. In this way, our work on social formations will combine the best insights of such seemingly divergent theorists as Louis

---

[33] Jonathan Z. Smith, "Social Formations of Early Christianities: A Response to
Burton Mack and Ron Cameron," *Method & Theory in the Study of Religion* 8/3 (1996),
pp. 271-278, p. 274.

Althusser, on the one hand (who, although coining the very notion of social formation, emphasized structure at the expense of agential human beings, whom he understood as mere "supports" for modes of production[34]) and, on the other, the historian E. P. Thompson (who disagreed quite publicly with Althusser's emphasis on structure and who, instead, understood social life as "unmastered human practice").

There may be no more apt way of communicating this complexity than to refer to the opening lines of Thompson's *The Making of the English Working Class*: what we are engaged in "is a study in an active process which owes as much to agency as to conditioning. The working class [a social formation, we might add] did not rise like the sun at an appointed time. It was present at its own making."[35] Borrowing a term from the British sociologist, Anthony Giddens, we can better get at this reciprocal process by talking about "recursive reproduction."[36] As explained by Braun, the

> key point is that social action, even in times of high degrees of social change, is bounded by and dependent on the structures (material, economic, political, etc.) and resources (means of communication, mythmaking, etc.). *The full package of a society's constitution thus is both means and outcome of social actions and practices.* Analogy: even a "novel" sentence is a reproduction of the rules of grammar and the repository of vocabulary.[37]

In Giddens' own words, "human beings act purposefully and knowledgeably but without being able either to foresee or to control the consequences of what they do."[38] The study of social formation, then, "is involved in relating action to structure, in tracing, explicitly or otherwise, the conjunction or disjunctions of intended and unintended consequences of activity and how these affect the fate of individuals.... For the permutations of influences are endless, and there is no sense in which structure 'determines' action or vice versa."[39] In studying social formation, then, we will have to attend to the interface of individual actors and the system wide constraints in which they live.

---

[34] Anthony Giddens, *The Constitution of Society: Outline of the Theory of Structuration* (Berkeley: University of California Press, 1984), p. 217.

[35] E. P. Thompson, *The Making of the English Working Class* (Harmondsworth: Penguin, 1963/1991), p. 8.

[36] Giddens, *The Constitution of Society.*

[37] Willi Braun, "Greco-Roman Schools and the Sayings Gospel Q," Discussion Paper Presented to the SBL Seminar on Ancient Myths and Modern Theories of Christian Origins (1997), pp. 1-22, p. 9, note 18 (emphasis added).

[38] Giddens, *The Constitution of Society*, pp. 217-18.

[39] Ibid., p. 219.

For purposes of scholarship, we will likely wish to arrive at a vocabulary capable of comparing and detailing what we take to be significant differences and similarities between, and developments within, analytically distinguishable social formations. In other words,
why does no one group themselves with reference to "Christendom"? Or in Braun's example, what makes this sentence "novel"
from that? I recently re-read parts of Kurt Rudolph's 1983-1984
Haskell Lectures, *Historical Fundamentals and the History of Religions*
(1985), where, over a decade ago, Rudolph anticipated our current
interest in pursuing a thoroughly redescribed, social theory of religion by rehabilitating some of our vocabulary.[40] In the last lecture,
entitled "Development as a Problem for the History of Religions,"[41]
after tracing the rich history of evolutionist thinking in the early
field, Rudolph nicely reclaims the category "development" to refer
not to a pre-programmed, unfolding process but to a complex set of
analytically separable, historical stages. In other words, because social formation is always under way, we will only be able to study its
strategies and movements by halting it artificially by means of analytic vocabularies. According to Rudolph, then, to be interested in
the development of any given religion—or, as we would say, social
formation—means one will likely examine a number of interrelated
sites:

> the beginning phase, the phase that gives to each its characteristic fe-
> atures or "habitus,"...that is, the stage of founding or consolidation;
> the stages of adaptation and assimilation ("syncretism"), of substitu-
> tion (as in the interpretation of the names of foreign gods), or of isola-
> tion; the stages of deformation and "encrustation"; of revolution or
> reformation; a stage of heresies and schisms; and stages of seculariza-
> tion and dissolution. The stage of dissolution, however, can also be a
> stage of transformation.[42]

Borrowing from the British Marxist literary critic Raymond
Williams,[43] we can simplify Rudolph's overly complex stages by
identifying three phases we would expect to find in the life of any social formation: dominant (when a social system reproduces its authority effectively in the midst of ongoing natural disruptions), residual (when, due to changing natural conditions, a social system

---

[40] Kurt Rudolph, *Historical Fundamentals and the History of Religions*, introduction by
Joseph Kitagawa (New York: Macmillan Publishing Co., 1985).
[41] Ibid., pp. 81-98.
[42] Ibid., p. 93.
[43] Raymond Williams, *Marxism and Literature* (Oxford: Oxford University Press,
1977), pp. 121-27.

formed in the past is no longer able to reproduce its authority and legitimacy but yet remains effective in the present), and emergent (when, in the wake of natural disruptions, novel or experimental forms of authority and attendant social organization are developing).

Although the first and last more than likely are self-explanatory, the middle term, residual, may require some brief explanation: since all social formations develop from chronologically prior groups and institutions, a social theory of religion will avoid questions of absolute origins, but will, instead, examine the social and natural conditions that attend the demise of one social formation and the role residual social formations play in the emergence of new forms of identity and organization (i.e., we only ask how this particular social formation emerged when and where it did). Therefore, dominant, residual, and emergent social formation will always be found to occur together. For example, I think of Jack Lightstone's comments concerning the role played by the turn-of-the-era residual, intellectually elite Jewish scribal class in the emergence of text-based Judaism: combining both Lightstone and Smith, Braun phrases it as follows:

> the end of the Temple in 70 CE meant that a large priestly-scribal sector lost not only jobs, but its fundamental social, intellectual, and ritual reason d'être. The sector's 'burden of alienation and deracination' can hardly be overestimated. We know the imaginative remaking of this group of itself as the formation of the rabbinic colleges which reconstituted a Judaism in which "temple" and judiciary values based on temple ritual becomes replacement ritual.[44]

I would like to suggest that scholars give some thought to developing increasingly sophisticated, nuanced, and—most importantly of all perhaps—cross-culturally based theories of the manner in which what we often call religion functions to provide the sufficient (possibly the necessary?) conditions of on-going social formation at all of its stages or phases. Although all social formations will undoubtedly share some characteristics and strategies (e.g., origins and endtime discourses are found in so-called religious and nationalist social formations; discourses on ahistorical founders are found as well),[45] we will certainly be able to distinguish the conditions of *establishment* for

---

[44] Braun, "Greco-Roman Schools and the Sayings Gospel Q." p. 15. See Jack Lightstone, "Whence the Rabbis? From Coherent Description to Fragmented Reconstruction," *Studies in Religion* 26 (1997), pp. 275-95.

[45] In a separate essay currently at press, I discuss the similarities between the hunt for the historical Jesus and the hunt for the historical Eliade, and the manner in which both discourses function to manufacture and authorize scholarly communities; see "Autonomy, Unity, and Crisis: Rhetoric and the Invention of the Discourse on *Sui Generis* Religion," *Pre/Text*.

social authority that grows out of contestation and dissolution as opposed to its *legitimation* within a dominant social formation. Some of this work is already going on; what we need to do is to organize ourselves and our research projects. As a start, I would like to finish this paper by bringing together several authors working on related topics.

A Natural History of Social Formation

To study the social formations we normally call religions or religious traditions amounts to writing their natural history, from their emergence to their eventual dissolution and, possibly, reconstitution. Related to Smith's comments on the incongruity of lived experience and the need to rationalize the disruptions and accidents that invade our systems of signification, is Gary Lease's attempt to delineate a life span for social formations. (The work of Bruce Lincoln and Burton Mack of course come to mind at this point as well). For Lease, religions, much like nationalisms, attempt "to be totally *inclusive* of all paradoxes by establishing *exclusive* meanings." Or, in the words of Lincoln, religion "is that discourse whose defining characteristic is its desire to speak of things eternal and transcendent with an authority equally transcendent and eternal."[46] Because historical life is rather more complex than the interpretive models of any totalized system, Lease predicts that, despite our best attempts to rationalize their appearance, the dissonances and conflicts that inevitably arise will eventually cause "the societal system to *breakdown* and the 'structures' which allowed such a paradoxical mutuality to dissolve."[47] In Lincoln's terms, authorizing systems inevitably have disjunctions and fracture points where contestation takes place. A natural history of social formations will therefore examine so-called religious systems not as stable realities but as historic products where legitimacy is generated; they are systems that have a specific history and a limited future.

If we follow Lease and Lincoln, then to write the natural history of a religion as a social formation would be to create a "catalog of

---

[46] Taken from his second thesis, "Theses on Method," p. 225.

[47] Lease, "The History of 'Religious' Consciousness and the Diffusion of Culture," p. 475. This is precisely what Lincoln's *Authority: Construction and Corrosion* is about. To the traditional historian of religions, the book is not about religion at all, since its chapters analyze rhetorical strategies employed in Norse myth, Greek epic, and Roman history; however, once religion is redescribed as a mechanism in social formation, the book is about the very heart of the authorized social systems scholars of religion study.

strategies for *maintaining* paradoxes, *fighting* over dissonances, and *surviving* [and recovering from] breakdowns."[48] Such a catalog would amount to a map of the many social sites where myths and rituals are developed and deployed for one of the primary ways in which social formations are constructed, maintained, contested, and rebuilt is through the active process of mythmaking. According to Mack:

> Social formation and mythmaking are group activities that go together, each stimulating the other in a kind of dynamic feedback system. Both speed up when new groups form in times of social disintegration and cultural change. Both are important indicators of the personal and intellectual energies invested in experimental movements.... [S]ocial formation and mythmaking fit together like hand and glove.[49]

Although he did not employ these specific categories in his early study of religion, the reciprocal relationship between social formations and mythmaking was made clear as early as Durkheim's *Elementary Forms*. To repeat a portion of one of this paper's epigraphs:

> A society can neither create nor recreate itself without creating some kind of ideal by the same stroke. This creation is not a sort of optional extra step by which society, being already made, merely adds finishing touches; it is the act by which society makes itself, and remakes itself, periodically.[50]

In keeping with, but improving upon, this Durkheimian tradition, we could say that a social formation is the activity of experimenting with, authorizing, and reconstituting widely circulated ideal types, idealizations or, better put, mythifications, that function to control acts and sites of signification.

Based on my readings, this is what Lease seems to imply by his notion of religions as totalized systems of meaning, what Smith seems to be saying about ritual functioning to classify and clarify by exercising an "economy of significance,"[51] and what Roland Barthes seems to be saying about myths authorizing contingent History as necessary Nature.[52] Moreover, these interrelated strategies of routinization, normalization, domestication, universalization, and idealization—all of which are ways in which significance is managed and

---

[48] Ibid., p. 475.
[49] Mack, *Who Wrote the New Testament*, p. 11.
[50] Durkheim, *The Elementary Forms of the Religious Life*, p. 425.
[51] Smith, *Imagining Religion*, p. 56.
[52] Roland Barthes, *Mythologies*, translated by Annette Lavers (London: Paladin, 1973), p. 11.

controlled by means of myth and ritual—are themselves ideological
mechanisms. This is precisely what Bruce Lincoln seems to mean
when, a decade ago in *Cosmos, Myth, and Society,* he employed some
classic Marxist vocabulary to note that

> an ideology...is not just an ideal against which social reality is meas-
> ured or an end toward the fulfillment of which groups and individuals
> aspire. It is also, and this is much more important, a screen that stra-
> tegically veils, mystifies, or distorts important aspects of real social
> processes. Like any other ideology, myth largely serves to create false
> consciousness in many members of society, persuading them of the
> rightness of their lot in life, whatever that may be, and of the total so-
> cial order.[53]

Therefore, mythmaking is none other than idealmaking, where
"ideal" is conceived not as an abstract, absolute value but as a contingent, localized construct that, by means of rhetorical, even ideological mechanisms, represents and simultaneously reproduces certain specific social values *as if they were universal.*[54]

Social formation, then, is explicitly caught up in the ideological
strategies of totalization, naturalization, rationalization, and universalization; to appeal to Benedict Anderson, we could say that social
formations are based on mythic "ontological reality [that is portrayed as] apprehensible...through a single, privileged system of representation."[55] Accordingly, Durkheim's thoughts on the creation
and authorization of "some kind of ideal" find their modern equivalent in the works of the authors just named. Social formations are
the ongoing results of mythmaking activity (where I see mythmaking
as a discourse involving acts and institutions as well as narratives), an
activity that unites into a totalized system of representation what
Mack refers to as the epic past, the historical past, the historical present, the anticipated historical future, and the hoped for epic future
in one narrative, behavioral, and institutional system. Where but in
so-called religions do we see this happening most effectively?

---

[53] Bruce Lincoln, *Myth, Cosmos, and Society: Indo-European Themes of Creation and De-
struction* (Cambridge: Harvard University Press, 1986), p. 164.

[54] For an application of mythmaking in the explanation of a more recent social
event, see Philip L. Tite, "Princess Diana, Mythmaking, and the Academic Study of
Religion," *Bulletin of the Council of Societies for the Study of Religion* 27/2 (1998), pp. 3-6;
see also Stephen Heathorn, "Underdogs and Englishmen: Diana and the Secular
Worship of the Nation," *Bulletin of the Council of Societies for the Study of Religion* 26/4
(1997), pp. 92-93; and Sarah McFarland Taylor, "Dianic Devotions and Manu-
factured Saints: Cultic Power, Institution, and Authority in the Death of Diana
Spencer," *Bulletin of the Council of Societies for the Study of Religion* 27/2 (1998), pp. 6-9.

[55] Benedict Anderson, *Imagined Communities: Reflections on the Origin and Spread of
Nationalism* (London: Verso, 1991), p. 14.

To return to Lincoln's thoughts, and as Mack has also suggested, mythmaking takes place from a specific socio-political position and supports a specific judgment about the here and now. Ideal, myths, and rituals therefore do not simply project consensually reached agreements that have been reached; each of these do not communicate some substance so much as give shape and authority (i.e., significance) to this or that message. Accordingly, myths present one particular, contested, viewpoint as if it were an "agreement that has been reached" by "we the people" (a phrase that is part of a powerful mythic rhetoric common in the history of the U.S.). For instance, to take up Mack's use of the contemporary American situation as an example, rhetoric that brings together references to the founding fathers (what Mack might refer to as the epic past), with the image of the patriarchal nuclear family of the 1950s (historical past), with current crime rates, teenage birth rates, abortion rates, and divorce rates (one particular present), with projections for budget reductions in the next ten years (historical future), all of which contributes to the future well being/security of the American experiment/idea/nation (epic future) is the consummate art of mythmaking. By means of mythmaking, the historicity and specificity of each of these is collapsed into one, monolithic, unfolding narrative. To appeal to Barthes once again, by means of myth, History has effectively become Nature. Or, to appeal to scholars as diverse as the American literary critic Frederic Jameson and the interpretive anthropologist Clifford Geertz, by means of a disguised or undetected ideological slippage, "is" becomes "ought," the myth of presence and self-identity is established, and value neutral "change" takes on the significance of being either good or bad.[56] And, even though the British Marxist literary critic, Terry Eagleton, sadly defines myth in a very traditional way (i.e., narratives about such things as "sacred times, places, and origins"), he nonetheless correctly understands myths to be "a particular *register* of ideology, which elevates certain meanings to numinous status."[57] All of these writers therefore appear to agree that by means of mythmaking local, symbolic worlds of significance are authorized and naturalized by being mistaken for, or actively portrayed as, universal, literal ones.

---

[56] Frederic Jameson, "The Ideology of the Text" in his *The Ideologies of Theory: Essays, 1971-1986. Vol 1. Situations of Theory* (Minneapolis: University of Minnesota Press. 1988), pp. 17-71, p. 17; Clifford Geertz, *Islam Observed: Religious Development in Morocco and Indonesia* (New Haven: Yale University Press, 1968), p. 97.

[57] Terry Eagleton, *Ideology: An Introduction* (London: Verso, 1991), pp. 188-89.

Because one of the premises of all social scientific scholarship is that all behavior is contextualized within historical (i.e., social, political, economic, gendered, etc.) pressures and influences, we must therefore understand all such perspectives and points of view as partial and linked to certain views and behaviors not shared by all members of a social grouping.[58] This ensures that we not lose sight of the fact that all social formation relies on a kind of sleight of hand whereby all-inclusive systems arise from premises that are fundamentally exclusive. Social formation, then, is the art of manufacturing and reproducing totalized systems of re-presentation. Because the social values, truths, and ideals are hardly universal, because, as Durkheim noted, the "mystery that appears to surround them is entirely superficial and fades upon closer scrutiny..., [when one pulls] aside the veil with which the mythological imagination covered them,"[59] there is an inherent contradiction embedded at the core of social formations. Accordingly, there is much at stake for members to maintain the mythic status of the system of representation and signification—their very self-identity is continually at stake! As Lease comments concerning the inherent contradictions of all totalizing practices, "a society cannot live without them, nor can it live with them."[60] It is precisely the mythmakers (in the academic study of religion we call them theologians) who develop discourses that obscure and thereby manage these contradictions.

Conclusion

Mythmaking, then, is the business of making "particular and contingent world-views appear to be ubiquitous and absolute."[61] Social formation by means of mythmaking is nothing other than reasonable responses to the inevitable social disruptions, contradictions, and incongruities that characterize the historical, human condition.

---

[58] As phrased by J. Z. Smith, "there is no primordium—it is all history" (1982, p. xiii). Or, as Marx and Engels put it in their eighth thesis on Feuerbach, "All social life is essentially *practical*. All mysteries which lead theory to mysticism find their rational solution in human practice and in the comprehension of human practice" (Karl Marx and Freidrich Engels, *The German Ideology*, translated by C. J. Arthurs [New York: International Publishers, 1988], p. 122, see also pp. 42 ff.).

[59] Durkheim, *The Elemementary froms of the Religious Life*, p. 431.

[60] Lease, "The History of 'Religious' Consciousness and the Diffusion of Culture," p. 475.

[61] William E. Arnal, "Making and Re-Making the Jesus-Sign: Contemporary Markings on the Body of Christ" in William E. Arnal and Michel Desjardins (eds.), *Whose Historical Jesus? Studies in Christianity and Judaism*, No. 7 (Waterloo, Canada: Wilfrid Laurier University Press, 1997), pp. 308-19, p. 317.

Systems of social significance, encoded within narratives of the epic past and the anticipated future, coordinated within behavioral and institutional systems of cognitive and social control, characterize our responses to the various incongruities and disruptions that come with historical existence; "myth both unites the group and provides an interpretive framework for coping with the exigencies of, and threats from, the natural world;[62] so-called religious systems are perhaps the pre-eminent site for creating such continuity (cognitive as well as social) amidst the discontinuities of life. In setting out to re-describe religion as but one set of strategies for accomplishing the always completed yet never ending recursive reproduction of social formation—a project many of us are already working on—we will be able to communicate with other scholars about an observable, public, and enduring aspect of human behavior rather than isolating ourselves within a privileged discourse concerned with studying non-empirical numinous experiences.

---

[62] Giddens, *The Constitution of Society*, p. 265.

CHAPTER SIX

THE EXEMPLARY LIFE

Dan Merkur

In 1932, in an article entitled, "The Sensus Numinis as the Historical Basis of Religion," Rudolf Otto took exception to theories
that distinguished magic and religion. Using historical evidence,
Otto demonstrated that the sense of the numinous is found in so-
called magic no differently than in religion. Otto's argument was
framed within the context of the theory of religious evolutionism but
contributed importantly to its abandonment. For the phenomenological school of the history of religions (*Religionswissenschaft*), Otto
had demonstrated the presence of the sense of the numinous in all of
the varieties of cultural institutions that scholars had discussed as religion. Many phenomenologists were subsequently content to define
religion by stipulating the converse. Wherever one finds the sense of
the numinous, one is dealing with religion. Whatever ideas, behavior, stories, experiences, and so forth contribute to, derive from, or
otherwise pertain to the sense of the numinous is the stuff that religions are made of.[1]

In *The Living God*, Otto's student and colleague, Nathan Söderblom, added that scriptures and other texts are religious in so far as
the gods they discuss attract the sense of the numinous. Living religious beliefs pertain not to ideas in books, but to numinous experiences to which the literary ideas refer.[2] I have argued elsewhere that
the case for myths is parallel. Stories are religious in so far as their
characters or events are numinous. Disconnected from a living sense
of the numinous, the same tales become fanciful fictions of no religious significance.[3] More generally, I have argued that the sense of

---

[1] Rudolf Otto, "The Sensus Numinis as the Historical Basis of Religion," *Hibbert
Journal* 30 (1932), pp. 283-97, 415-30.
[2] Nathan Söderblom, *The Living God: Basal Forms of Personal Religion* (London:
Oxford University Press, 1933).
[3] Dan Merkur, "Adaptive Symbolism and the Theory of Myth: The Symbolic
Understanding of Myths in Inuit Religion" in L. Bryce Boyer & Simon A. Grolnick
(eds.), *The Psychoanalytic Study of Society* 13 (Hillsdale, NJ: The Analytic Press, 1988),
pp. 63-94.

the numinous is a variety of existential experience, akin to the senses of moral virtue and beauty. Numinosity is a category of value that the psyche or soul has the capacity to endow to certain of its experiences. Numinous experiences should not be treated as a history-of-religions euphemism for theistic experiences that may be contrasted with the mystical or unitive experiences. Otto explicitly described mystical states as numinous. Numinous experiences are instances, in Paul Pruyser's phrase, of "limit situations"—points of reasoning at which the mind boggles, or ceases to be able to compute. Pruyser pointed to the origin, meaning, and end of existence as cognitive limit-situations that organized religions typically address. Otto emphasized the experience of mystery at the postulation of the wholly ineffable and Transcendent; but I would add "moments of truth" such as the life crises to which rites of passage may accrue, moments of wonderment at the splendor of natural phenomena, the solemnity of moral deliberation and conviction, and so forth. Some human experiences tend to elicit a sense of numinosity more readily than others do, but the response depends on an innately human capacity for judging values.[4]

Most academics writing on the definition of religion either opt for Otto's criterion or advocate a preference for a functional equivalent. Whether it is a sense of the numinous, or belief in an invisible world, or greater-than-human beings, or transcendent states and beings, the practice of defining religion in terms of an essential and distinguishing criterion represents a fundamentally different point of view than that which defines religion as a social institution. Essentialist definitions inevitably privilege whatever is postulated as religion's essence, while treating all else as secondary, adventitious, and potentially expendable. One problem with essentialist definitions is that a person may belong to an institutionalized religion without meeting any of the criteria of essentialist definitions.

Essentialist definitions of one sort or another have dominated the academic debate because their implicit concern is the legitimation of religion as a subject of academic study. If something—anything—can be shown to be distinctively and essentially religious, specialists in its study have an institutional claim to academic chairs and departments. Students of religion might otherwise be appointed to departments of history, sociology, psychology, and philosophy.

---

[4] Dan Merkur, "The Numinous as a Category of Value," in Thomas A. Idinopulos and Edward A. Yonan (eds.), *The Sacred and Its Scholars: Comparative Methodologies for the Study of Primary Religious Data* (Leiden: E. J. Brill, 1996), pp. 104-23.

Because I consider the sense of the numinous to be *sui generis*, in a manner closely analogous to the distinctiveness of moral and aesthetic sensibilities, I have no difficulty with historians of religions' traditional reliance on Otto's criterion for the definition of religion. Because any and all such essentialist definitions are aimed at academic budgets and politics, I do not see the profit (beyond merit pay raises) in hair-splitting about one essentialist definition as against another, as long as they are equally beneficial for the profession.

The business of defining religion has also a second major function, however. The study of religion is situated in the humanities in the belief, right or wrong, that learning about religions is beneficial to postadolescent and adult students. Religion is not taught as Freud, for example, might have encouraged: as an education in cultural pathology. Religion is supposed to be a Good Thing. Importantly, it is not religious tolerance, nor a postmodern religious relativism, but religion itself that is supposed to have this pedagogical virtue. Else it would suffice to teach tolerance or relativity, while regarding religion as cultural pathology. Under the circumstances, I think it appropriate to attempt to identify what this Good Thing is.

Even ignoring the teaching time and effort that is devoted to the Unmentioned Practice of disabusing true believers of errors in their own religious tenets and history, one may ask the value of presenting students with cultural points of view that are so alien to their own assumptions that the majority of them recoil in amazement, astonishment, incomprehension, alarm, or hilarity. Time and again, in teaching world religions, one sees large numbers of students for whom the course is a travelogue in the exotic, the bizarre, and the strange. The phenomenological exercise, to explain how each religion makes sense from the perspectives of its own devotées, does not mitigate students' sense of the religions' strangeness. It intensifies it. Whatever the Good Thing is, the phenomenological program does not teach it.

When C. Jouco Bleeker and Geo Widengren edited the encyclopedic *Historia Religionum* under the auspices of the International Association for the History of Religions, they invited the authors of the chapters on individual religions to follow the same basic scheme. Here is their inventory of the components of religions past and present.

1   Short Description of the Essence of Religion.
2   Historical Development.
3   Conception of Deity.
4   Worship (Cult, Ethics, Myth or Doctrine).
5   Conception of Man (Creation, Nature, Destiny, Path of Salvation, Personal and General Eschatology).

6   Religions of the Past: Subsequent Influence and Religions of the
     Present: Present Religious Situtation.
7   Short History of the Study of the Religion.
8   Selected Bibliography.[5]

The inventory assumes that a religion consists of a belief-system or
ideology that devotées may express either in so many words, or in
the symbols of myths, rites, art, architecture, and so forth. Mircea
Eliade happened to be introducing a book on alchemy when he self-
consciously articulated this methodological point of view.

> There is, indeed, only one way of understanding a cultural phenome-
> non which is alien to one's own ideological pattern, and that is to
> place oneself at its very center and from there to track down all the
> values that radiate from it. Only by looking at things from the stand-
> point of the alchemist will we succeed in gaining an insight into his
> mental world and thereby appraise the extent of its originality. The
> same methodological requirement would apply to any primitive or ex-
> otic cultural phenomenon. Before we proceed to judge it we must
> fully understand it and become imbued, as it were, with its ideology,
> whatever form it may take—myth, symbol, rite, social attitude...[6]

I am in complete agreement that the task of a historian is always finally an exercise in empathy. By immersing oneself in the historical
data, one hopes to empathize so very fully with religious devotées
that one is able to articulate their religiosity from their point of view.
As a rule, I feel that I understand a religious perspective adequately
only when I come to feel that if I had been raised in a given culture
and era, I too would have found the religious usages congenial. As
long as my empathy is incomplete, I remain uncertain of the validity of my results.

However, I suggest that Bleeker and Widengren's basic scheme,
and all similar commonplace ways of approaching "religions," are
modelled on mainline Protestant theology and church history, with
a bit of anthropology and perhaps ritual studies added in for com-
pletion. Bleeker and Widengren's program for the analysis of religions does not reflect the way that living religion is discussed by
adult practitioners, or taught to children. Their program is, I suggest, a secularization of a sectarian Christian religious act.

James Michael Lee argued that doing theology is a specifically
Protestant ethnocentricity. Protestantism rejected both the real pres-

---

[5] C. Jouco Bleeker & Geo Widengren (eds.), *Historia Religionum: Handbook for the History of Religions*, 2 volumes (Leiden: E. J. Brill, 1969), Volume I, p. v.
[6] Mircea Eliade, *The Forge and the Crucible: The Origins and Structures of Alchemy*, translated by Stephen Corrin (London: Rider and Company, 1962; New York: Harper & Row, Publishers, 1971), p. 11.

ence of Jesus in the Eucharist and the types of mystical experiences that Catholics exalt. The mainline churches also rejected the personal born-again experiences that Evangelical Protestantism prioritizes. "Mainline Protestant religious educationists...and officially church-sanctioned curricula eschew religious experience as a content to be taught or learned."[7] The result has been a falling back on theology as a cognitive content that is to be "transfer[red]...as safely and as purely as possible to the ears of waiting students in a school setting."[8] Mainline Protestant Christians behave as though it were an act of piety or devotion to fuss over theology, much as it is an act of devotion for Jews to study Talmud. Protestants do not fuss over canon law, nor Jews about theology, with anything approaching equal interest—or confidence in God's interest in their efforts.

Bleeker and Widengren's first two categories, the essence of the religion and its historical development, unwittingly reflect the two basic categories of Martin Luther's analysis of Christianity. Luther claimed that (his reconstruction of) the essence of primitive Christianity was true and salvific, while the subsequent history of institutionalized Catholicism was an unforgivable departure into heresy. Is this prejudice a paradigm that academic students of religion should be applying cross-culturally?

One may readily imagine that Bleeker and Widengren's program arose innocently when Protestant seminarians decided to study comparative religions and went about their studies by extrapolating from what they were already doing as seminarians. One may look to Rudolf Otto, Nathan Söderblom, Joachim Wach, and Gerardus van der Leeuw as prominent examples of the bridge between Protestant theology and the phenomenological school of the history of religions. The location of the history of religions in American divinity schools has contributed further to the conflict of interests. The result has been a skewing of the study of religion that today pervades textbooks and courses throughout the field. Treating ideology as the central element of a religion is a secularization of doing Protestant theology.

Privileging ideology as the essence of religion has aesthetic appeal as a program for the history of religions only as long as Protestant cultural expectations are treated as normative. Not only does it keep the study of religion from committing itself whole-heartedly to the

---

[7] James Michael Lee, "Religious Instruction and Religious Education," in Ralph W. Hood, Jr. (ed.), *Handbook of Religious Experience* (Birmingham, Alabama: Religious Education Press, 1995), p. 548.
[8] Ibid., p. 546.

humanities, but it imposes a methodological obstacle to the presentation of religion as a Good Thing. When the paradigm of ideological essence is applied to a religiosity that a scholar does not happen to share, the act of doing its theology ceases to be an act of homage to its god(s) and becomes something else entirely. In most cases, historians' inventories of the components of religious stereotypes are autopsies done on corpses. They are not portraits of any kind of living religiosity, and they do not arrive at results with which anyone could possibly empathize. They are not, in any full sense of the term, phenomenological studies. In other cases—and here I am thinking of works by Mircea Eliade,[9] Walter Otto,[10] and David Kinsley,[11] as well as a never-to-be-finished manuscript of my own— the doing of phenomenology in which one does not oneself believe can become a kind of poetic fantasizing. It is an ethnocentric projection of the Western academic pre-occupation with ideology onto a religiosity whose devotees may approach it quite differently. What is achieved may be charming. It may be challenging of the reader's ethnocentricity. But it is more an ethnocentric projection than a genuine engagement with other people's sensibilities.

Religion, as Wilfred Cantwell Smith has taught us, is a modern Western construction. Smith traced the term from its pagan Roman and early Christian uses, through its Renaissance revival in a Neoplatonic sense that was historically antecedent to perennial philosophy. The term was subsequently appropriated by Christianity, contrasted with false religion, pluralized into the world's religions, subdivided into natural and revealed religion, and so transformed into a generic concept of "religion in general."[12] An early and naively blatant example of the usage that the Enlightenment bequeathed to the academic study of religion may be found in Dr. James Anderson's *The Constitutions of Freemasons* of 1723.

> A Mason is obliged, by his tenure *to obey the Moral Law*; and if he rightly understand the Art, he will never be a stupid ATHEIST, nor an irreligious LIBERTINE. But though in Ancient times Masons were charg'd in

---

[9] The methodological flaw pervades Eliade's oeuvre. The most egregious instance is perhaps his *Patterns in Comparative Religion*, translated by Rosemary Sheed (1958; reprint New York: New American Library, Inc., 1974).

[10] Walter F. Otto, *The Homeric Gods: The Spiritual Significance of Greek Religion*, translated by Moses Hadas (1954; reprint London: Thames & Hudson Ltd., 1979).

[11] David R. Kinsley, *The Sword and the Flute: Kali and Krsna, Dark Visions of the Terrible and the Sublime in Hindu Mythology* (Berkeley: University of California Press, 1975).

[12] Wilfred Cantwell Smith, *The Meaning and End of Religion: A New Approach to the Religious Traditions of Mankind* (New York: Macmillan Company, 1962), pp. 15-50.

every country to be of the Religion of that Country or Nation, whatever it was, yet 'tis now thought more expedient only to oblige them to that religion in which *all men agree*, leaving their particular opinions to themselves; that is, to be *good Men and true*, or Men of Honour and Honesty, by whatever denomination or persuasion they may be distinguish'd—whereby Masonry becomes the *Center of Union* and the means of conciliating true Friendship among persons that must have remain'd at a perpetual distance.[13]

Alexander Piatigorsky commented that "we have here two different concepts of Religion. The first is absolute, universal, and general....The second is relative and particular. Particular, because it embraces every concrete religion in the world, the whole world of religious variety. Relative, because on the one hand it is always related to the first, just as the particular is related to the general, while on the other, it is opposed to the first, in the sense that that which differentiates is opposed to that which unites....while 'the Moral Law' and that 'Religion [undefined] in which all men agree' remain *summum bonum*, any particular religion, though always 'relatively good' when opposed to 'stupid atheism and irreligious libertinism,' appears to be 'relatively bad' in the context of Masonic universalism."[14]

Perhaps because they have Anderson's religious universalism in mind, many scholars are fond of stating that they can talk about religions in the plural, but want nothing to do with religion in the singular. In my view, their concern to avoid universalism presupposes a covert theological agenda that is inappropriate for the location of the study of religion in the humanities. The concept of "religion" in the singular is neither more nor less objectionable than the concept of "language" in the singular. The human species has a capacity for religion precisely as it has a capacity for language.

It is a category mistake to contrast "religion" in the singular with "religions" in the plural. One might as well contrast "language" with French, German, and Italian, or make the claim that philology is valid but linguistics unworthy of academic interest. "Religions" in the plural are simply not the same sorts of thing as "religion" as such. To speak of "religions" in the plural implies a reification of ideal types. Scholars acknowledge this fact whenever they lament that students in introductory courses are regularly taught generalizations that are so broad, so categorical, and so little nuanced as to misrepresent the religions discussed. "Everything we teach is lies," I

---

[13] James Anderson, *The Constitutions of Freemasons, 1723*, with an introduction by L. Vibert (London, 1923), p. 50; as cited in Alexander Piatigorsky, *Who's Afraid of Freemasons? The Phenomenon of Freemasonry* (London: Harvill Press, 1997), p. 65.

[14] Piatigorsky, *Who's Afraid of Freemasons?* , pp. 65-66.

heard one distinguished scholar remark at the 1997 meeting of the American Academy of Religion. In teaching religions, we teach *stereotypes*—with all the dangers that stereotyping entails. The issue should not be lightly brushed aside. Ideal types may be unobjectionable when they are consciously employed as heurisms. However, they are inevitably reified when they are made objects of research, rather than utilized as tools in the process of studying something else whose existence is empirical. To study Buddhism, for example, is not the same as to study how Buddhists go about being religious. Either the heuristic character of ideal types is built into the research, or the research will inevitably reify the ideal types. Moreover, much that deserves to be interrogated is instead glossed over through references to "religions" in the plural. Because Buddhists, Muslims, Hindus, Jews, Christians, and so forth, are not invariably religious, Buddhism, Islam, Hinduism, Judaism, Christianity, and so forth, are not always religions. They are something else, for which we do not have a term, and calling them religions is misleading.

Thirty-five years after Wilfrid Cantwell Smith made his case against "religions" in the plural from his perspective as a theologian, it is shameful that cultural stereotypes are still being mass-produced in undergraduate courses everywhere. What has become of the Good Thing that undergraduate students are supposed to be learning? What are academics trying to teach when we teach religion? What is religion? And how must we redesign curricula in order to teach it?

It is because doing Protestant theology has been secularized as doing world religious phenomenology that scholars have been unable to articulate the sense in which religion is a Good Thing for students in the humanities. The curriculum has been constructed on the unexamined assumption that if it is good for Protestants to do theology, it must be good for students in general to learn religious ideologies in general. However, the covertly theological syllogism does not hold water. The God who validates Protestant theology can scarcely be held to validate religious ideological pluralism. Either the academic study of religion must opt explicitly for Dr. Anderson's universalism, or we need to define our academic Good Thing on exclusively humanistic criteria.

I have mounted this critique of the scholarly tradition in which I was trained and have published and taught, because the critique may finally be of greater value to the reader than the particular solution at which I have presently arrived. I have greater confidence in the road I have come than in the direction in which I have only begun to head.

In his methodological essay on "Religion as a Cultural System," Clifford Geertz defined religions in terms of the relation of two major elements, their ethos and their worldview. "Sacred symbols function to synthesize a people's ethos—the tone, character, and quality of their life, its moral and aesthetic style and mood—and their worldview—the picture they have of the way things in sheer actuality are, their most comprehensive ideas of order."[15] Geertz expressed the same point somewhat more elegantly in his book *Islam Observed*:

> The heart of...the religious perspective...is the conviction that the values one holds are grounded in the inherent structure of reality, that between the way one ought to live and the way things really are there is an unbreakable inner connection. What sacred symbols do for those to whom they are sacred is to formulate an image of the world's construction and a program for human conduct that are mere reflexes of one another.[16]

By contrast with the seminary-derived methodology that has dominated the academic study of religion, I see religious people educating children and other neophytes (converts, and so forth) firstly in how to behave properly, and secondly in traditional narratives and brief statements of beliefs. Only in a minority of cases do religious people go on to trouble themselves about the kinds of intellectualism that pre-occupy seminarians and many academics. Geertz provided a partial corrective by suggesting that religion blends religious behavior (the ethos) with religious beliefs (the world view) in a way that is mutually reinforcing, but his formulation continues to give too much attention to the intellectual contents of the worldview, and too little to the worldview's function.

I would like to suggest that every religious life is lived in the midst of creative tension. On the one hand is the actuality of the ethos, the reality of the religiosity lived. On the other is the postulation of the worldview, the image of the religion as it ideally ought to be. We are forced to creativity, we are obliged to exercise our wills, because we find ourselves situated in the discrepancy between what we have done and what we believe that we ought to do. To portray living religion, it is necessary somehow to capture the creative tension of the plight and opportunity of the human condition.

---

[15] Clifford Geertz, "Religion as a Cultural System," in Michael Banton (ed.), *Anthropological Approaches to the Study of Religion* (London: Tavistock Publications, 1966), p. 3.

[16] Clifford Geertz, *Islam Observed: Religious Developments in Morocco and Indonesia* (Chicago: University of Chicago Press, 1968), p. 97.

What unifies religious lives, so it seems to me, is not ideas about the numinous and the behavior that arises in consequence. Rather, it is a holistic concern to be a good person: a good shapeshifting hunter, a good shamanic healer, a good garden magician, a good Muslim, a good Christian, a good Jew, a good Chinese, a good Buddhist, and so forth. "Good" is in each case partly utilitarian (good at...) and partly ethical (intrinsically good). In each case, a goodly life has its values shaped by a sense of numinosity. Virtue is defined in numinous terms. What is at stake is not ideas about numinous beings or states of existences, treated as intellectual objects, but the integration of a sense of the numinous within the conduct of a human life. I am suggesting a shift in emphasis that is analogous to the distinction between an artist's life and the art objects that the artist produces. Art is not limited to art objects alone, but encompasses the entire process by which the objects are produced. The circumstance of religion is comparable. What is religious is not reducible to the objects of numinous experiences. Religion is more fully, accurately, and meaningfully appreciated as the entire process, the way of life that sustains, facilitates, induces, or accommodates a sense of numinosity. For the vast majority of humanity throughout time, instruction in how to live a goodly life is the content of religious education. Religion is the living of a numinously virtuous life.

The popular expectation that religious leaders and teachers exemplify the goodly life, without human compromise, fault, or failure, points to the importance of role modelling in the institutional life of religion. Many communities attribute a formal status to religious virtuosos who live extreme cases of the goodly life: the shaman, spirit medium, and prophet, the sinless Christ and the perfect man Muhammad, the saint, the tsaddik, the arahat, and the boddhisatva. Other religious roles may be more immediately accessible: priest, missionary, volunteer worker, teacher, and so forth. In other instances, religious aspirations are expressed in terms not of role models, but of goals for attainment.

In living practice, the ostensible goal of the religious life (*nirvana*, *moksha*, salvation, redemption, liberation, magical power, and so forth) is culturally shared metaphysical language for discussing a variety of different senses of the numinous. *Moksha*, salvation, and so forth, are religiously important not as phenomena post mortem, but for orienting or shaping the living of religious lives. The ostensible goal is, I suggest, a means to the end. The real end, the end that is lived and felt, is not metaphysical. It is numinous experience. Whatever it takes to have a sense all day long, day in and day out, of being a good Christian, or a good Hindu, and so forth, seems to me to be how religions constitute themselves.

Given my definition of religion as the pursuit and promotion of a numinously virtuous life, it is not ideology but religious pedagogy to which I would accord a central place in the academic analysis of religion. Equally important, from my point of view, is a recognition that religious communities invariably seek to transform their devotées, by guiding them from infancy onward to seek and to achieve goodly lives. To bring out the transformative character of religion, it might be appropriate to portray religious lives in developmental terms by articulating the ideal and actual religious expectations of people at different times in their lives, and in different walks of life. How people move from one set of expectations to another, why some fail to do so, and so forth, would be examples of the questions that such a research program might ask.

It is fair to characterize my proposal as an invitation, in some sense, to psychologize the study of religion in general. I suggest, however, that the psychologizing of religion today is analogous to the impact of Hellenistic philosophy on Western religions in late antiquity and the early middle ages. Just as late antique paganism and the three Western monotheisms each rationalized their existing beliefs and customs, so far as possible, in fashions consistent with Neoplatonic and/or Neoaristotelian philosophy, so religious self-understanding is embracing psychology today. We live in an era when the impact of psychology is being felt throughout the world's cultures. In North America, the "Baby Boom" generation has shown a statistically significant demand that religion provide opportunities for personal fulfillment;[17] and an increasing number of people are explaining their religion in increasingly psychological terms. Religious people have learned the concept of psychological functionalism from the academy and recognized that a great deal of traditional teaching can be articulated in appropriately modern terms, without doing violence to the tradition.

For example, writers on the Desert Fathers of Christianity are conceptualizing their traditional teachings as having always had a transformative character.

> Human transformation, union with Christ, and divinization (*theosis*) are, for the Desert Fathers and the Eastern Fathers in general, the fundamental goals of Christianity...The very consensus of the Fathers

---

[17] Wade Clark Roof, *A Generation of Seekers: The Spiritual Journeys of the Baby Boom Generation* (San Francisco: HarperCollins Publishers, 1993).

rests in their exposition of the process by which man, in the Grace of God, becomes a "god," a participant in the divine, a partaker of the energies of God...If man remains *wholly himself* in union with Christ— in union with the Redeemer or Restorer of man's fallen nature—it is his person, his very self, which is renewed.[18]

Tu Wei-Ming, who is attempting to revive Confucianism in Taiwan, argues that the traditional Confucian goal of self-cultivation is implicit throughout East Asian religiosity.

> The Confucian ideal of sagehood, the Taoist quest for becoming a "true person," and the Buddhist concern for returning to one's "original mind" are all indications that to follow the path of knowledge backward, as it were, to the starting point of the true self is the aim of East Asian thought...Since presumably a genuine knowledge of the self entails a transforming act upon the self, to know in this sense is not only to reflect and comprehend, but also to shape and create. To know oneself is simultaneously to perfect oneself. This, I think, is the main reason that East Asian thought lays as much stress on how to cultivate oneself as on who and what the true self is. To the Confucians, Taoists, and Buddhists, self-knowledge is predominantly an ethico-religious question, although it is inevitably laden with epistemological implications.[19]

I would like to suggest that this argument holds on a global basis. Whether or not religions consciously acknowledge their engagement in human transformation, their primary concerns have always been the idealization, promotion, and pursuit of goodly lives.

It is not necessary to go so far as the mystics for one's examples. A colleague informs me, for example, that he was taught as a Mennonite child to cultivate and maintain an inner sense of the presence and love of Jesus. He avoided sin in order to avoid a devastating sense of alienation from Jesus. Interestingly, a parallel argument could be drawn with the significance of vision quests among Algonkian Indian children.[20] Spirits traditionally served both children and adults as helpers on the condition that numinously virtuous standards were adopted and maintained.

One starts, as a small child, being enjoined to keep the outer forms of the religion. As children, we are all "extrinsically religious,"

---

[18] Bishop Chrysostomos of Oreoi, "Toward a Spiritual Psychology: The Synthesis of the Desert Fathers," *Pastoral Psychology* 37/4 (1989), p. 257.

[19] Tue Wei-Ming, *Confucian Thought: Selfhood as Creative Transformation* (Albany, NY: State University of New York Press, 1985), pp. 19-20.

[20] For examples of self-reports, see Paul Radin, "Ojibwa and Ottawa Puberty Dreams," in *Essays in Anthropology Presented to A. L. Kroeber* (Berkeley: University of California Press, 1936), pp. 233-64.

to use Gordon Allport's term.[21] We do what we are told, because we wish to gain social approval. It is Mummy and Daddy whom we wish to please, not Truth that we seek to pursue. Some people remain extrinsically religious all their lives, conforming with their culture-mates in abiding by a way of religion that in some profoundly existential way does not touch them. The sense of the numinous does not enter their experience.

In other cases, people undergo spiritual awakenings. They become, in Allport's phrase, "intrinsically religious." Their religiosity is a matter of personal belief and conviction. The Mennonite and Algonkian examples that I have used pertain to this developmental milestone. In all cultures, some children become intrinsically religious in a spontaneous and uncomplicated way. In many cultures, rites of initiation are designed in order to induce numinous experiences. When numinous experiences are accepted as proof of the validity of a religious worldview, they awaken intrinsic religiosity. Religion is no longer a matter of social conformity alone. It becomes an existential concern, integrated within the sense of self. Self-approval motivates its observance, whether social approval is forthcoming or not.

Approaching religion in terms of extrinsic and intrinsic religiosity permits unification of the divergent methodological approaches to religion as a social institution and as a personal orientation.[22] Political, economic, environmental, and social considerations profoundly shape extrinsic religiosity, which intrinsic religiosity takes as its point of departure. It is not a question of contrasting extrinsic and intrinsic, group behavior and personal devotion, or sociological and psychological methods. The extrinsic/intrinsic relationship does not mirror the Christian antinomy of law and spirit that has traditionally marginalized sociological methods in the study of religion. Over the course of a religious life, extrinsic and intrinsic religiosity instead compare with the booster and payload that together comprise a functioning rocket.

For many people, certainly in the monotheistic religions of the West, intrinsic religiosity entails a lifelong experience of conflict. For rabbinical tradition, the conflict pertained to humanity's natural endowment. The twin inclinations to do good and to do evil were both to be included when fulfilling the obligation to "love the Lord your

---

[21] Gordon W. Allport, "The Religious Context of Prejudice," *Journal for the Scientific Study of Religion* 5 (1966), pp. 447-57.

[22] On the two approaches, see Larry D. Shimm, *Two Sacred Worlds: Experience and Structure in the World's Religions* (Nashville: Abingdon, 1977).

God with all your heart and with all your soul and with all your
might" (Dt 6:5). Michael Fishbane explained:

> One possibility, urged by the sages, is for the true devotee to subli-
> mate base instincts to divine ends. The clash of opposing *yetzers* [incli-
> nations] would of course still remain, but the negative effects of the
> evil inclination would be overcome. Such a religious psychology strik-
> ingly softens the stern duality of two opposing *yetzers* and suggests the
> possibility of self-mastery.[23]

Through self-mastery, the rabbis held, it was possible for any Jew to
attain righteousness. It was necessary only to make oneself fulfill all
of the observances of Judaism. Gershom Scholem explained:

> The righteous person, who seeks to meet the demands of the Torah,
> is caught in a never-ending struggle with his Evil Urge, which rebels
> against these demands; he must constantly wage battle with his own
> nature. But even this struggle between the Good Urge and the Evil
> Urge, in which he emerges as the "hero who conquers his own
> drive," never goes beyond the demands placed upon every human
> being.[24]

Early Jewish tendencies to develop self-mastery into asceticism were
resisted by the rabbis,[25] but flourished in the Christian concept of
the monk as a "spiritual athlete," constantly engaged in training and
competition.[26] The conflict was also traditionally discussed as a
"spiritual warfare" with Satan.[27] The monastic idealization of interi-
or conflict was taken over by Muslim Sufis. A saying attributed to
Muhammad states: "The true Flight or Hijrah is the flight from evil,
and the real Holy War or Jihad is the warfare against one's passions."[28] Al-Ghazali termed "the mystics, those men of piety whose
chief occupation is to meditate upon God, to oppose the passions,
and to walk in the way leading to God by withdrawing from world-

[23] Michael Fishbane, *The Kiss of God: Spiritual and Mystical Death in Judaism* (Seattle:
University of Washington Press, 1994), p. 5.

[24] Gershom Scholem, *On the Mystical Shape of the Godhead: Basic Concepts in the
Kabbalah*, translated by Joachim Neugroschel (New York: Schocken Books, 1991), p.
91.

[25] Steven D. Fraade, "Ascetical Aspects of Ancient Judaism," in Arthur Green
(ed.), *Jewish Spirituality: From the Bible Through the Middle Ages* (New York: Crossroad,
1987), pp. 253-88.

[26] See, for example, Richard Blum and Alexander Golitzin, *The Sacred Athlete: On
the Mystical Experience and Dionysios, Its Western World Fountainhead* (Lanham: University
Press of America, 1991).

[27] Dom Lorenzo Scupoli, *The Spiritual Combat and A Treatise on Peace of Soul*, translated by William Lester & Robert Mohan (Westminster, MD: Newman Bookshop;
reprint Rockford, IL: TAN Books and Publishers, Inc., 1945).

[28] William Montgomery Watt, translator, *The Faith and Practice of Al-Ghazali* (1953;
reprint Oxford: Oneworld, 1994), p. 145.

ly pleasure. In their spiritual warfare they have learnt about the virtues and vices of the soul and the defects in its actions."[29]

From the late Second Temple period, Judaism knew also a second standard. Scholem characterized it as follows:

> The *Hasid*...the pious man is the extraordinary type....the *Hasid* carries out not only what is demanded of him, that which is good and just in the eyes of the Law, but goes beyond the letter of the Law...He demands nothing of his fellow, and everything of himself. Even when carrying out a prescription of the Law, he acts with such radical exuberance and punctiliousness that an entire world is revealed to him in the fulfillment of a commandment, and an entire lifetime may be needed to carry out just one commandment properly.[30]

Rabbinical sources provide no indication that anyone could voluntarily develop into a *Hasid*. It is clear, however, that a minority view conceptualized an unconflicted life. In *Sifrei Deuteronomy* 32, a midrash suggests that the noun *lebabekha*, "your heart," be read as two words, *leb bakh*, "heart in you." Fishbane commented:

> In this way Moses is made to urge the people to love God..."with your whole heart....the explication...follows: "that your heart not be divided [*haluq*] toward God." From this it would seem that the instruction is to love God with a perfect service and not be conflicted. The divided self must be brought in line, for the One God demands all one's heart.[31]

Equally limited but tantalizing cross-cultural evidence regarding the transition from conflicted to unconflicted intrinsic religiosity is presently available from a limited number of traditions. Self-cultivation in Confucianism aimed traditionally to bring the devotée into harmony with the inherently moral character of the universe.[32] In Mahayana Buddhism, the acquisition of uniform, that is, unconflicted, compassion is held to be a by-product of the pursuit of *nirvana*.[33] Christian sanctification, at least in the Wesleyan tradition, entails an experience of freedom from temptations to sin.[34]

---

[29] Ibid., p. 39.

[30] Scholem, *On the Mystical Shape of the Godhead*, p. 90.

[31] Fishbane, *The Kiss of God*, p. 5.

[32] Rodney L. Taylor, *The Confucian Way of Contemplation: Okada Takehiko and the Tradition of Quiet-Sitting* (Columbia, SC: University of South Carolina Press, 1988); Philip J. Ivanhoe, *Confucian Moral Self Cultivation* (New York: Peter Lang, 1993).

[33] Edward Conze, *Buddhist Scriptures: Selected and Translated* (Harmondsworth: Penguin Books Ltd., 1959), p. 72; Gen Lamrimpa, *Samatha Meditation: Tibetan Buddhist Teachings on Cultivating Meditative Quiescence*, translated by B. Alan Wallace and edited by Hart Sprager (Ithaca, NY: Snow Lion, 1992), pp. 113-14.

[34] Donald L. Alexander (ed.), *Christian Spirituality: Five Views of Sanctification* (Downers Grove, IL: InterVarsity Press, 1989).

The optimal life in Mahayana Buddhism, Confucianism, Judaism, and Christianity is not only goodly, but unconflicted about its good-liness. These achievements of characterological resolutions of inner conflict correspond, in secular terminology, to the psychoanalyst Marjorie Brierley's concept of personality integration[35] and to the humanistic psychologist Abraham Maslow's concept of self-actual-ization.[36] Let me underscore this point. What is considered most ex-emplary in at least four major approaches to religiosity is the achievement that psychologists call self-actualization.[37]

To my mind, the study of the exemplary life may be the Greatest Good Thing that the academic study of religion has the present po-tential to contribute to the humanities. What is more, the standard of an unconflicted religious life can be used as a cross-cultural crite-rion for adjudicating not necessarily the truth-claims, but certainly the comparative health-value of different religiosities. We may leave it to spiritual directors and psychotherapists to do the hands-on clin-ical work. The academic task is to organize historical and ethno-graphic findings in manners that help explore and explain the hu-manistic Good Thing that religion is.

In closing, let me repeat that I endorse Otto's definition of reli-gion in terms of the sense of the numinous. In so far as the academy pursues knowledge for the sake of knowledge, I welcome within the study of religion any contributions that bear on the topic. I never-theless suggest that religion functions above all else to promote the living of what religious devotées consider to be exemplary lives and that some forms of religion knowingly promote optimal lives as de-fined by the resolution of inner conflict. Religious people do not seek only to be religious; they seek to be good at being religious. There is no reason not to adopt their priority as a priority for the academic study of religion. It is not religions but religious ways of life that we ought to be studying—not ideology, but the processes of human reli-gious development that we ought to be popularizing in courses and texts.

---

[35] Marjorie Brierley, *Trends in Psycho-Analysis* (London: Hogarth Press & Institute of Psycho-Analysis, 1951).

[36] Abraham H. Maslow, *Motivation and Personality*, 3rd ed. (New York: Harper-Collins, 1970).

[37] On self-actualization, see Dan Merkur, "'And He Trusted in Yahweh': The Transformation of Abram in Gen 12-13 and 15," *Journal of Psychology of Religion* 4-5 (1995-96), pp. 65-88; *idem*, "Transpersonal Psychology: Models of Spiritual Awakening, "*Religious Studies Review* 23/2 (1997), pp. 141-47; *idem, The Creative Imagination: Psychedelic Experiences and the Psychoanalysis of Self-Actualization* (Albany, NY: State University of New York Press, 1998).

It is only because the pursuit of knowledge for the sake of knowledge is a political and moral agenda that pretends not to be, that
most work in the academic study of religion is profoundly conflicted.

CHAPTER SEVEN

RELIGION, WORLD, PLURALITY

William E. Paden

Religion is not an *object* for which one can have an explanation, but a *word* which points to a variegated domain of different but related phenomena, each of which may appropriately require explanation—or multiple explanations—of a different kind. "Religion" is then not a thing but a start-up category pointing to a general realm or zone of cultural behavior, and that realm may conventionally be described as something like, "behaviors (whether verbal or nonverbal) that refer to and engage culturally postulated superhuman powers deemed to be sacred." While this initially distinguishes religion from science, morality, art and politics as various zones of culture that one may want to look into, it does not essentialize or entify religion. As a region of behavior, types of religion may then be examined just as one might analyze types of military, gaming and courtship behaviors and symbolisms. We, the interpreters, are the ones who postulate these distinctions, for purposes of analysis, and create models or prototypes by which to define and explore them.[1]

In this approach, religion is a broad area that includes not one but innumerable kinds and contexts of relationships with superhuman objects. A topic like this is not an object or datum for explanation any more than "America" or "Asia" is an object for explanation. It is rather a large region with much dimensionality and internal contextuality, with many significations and functions to insiders and outsider-interpreters, with permeable and contested definitional boundaries, a site where one may begin to investigate complexity, form sub-mappings, make discoveries, and, indeed, create new maps and discard old ones.

If religion is understood in this way, it is pointless to contend so wearisomely over what "it" "essentially is." Yet if a singular explanation of religion makes no sense, and the same could be said of

---

[1] A useful introduction to prototype theory as applied to religion is Benson Saler, *Conceptualizing Religion: Immanent Anthropologists, Transcendent Natives, and Unbounded Categories* (Leiden: E.J. Brill, 1993), pp. 197-226.

music or art, there can certainly be theories of controlled, contextualized aspects of religion. And the aspect we choose to look at already prefigures the kind of explanation one may expect. The primary need today for the secular study of religion is to clarify the relationship of various theoretic frames by making clear the aspect of religion they describe, while also generating more adequate cross-cultural categories and perspective.

An Aspectival Approach to Religion

Religious behavior is simply not monolithic: engagement with superhuman objects takes place at every cognitive level of human consciousness and in every cognitive domain, in every form of social dynamic and causality, in every conceivable historical environment and cultural context, in every type of mythological discourse and meaning-attribution, in every imaginable form of ritual performance and sensory environment—in short, through every genre of human behavior. By the same generic definition stated above, it would be religious to be possessed by a god in a trance state but it would also be religious to maintain fidelity to divinely endowed moral precepts. It would be religious to exercise altruistic care for others in the name of the teachings of the faith and also religious to abandon social attachments to others in order to seek other-worldly communion. For those under threat of chaos, it may be religious to see the "superhuman" as absolute order and stability, but for those bound and suppressed by their social identities, it may appear in the form of liberation from a given, corrupt order. "Religion," then, may either bind or unbind, separate or bring together, invite ascetic constraint or ecstatic dance. It draws on many trajectories of basic behaviors—like territorial marking, submission to authority, bonding, offering and gift-giving, atoning for offenses, sacrificing, communal sharing, and acts of loyalty.[2] Even what seems like a specific categorical theme like sacrifice turns out to not be unitary but quickly breaks down into quite different modalities and collocations.[3] The reason we have dozens of fairly reasonable theories of religion, myth, ritual and gods, is because each addresses an important aspect of the subject.

---

[2] Walter Burkert's *Creation of the Sacred: Tracks of Biology in Early Religions* (Cambridge: Harvard University Press, 1996) does an admirable job of examining several of these modalities in relation to specific biological, evolutionary contexts.

[3] Ivan Strenski, "Between Theory and Speciality: Sacrifice in the 90s," *Religious Studies Review* 22/1 (1996), pp. 10-20.

There is no apparent way out of this embarrassingly simple common-sense circularity in which explanations of religion are driven by chosen prototypes. Where "religion" is understood as social belonging, or as ecstatic apparitions, or as ritual, theory must follow suit. The gender dimensions of religion invite gender-factor explanation, out-of-body experiences invite theories of sleep-paralysis and brain-states, and historical changes and syncretisms invite historical expertise and analysis. Thus, Gananath Obeyesekere examines the susceptibility of Sri Lankan women to enter into orgiastic possession trances and applies Freudian theory about repressive sexuality. C.G. Jung looked at mandalic symbols and found emblems of psychological wholeness and polarity. Emile Durkheim studied totemic objects and, behold, found his theory of the totemic principle. Likewise, scholars explain variations on church attendance through notions of suburban change, explain religious submission through evolutionary concepts of authority deference, explain ceremony as a form of display behavior, explain the persistence of tradition by theories of cognitive transmissibility and memory-filters, explain millennialist cults by theories of social marginality, explain prayer by theories of object-relations, explain the rise and fall of cult leaders by theories of ego-inflation and paranoia, explain altruism and self-abnegation by sociobiological theories of group survival, and explain religious conversions by psychological theories about identity transformation.

When theory works well at one site, the tendency is to hegemonize it, even though rightness and fit applied to one set of behavioral constraints and defined conditions may be misplaced or irrelevant elsewhere. As theory, after all, is itself a form of political behavior, a kind of struggle for control of the ideological center, we do well to remember its coercive nature. Nor is it unnatural in itself to totalize, to make one's particular theoretic worlds into "the" world, to reduce chaos and complexity by unifying and ultimately inhabiting a world filled with one's own semantic field, a world "good to perceive,"[4]—in this case, one's invested theory.

The Sui Generis *Issue and Beyond*

Critics of the idea that religion is a privileged, *sui generis* datum have challenged the discourse of the phenomenology of religion tradition and have attempted to replace it with more scientific,

---

[4] Burkert, *Creation of the Sacred*, p. 165.

analytical agendas.[5] Their view is that religion and "the sacred" are not unique, autonomous or privileged categories, or something with a supernatural content that requires spiritual intuition on the part of the scholar to be understood. The tradition represented by Rudolf Otto and Mircea Eliade, the argument runs, epitomizes this privileging and is thus unworthy of the secular academy.

But exposing the theological and political rhetoric of ontological and administrative autonomy should not be an excuse to cease paying attention to what is "different" about the subject matter. All forms of behavior have their own features, their "own kinds" of traits. Moreover, the meanings attributed to actions by their performers—for religion, read "believers"—are part of the data of difference that the outside interpreter must pay attention to.

William James saw both sides of this issue well. On the one hand, he showed that one does not need to posit a special, distinct religious feeling or behavior as a category in its own right, as there is rather a "common storehouse of emotions"—and presumably, actions—"upon which religious objects may draw...".[6] On the other hand, "[A]s concrete states of mind, made up of a feeling *plus* a specific sort of object, religious emotions of course are psychic entities distinguishable from other concrete emotions...".[7] Religious behavior does not have to be theologically privileged and essentialistically "separate" to be simply different.

Religious humility and praise, then, are homologous with other forms of humility and praise, and yet are "different" from nonreligious humility and praise by virtue of the role of the postulated superhuman object and its significatory context in the mind of the participant. Any behavior, like kneeling, running, shouting, or submissiveness can have a different meaning depending on the context, and religious models function as differential contexts or frames for behavior just like any nonreligious setting does, e.g. athletics, war, or love.

While the behaviors which religion draws upon are from the same fund of general conduct available in nonreligious contexts, conduct

---

[5] Robert Segal, *Religion and the Social Sciences: Essays on the Confrontation* (Atlanta: Scholars Press, 1989); Hans H. Penner, *Impasse and Resolution: A Critique of the Study of Religion* (New York: Peter Lang Press, 1990); Russell T. McCutcheon, *Manufacturing Religion: The Discourse on Sui Generis Religion and the Politics of Nostalgia* (New York: Oxford University Press, 1997).

[6] William James, *The Varieties of Religious Experience* (New York: Penguin Books, 1985), p. 28.

[7] Ibid., p. 28.

which may occur without any superhuman objects—e.g. deference, trance, gift giving, contemplation, and protocols of purification—the superhuman factor in the equation generally adds authority and consequentiality, thus enhancing the intensity and commitment of the human response. In Peter Berger's words, "To go against the order of society is always to risk plunging into anomy. To go against the order of society as religiously legitimated, however, is to make a compact with the primeval forces of darkness."[8]

At the same time, religious activity is more than just structures and analytical features of object-relations and enhanced empowerments. It is typically a way of living and perceiving the world that is invested with values and networked, textured significances conveyed by the participant's mythic tradition and mindset—in short, a form of world habitation. Again, to point this out is not to elevate or idealize the subject matter per se, for the same could be said of the world of psychotic depression or the world of crime. Every domain of experience and culture has a life and logic of its own and constitutes a piece of theater where roles are played out.

In that regard, the critics of the idea that religion is "its own kind," in lumping Otto and Eliade together as essentialists, have tended to obscure the very significant contributions Eliade made to the analysis of characteristically religious world formations and behaviors. While Otto clearly emphasized the non-natural character of the numinous and capacity to apprehend it, Eliade, while occasionally speaking broadly about the spiritual implications of studying the history of religions, for the most part saw sacrality as a category of religious life bearing on the construction of religious universes and thus a structural element in behavior that needed descriptive attention. In this sense Eliade is closer to the Durkheimians, who developed a discourse about the "irreducible" role and character of sacred objects within collective systems, and did so within a decidedly secular conceptual frame.[9]

---

[8] Peter Berger, *The Sacred Canopy: Elements of a Sociological Theory of Religion* (New York: Doubleday, 1967), p. 39.

[9] William E. Paden, "Before 'the Sacred' Became Theological: Durkheim and Reductionism," in Thomas A. Idinopulos and Edward A. Yonan (eds.), *Religion and Reductionism*, Studies in the History of Religions, LXII, (Leiden: E.J. Brill, 1994), pp. 198-210.

Religious Worlds

These considerations lead to the important concept of "worlds."[10] The concept of world assumes that existence or "the universe" is not a given, known, already agreed upon referent, but always a concomitant of interpretation, a product of particular ways of representing and inhabiting it.

> World thus describes versions of life-space without reducing those versions to an independent norm. The idea of world acknowledges these multiple orderings of reality by not assuming a single, a priori system of knowledge in terms of which all human experience should be described. For example, rather than viewing religions in terms of a given standard, religious or nonreligious, of what "the" world is and then seeing how they, the religions, represent it, the assumption is rather that religions themselves create their own versions of world. It is their central function to do so..."[11]

The concept of world is then non-metaphysical. It is isomorphic with system, environment, place of habitation, horizon. It has no structural or thematic content. It is a category that directs attention to context while placing no categorical imposition onto cultural data. Rather, it is an orientational, comparative tool for asking about and identifying the very different contexts that may bear on the import of any particular object or event.

A world is the operating environment of behavioral and linguistic options which persons presuppose, posit and inhabit at any given point in time and from which they choose courses of action. Culture, accordingly, is not a single horizon of linguistic and behavioral expectations, but the entire set of shifting horizons and world-versions available to its members. Humans may act out or encounter many such worlds, even in the course of a day.

Religions provide a conspicuous instance of worldmaking because of the ontological character of their language. It is the nature of religious language to name and script the ultimate powers that determine, ground and empower existence itself, and to fill world-experience with their meaning, agency, presence and authority. Religion is a primary cultural/linguistic instrument for

---

[10] Nelson Goodman, *Ways of Worldmaking* (Indianapolis: Hackett Publishing Co., 1978); William E. Paden, *Religious Worlds: The Comparative Study of Religion*, 2d ed. (Boston: Beacon Press, 1994); William E. Paden, "World," in Willi Braun and Russell T. McCutcheon (eds.), *Guide to the Study of Religion* (London: Cassell, forthcoming).

[11] Paden, "World," pp. 1-2.

defining and explaining identity, fate, time, space, cosmic order, suffering, danger and other meta-categories. While ontologies can also be shaped by secular and scientific concepts, religious world horizons continue to abound with a vigorous cosmizing and nomizing life, to use Peter Berger's terms.[12]

Broadly speaking, one might say that world habitation rather than "manifestations of the Holy" becomes here the more appropriate conceptual referent for describing religion. The hermeneutical shift is from a version of political monarchy ("the Sacred" as God), within the context of religious edification, to a decentered, pluralistic set of coexisting universes—reflecting a turn from the theological interests of divinity schools to those of the secular academy. But note that as a concept, world has a particularly open-ended character. It can refer to any world-version, religious or nonreligious. It may include the data of postulated experiences of otherness and superhuman powers as it may also feature the data of physical life. It can have virtually any content. It calls attention to the many matrices of experience such as ethnicity, geography, gender and social class that contextualize religious life so diversely. World is both something represented and something practiced; it is imaginal objects and bodies-in-performance; it can be static or mobile. It allows these not only as data expressive of the insider's realities, but at the same time as data for the interpreter to analyze, compare and explain. In its acknowledgement of religious content combined with the endless contextual variables constituting any system, it here reconciles at least some of the traditional concerns of the so-called phenomenology of religion with a socio-anthropological program, and also creates a matrix both for reformulating the notion of sacrality in a non-theological, non-foundationalist sense, and for regrounding comparativism.[13]

Sacrality

The term "sacred" is typically used as a noun, amounting to a kind of generic label for the transcendent, divine, or "wholly other" object of religious experience. But apart from the problem that this tends to foundationalize the referent of religion, it also

---

[12] Berger, *The Sacred Canopy*, pp. 19-28.

[13] On the issue of a "new comparativism" see the panel on that subject published in *Method and Theory in the Study of Religion* 8/1 (1996), pp. 1-49, with contributions by Luther Martin, Marsha Hewitt, Donald Wiebe, E. Thomas Lawson and myself, William E. Paden, "Elements of a New Comparativism," pp. 5-14.

limits the concept to substantive use rather than allowing it to have adjectival and adverbial meanings which draw attention to *how* insiders behave in relation to religious objects. Sacredness and holiness are not just attributes of objects, but also forms of behavior in relation to objects. The organizing factor in the constitution of religious domains is the constraining relationship between sacred objects and appropriate human responses to them, and "sacrality" can serve as a polythetic, umbrella term for those relational behaviors.

There are any number of ways of identifying these kinds of relationship to such objects. One might say that the superhuman is a realm that humans *receive* through states of possession, awe, gratitude, divination and fate, but also *give to* through acts of offering and sacrifice, and *interact with* through acts of exchange, prayer and communion, and *defend* through acts of protection, adherence to moral and ritual laws, and exorcism of impurities. Any sacred object may elicit any of these actions. Thus, superhuman objects in different religious systems may evoke similar behaviors; objects in the same religious system may evoke different behaviors; and the same object in a single system may evoke different behaviors at different times. Sacrality here refers to the place and requirements of an object within interactive systems, not just to a vague "transcendence."

It also follows that the experience of otherness or numinousness is understood here as *one* modality of religious objects (or relationship to them) rather than as a foundationalist entity hegemonized or essentialized as the single, dominant mode and reified as a phenomenological epithet for God. The superhuman realm may appear as mana-laden and revelatory, as an active agency, but *also* as an object to be kept from violation or defilement—a particularly salient distinction I have elaborated on elsewhere.[14] The concept of sacred, superhuman objects needs to be emancipated both from a restrictive revelational model, and from a model that reduces these objects simply to referents of basic, counterintuitive "belief."

It is certainly the case that we need a wider, more complex accounting of superhuman objects and relationships to them. These objects of course not only include deities, ancestors, spirits,

---

[14] William E. Paden, "Sacrality as Integrity: 'Sacred Order' as a Model for Describing Religious Worlds," in Thomas A. Idinopulos and Edward A. Yonan (eds.), *The Sacred and its Scholars: Comparative Methodologies for the Study of Primary Religious Data*, Studies in the History of Religions, Vol. LXXIII (Leiden: E.J. Brill, 1996), pp. 3-18.

buddhas, holy persons, and so forth, but also places, writings, signs, icons, words, principles and symbols that represent any of these. While anything can function as a superhuman object, religious objects are constituted as much by the behaviors they require as by any self-defining mythologizations about their superhuman nature per se. If the objects can do what humans cannot, they start to qualify as superhuman, but this is not enough since cartoon and popular figures like Superman or space aliens can do what humans cannot yet they are ordinarily not objects constraining sacred behaviors.

While the modes of sacrality are not culture-specific, because they draw on human capacities, the content of sacrality is entirely system-specific. The office of the papacy is sacred to Catholics but not to non-Catholics; the Ganges river is sacred to Hindus but not to Jews; the history of the Emperors of Japan is sacred to Shintoists but not to Swiss Protestants; the Jiba in Tenri, Japan, is not the center of the world to those outside the Tenri-Kyo faith. Religious systems crystallize around their own objects, their own linguistic, ritual, historical and geographic "places," reciting quite different histories of the world, observing alternative world calendars, and making unequivocal allegiance to disparate systems of authority and lineage.

Comparative Perspectives

Understanding the realm of religion means being grounded in comparative perspective. Comparative concepts show common, human processes amidst otherwise diverse cultures, while also allowing us to perceive and explain differences relative to those common forms, so that the study of religion develops by identifying both what is generic and what is specific in the subject matter. Generalizations about religion therefore issue from, and are accountable to, the kind of conceptual analysis that issues from responsible, controlled comparative work. Today comparison is not limited to marshalling parallel religious motifs, much less comparing religions as wholes, but analyzes religious factors as they interact with *any* of the patterns and variables that comprise the human situation.

Comparativism builds a vocabulary not available in the limited language of the religious insiders—just as economics builds a language beyond the vocabulary of any particular system, or comparative literature builds analytical terms beyond the poetics of any one tradition. This is at once the great de-provincializing achievement of religious studies and one of its most serious, ongoing problems, given the issues of commensurability between different cultural contexts. Yet one cannot even begin to describe and explain human behavior at any historical or ethnographic level without conceptualizations, which are themselves comparative formations. The issue is not whether to compare, but what to compare and how to get the comparability factor right.

Cross-cultural study certainly shows common features of religious worldmaking activity. Nor does connecting these features with generic human activity disregard their religious form. Humans *do* religious worlds. They make them as naturally as birds build nests. While every spider has a distinctive pattern of webmaking, they all build webs. All religious worlds make pasts by transmitting memories of sacred, founding events and mythic histories; they all cosmicize or absolutize their own sacred symbols and authorities; they protect these symbols from violation; and they always renew their sacred objects and categories through periodic observances.

The discovery of otherwise unnoticed commonality and the discovery of otherwise unnoticed difference are therefore both functions of comparison. If religious cultures commonly conduct periodic rites of world-renewal, linking their community with "the Great Time" of myth, each one does so by giving a different content to what it is that is being renewed, e.g. hierarchic family relationships, or the dependency of laity and monks, or economic exchange alliances between villages, or the prestige of the founder. Moreover, if classic phenomenologies tried to illustrate the ubiquity of versions of sacred space and time, contemporary historians of religion are more interested in the way myth and ritual reveal particular, cultural worlds of gender, class, power, sexuality and "local knowledge." At the same time, differences do go all the way down to the individuals in the culture, and we should beware of essentialist projections onto what cultures think or do as wholes.[15]

The significant common factor in comparison here is that it is in every case *human beings* that are engaging in religious actions. An era of emphasis on cultural differences has either obscured or trivialized this bedrock, bioanthropological referent.[16] Religions share

---

[15] Wendy Doniger, "Minimyths and Maximyths and Political Points of View," in Laurie Patton and Wendy Doniger (eds.), *Myth and Method* (Charlottesville: University of Virginia Press, 1996), pp. 109-27, pp. 114-15.

[16] Donald Brown's *Human Universals* (Philadelphia: Temple University Press, 1991) is a useful account of the history of the question of anthropological universals, and a compelling case for reconsidering the issue. It includes an extensive annotated bibliography on the subject.

certain features because it is humans who are the actors, just as in every culture there are common factors in the way humans eat, work, sleep, make love, bring up families, play, and make art. Likewise, humans recite myth, offer to gods, and perform rites of purity. Again, if previously comparative religion abstracted out and focused on the religious content of these, we are today equally interested in the nature of recitation (who recites, and why, and how, and in what context), the politics of exchange, and the sociology of purity.

We therefore need not limit comparative religion to juxtaposing only religious material per se, but also see religious behaviors in the context of the kind of human behavior they are drawn from, not isolating religious versions as being "outside of nature's order altogether."[17] Comparativism enlarges its notion of patterns by not limiting them to an inventory of religious genres (prayer, priesthood, deity), because religion as a subject matter is filled with all the same "patterns" as found in human culture generally, e.g. authority, order, freedom, economic status, class and gender interests, types of environment, ego development and types of personality. This generates more complex templates of comparison, differentiated typologies, and thus more variations and bases for showing difference. Comparativism builds and extends its vocabulary by using all these crisscrossing matrices of understanding and explanation, thus acknowledging and addressing religion's complexity (indeed, the world's complexity), showing the relationship between religious and nonreligious realms, checking our propensity for conceptually monolithic packagings and reductions, and providing a zone of integration that joins the interests of the history of religions and the social sciences.

Finally, in all this connectedness of "religion" with comparative themes, all comparativism should be conducted by controlled, delimitative aspectual focus. Fitz John Porter Poole states this well: "Comparison does not deal with phenomena *in toto* or in the round, but only with an aspectual characteristic of them. Analytical control over the framework of comparison involves theoretically focused selection of significant aspects of the phenomena...".[18] Two or more objects may then be comparable in one respect, but not in others; they may have some point of commonality, but be

---

[17] James, *The Varieties of Religious Experience*, p. 24.

[18] Fitz John Porter Poole, "Metaphors and Maps: Towards Comparison in the Anthropology of Religion," *Journal of the American Academy of Religion* 54/3 (1986), pp. 411-57, p. 414.

unlike in every other way. Comparison has the right to pick out single points of analogy for its own theoretic purposes. In this way, comparative method is itself a tool of the general approach to religion outlined above that shows the subject matter to be modal and domain oriented. These domains, thematizations or conceptual zones may be large ("world," "authority"), small (hand-washing rites in Moroccan Muslim villages), and complex or formulaic (correlations between urbanization, kinship solidarity and Passover observance in industrial North America).

Religion and Nature: The Broad View

Negotiation with postulated superhuman objects and the sacralization of life environments in relation to sacred objects apparently count among the natural dispositions of human behavior. It is natural to bond reciprocally with these ostensible ruling forces of the environment, to give to them in order to receive from them. It is natural to defend these objects from any violation and to sense guilt, impurity or the need for atonement if infraction of their order occurs. It is natural to see the whole of time and space in terms of one's own ancestries and ritual categories, just as it is natural to equate one's moral order with the ultimate order of the universe and it is natural to find "the absolute," centripetally, in one's own communal shrine. It is natural to form boundaries of kosher and nonkosher, and it is natural to draw contemporary meaning from the founders and other mythic exemplars of one's collective memory. Likewise, the "doing" of myth and theology can be understood not just as disembodied speculation, but as a natural activity, a behavior, namely the behavior of meaning-giving, orienting, reciting, and performing. In such ways, the study of religion is the study of the variety and relativity of human world-making and the variety of cognitive situations that transmit or undergird both religious and nonreligious behaviors.[19]

These sacred, superhuman objects will have multiple functions both for insiders and according to interpreters. Any one function may be more or less relevant or operable depending on context. Thus, sacred objects: a) give focus and explicitness to values and worlds that would otherwise remain unfocused and implicit, b) give status, dignity, objectivity and stability to what would otherwise

---

[19] Pascal Boyer, *The Naturalness of Religious Ideas: A Cognitive Theory of Religion* (Berkeley: University of California Press, 1994).

only be taken as transient human invention, c) provide an expand-
ed, surplus repertory of imagination for the psyche and thus its
capacity to express many voices, d) provide an alter-ego, an
"other," in relation to which participants can form behaviors and
attitudes that would be unexpressed without such a compelling
object-relation, e) call forth more authoritative forms of respect,
accountability, dependability and disciplined performance than
would obtain through nonreligious conceptions, f) give a name to
the forces of the adherent's world that appear to bear upon heal-
ing, strength in adversity, liberation, destiny and fate, and g) ritual-
ize and anchor, at a postulated transhuman level, practices of
social solidarity, status, and difference. Likewise, in the name of
the superhuman, religion gives enhanced value and exemplary
standards to particular behavioral qualities that vary from system
to system but include, for instance, devotion, respect, honor, sense
of purity, humility, courage, fortitude, integrity, capacity for selflessness, self-criticism, and the many versions of holiness generally.
Other cultural forms like nationalism, ideologies, educational systems, and philosophies do some of this "virtue-enhancing," and
certainly maintain some of the functions listed above, but it could
be said that religion in its more conspicuous forms virtually spe-
cializes in it.

Yet none of this means "religion" is necessarily good or desir-
able or that "the sacred" is by definition simply a benign force in
culture that radiates transcendental truths. The same force which
mythicizes positive qualities can foster negative ones. Religious
world views manifest the same human problems as any world
views, and thus can become systems of aggression and violence,
discrimination and subordination, fear and ignorance, colonialism
and racism, paranoidal inflation and banal trivialization. The gods
may be masks for fickle political honor, and the fact that they are
deities does not mean they cannot be tyrants. Religious authorities
are themselves subject to destructive paranoias. In these senses,
religion attracts all that human nature has to offer, functional or
dysfunctional, showcasing the range of human conduct. It is not
something that simply shows us a divine, cosmic transcendence
(classically, "the sacred"), but a part of the world that blends
sacrality with webs of social power and political legitimation.

In this last regard, religious objects and behaviors are not only
reflections of nonreligious objects and behaviors, but also the other
way around. That is, religion throws perspective on our ordinary
nature because it amplifies or intensifies features of behavior that
are already there and implicit in quasi-religious forms. Both

Durkheim and Eliade saw this well—the way societies elevate and idolize their heroes and give them a "supernature," construct social and political mythologies, and indulge in secular initiatory schemas and rites. So it is not just that religious praise is "like" ordinary praise, but also that ordinary praise is "like" religious praise. The analogies go both ways. In this way, religion shows us dimensions of humanity.

Final Points

In its pluralistic stance, this essay implicates certain notions of reflexivity and constructivism. Some clarification is in order. I am not advocating that every interpretation of religion is merely an arbitrary selection from endless possibilities. That there is no uninterpreted world does not mean there is nothing out there. Agreeing with Byron Good's statement that "perspectivism is rooted in reality itself,"[20] my view is not that everything is an invention of the interpreter or that the world is "only" or "merely" in the eye of the beholder, but rather that the world is a multi-dimensional immensity that the interpreter selects from and observes in some particular context, and that one should be aware of the way interpretation both gains and limits access to what is there, and thus become accountable for why we choose to look at what we do. The study of religion can become a vast lesson in such reciprocities and positionalities—which is to say, in methodological reflexivity.

Because I am impressed by the relational, reciprocal nature of meaning and the way objects and world take place and form through human positionings, I prefer neither the objectivist view that reality is there simply to be represented by subjects, nor the subjectivist view that human interpretation makes it all up, but rather a reciprocity model wherein the world gives itself through the receiving and configuring acts of the subject. The approach is addressed more fully in my *Interpreting the Sacred*.[21]

Are religious worlds "just" constructs? We speak of worlds as constructions at one level of generalization in order to point to the plurality and cultural relativity of reality-versions and the strong role of human activity in the formation of environments. But

---

[20] Byron Good, *Medicine, Rationality, and Experience: An Anthropological Perspective* (New York: Cambridge University Press, 1994), p. 177.

[21] William E. Paden, *Interpreting the Sacred: Ways of Viewing Religion* (Boston: Beacon Press, 1992), pp. 110-35.

worlds, including religious worlds, are also environments to which one attends and responds.[22] In that setting, "making" a world is only one aspect of the process. Humans, as Paul Ricoeur puts it, also "render" a world, like an artist.[23] They also surrender to it, discover and receive it, and give it back. Even to the extent that worlds are our creations, our cultural artifacts, they nevertheless present themselves already externalized to individuals and thus as non-arbitrary, given objectivities.[24] This externalization and objectivation is certainly the case with language, knowledges, and all the arts and categories of any civilization. From this angle, worlds come to individuals already weighted with a certain ontological authority.

It follows that I would not restrict the notion of world to metaphors of building. Worlds are not just constructions, but habitations; not just inventions, but expressions; not just projections, but performances and engagements; not just fabrications but ways of seeing, doing and behaving.

It is not, then, that religious systems are without reality, without foundation, without reference, but rather that they posit and mediate their own realities, foundations, and references. Such a view takes every world as its own performance, voices and renderings. Indeed, these expressions are what we are trying to learn about. They are "the data." What we do with them is the work of analysis, comparison, explanation and evaluation, and the twofold process of finding religion and interpreting it, a process that does always proceed in that order, is the work of our field. In all, the huge domain of the history of religion—that interesting space of human possibilities—is not only a lesson in the nature of world-making, the mutually constitutive nature of human subjects and their sacred objects, and the revealingly various regimens and contents of those objects, but also an occasion for coming to clarity about how our categories both occlude and reveal what is there.

---

[22] I draw the distinction of "attending" to the world vs. "constructing" the world from Tim Ingold, in Tim Ingold (ed.), *Key Debates in Anthropology* (London: Routledge, 1996), p. 115. A section of this volume (pp. 99-146) includes a useful debate among anthropologists on the concept of the cultural construction of human worlds.

[23] Paul Ricoeur, "Review of Nelson Goodman's *Ways of Worldmaking*" in *Philosophy and Literature* (Spring, 1980), pp. 107-20, pp. 116-20.

[24] Berger, *The Sacred Canopy*, pp. 3-28.

CHAPTER EIGHT

DIAGNOSING RELIGION

Robert Segal

Richard Rorty distinguishes epistemology from hermeneutics on
the grounds that epistemology assumes that "all contributions to a
given discourse are commensurable," whereas hermeneutics "is
largely a struggle against this assumption."[1] By "commensurable,"
Rorty means "able to be brought under a set of rules which will
tell us how rational agreement (if not the truth, then on what
would be needed to settle the issue) can be reached on every point
where statements seem to conflict."[2] The assumption is not that
disagreements will be resolved but that there is agreement on the
rules by which they can or may be resolved. In the interim, "the
interlocutors can agree to differ—being satisfied of each other's
rationality the while."[3]

In hermeneutics, the quest is likewise for common ground, but
hermeneutics does not require the existence or even the prospect
of it. Hermeneutics "sees the relations between various discourses
as that of strands in a conversation, where there is no disciplinary
matrix which unites the speakers, but where the hope of agreement is never lost as long as the conversation lasts."[4] Moreover,
the hope is not for "the discovery of antecedently existing common
ground"—the rules for securing agreement—but for agreement
itself, or at least for "exciting and fruitful disagreement":

> Epistemology sees the hope of agreement as a function of the discov-
> ery of the implicit common ground which does, perhaps unbeknownst
> to them, unite the speakers in a common rationality. For hermeneu-
> tics, to be rational is to be willing to refrain from epistemology—from
> thinking that there is a special set of terms in which all contributions
> to the conversation should be put—and to be willing to pick up the
> jargon of the interlocutor rather than translating it into one's own.

---

[1] Richard Rorty, "From Epistemology to Hermeneutics," in Jaaka Hinitikka
(ed.), *Acta Philosophica Fennica*, **XXX** (Amsterdam: North-Holland Publishing,
1979), p. 11
[2] Ibid.
[3] Ibid.
[4] Ibid., pp. 13-14.

> For epistemology, to be rational is to find the proper set of terms into
> which all the contributions should be translated if agreement is to be-
> come possible. For epistemology, conversation is implicit inquiry. For
> hermeneutics, inquiry is routine conversation.[5]

Rorty denies that the difference between hermeneutics and epistemology is the difference between the humanities and the sciences.
On the contrary, he argues that both the humanities and the sciences have fluctuated between hermeneutical phases and epistemological ones. Using his terms, I suggest that the modern study of
religion has been less a fluctuation than a clash between a hermeneutical approach and an epistemological one. The hermeneutical approach, which commonly regards itself as the guardian of
the subject of religion, takes the form of conversation, for which
religious studies prefers the term "dialogue." While the term is
usually applied intramurally to conversations between representatives of different religions, it is also applicable to the hermeneutical
relationship between students of religion and practitioners. Here
the student, who corresponds to the anthropological observer,
seeks simply to converse with the adherent. As Rorty characterizes
the process,

> [C]oming to understand is more like getting acquainted with a person
> than like following a demonstration.... [O]ne plays back and forth be-
> tween guesses about how to characterize particular statements or
> other events, and guesses about the point of the whole situation, until
> gradually one feels at ease with what was hitherto strange.[6]

The adherent is not merely the passive subject of study but a full
conversation partner. The student of religion does not presume to
persuade—to "convert"—the practitioner but merely to grasp, as
they used to say, where the practitioner is coming from. Should
agreement be achieved, all the better, but respectful disagreement
is both typical and sufficient.

    Indeed, what is often sought is even less than disagreement:
empathetic listening, as in Rogerian therapy. Here dialogue is
demoted to interview. The interviewer may be the one asking the
questions, but the questions take the form of "Tell me about your-
self." The interviewer may probe, but only to ascertain what the
adherent is willing to divulge. The interviewer has no independent
source of information about religion and dares only prod, not challenge or second-guess, the adherent. Interviewing here is in the

---

[5] Ibid., p. 13.
[6] Ibid., p. 14.

manner of "20/20," not "Sixty Minutes."

Whether as conversation or as interview, the hermeneutical approach need not be confined to living adherents of religion. It can be conducted with dead religions or with the inanimate artifacts of living ones. Whatever format the encounter takes, the assumption is of not mere disagreement but of partial incommensurability between student and practitioner. As Rorty puts it, "One will be epistemological where one understands perfectly well what is happening but wants to codify it in order to extend, or strengthen, or teach it. One must be hermeneutical where one does not understand what is happening but is honest enough to admit it...".[7] The student still strives to figure out what makes the believer tick, but takes for granted that the religious discourse will prove at least partly indecipherable. For that discourse assumes a reality that the student cannot fathom save by becoming a believer: the reality of the sacred.

The hermeneutical approach does not just grant but outright celebrates the impenetrability of the sacred. That impenetrability safeguards the autonomy of religious discourse, keeping it from being dissolved into the discourse of the student. Religion can be discussed endlessly but neither refuted nor subsumed under the student's discourse. The student and the practitioner are conversational equals, however much the conversation proves to be a dual monologue.

By contrast to the hermeneutical approach, the epistemological approach to religion does not defer to the adherent. On the contrary, the epistemologist presumes to know more than the practitioner. The epistemologist claims to know what makes religion tick. In contrast to the hermeneut, who dutifully respects the autonomy of religion, the epistemologist subsumes religion under another category—usually, one of the social sciences. The rationality of epistemology is exactly, as Rorty says, the "disciplinary matrix which unites the speakers." An epistemological approach views religion as a case of anthropology, sociology, economics, or psychology. There is no divide between student and practitioner, not because the anthropologist or sociologist is religious but because religion is anthropology or sociology. The common ground underlying religion and social science is not the meeting place of the two—the hermeneutical approach—but the incorporation of religion in social science. Rather than sacrosanct, religion is open to the same

---

[7] Ibid., p. 15.

scrutiny as any other phenomenon that social science undertakes to analyze.

Just as the most telling metaphor for hermeneutics is conversation, so the most apt metaphor for epistemology is medical diagnosis. The social scientist is the counterpart to the doctor; the believer, the counterpart to the patient. Just as the patient is not the arbiter of illness, so the believer is not the arbiter of religion. The patient may come to the doctor complaining of pain, but it is the doctor who makes the diagnosis. The doctor listens attentively to the patient's report but does not engage in a dialogue with the patient. The results of any tests taken do not quite depend on the patient's concurrence. The doctor knows both an array of cases, where the patient knows only one, and, even more, knows a theory, which links the complaint to a disease. The pain becomes a symptom of a disease, not the disease itself. The patient need not even be seeing the doctor with a complaint but may be going for a general physical examination or for some other ailment altogether. Some diseases are asymptomatic—that is, to the patient. In sum, the patient is the subject of study but not thereby the student.

Ironically, it is Clifford Geertz, advocate par excellence of a hermeneutical rather than an epistemological approach to culture, who invokes medical diagnosis as the model for hermeneutics. For him, diagnosis is different from explanation. Diagnosis is classification: it is the identification of a set of symptoms as a case of a disease. A diagnosis differs from an explanation because symptoms are neither the cause nor even the effect of a disease but instead part of the meaning of the disease: to have skin cancer is to have discolored skin. The diagnosis of any aspect of culture means the identification of it as a case of, say, religion rather than an account of how religion arises or functions:

> To generalize within cases is usually called, at least in medicine and depth psychology, clinical inference. Rather than beginning with a set of observations and attempting to subsume them under a governing law, such inference begins with a set of (presumptive) signifiers and attempts to place them within an intelligible frame. Measures are matched to theoretical predictions, but symptoms (even when they are measured) are scanned for theoretical pecularities—that is, they are diagnosed. In the study of culture the signifiers are not [to be sure] symptoms or clusters of symptoms, but symbolic acts or clusters of symbolic acts, and the aim is not therapy but the analysis of social discourse. But the way in which theory is used—to ferret out the unapparent import of things—is the same.[8]

---

[8] Clifford Geertz, *The Interpretation of Cultures* (New York: Basic Books, 1983), p. 26.

Yet even if diagnosis itself merely classifies—interprets—symptoms as a case of a disease, every disease has an explanation, and the diagnosis is surely a clue to it. To identify a mole as cancerous is surely to suggest an explanation of both its cause and its effect. Diagnosis is not like conversation: the aim is not to appreciate the patient's perspective on a symptom but to determine what it is a symptom of. Diagnosis fits the epistemological approach far better than the hermeneutical one.

Like any other metaphor, religion as illness is inexact. It is intended not to make religion like an ailment but to make the believer like a patient, who harbors the illness but is not thereby the authority on the illness. The metaphor is intended not to make social science like a cure but to make the social scientist like a doctor, who is not beholden to the patient in diagnosing and treating the illness. Where the hermeneutical approach makes believers the equivalent of their own doctors or at least the equal of doctors, the epistemological approach is prepared to ignore patients, not as a source of data but as a source of theory.

The epistemological approach to religion by no means presumes to have accounted for all of religion. It presumes only the potential to do so and, more, the obligation to do so. Where the duty of the hermeneut is to "appreciate" religion, the duty of the epistemologist is to account for it. The hermeneut does not assume that religion is true, only that it is distinctive, and that one must try to imagine what it is like to be religious. Conversation works when those engaged in it do their best to imagine what, from the religious point of view, the world is like. By contrast, the epistemologist, far from trying to imagine what it is like to be religious, presumes to know what it is like, for religion is simply an instance of the discipline from which the epistemologist hails. Diagnosis works exactly when the doctor recognizes symptoms as a case of a known disease.

Put another way, hermeneutics revels in difference; epistemology, in similarity. By no coincidence, Geertz and other advocates of a hermeneutical approach to culture emphasize the particularity of each culture:

> [T]he notion that the essence of what it means to be human is most clearly revealed in those features of human culture that are universal rather than in those that are distinctive to this people or that is a prejudice that we are not necessarily obliged to share. Is it in grasping such general facts—that man has everywhere some sort of "religion"—or in grasping the richness of this religious phenomenon or that—Balinese trance or Indian ritualism, Aztec human sacrifice or Zuni rain-dancing—that we grasp him? Is the fact that "marriage" is

universal (if it is) as penetrating a comment on what we are as the facts concerning Himalayan polyandry, or those fantastic Australian marriage rules, or the elaborate bride-price systems of Bantu Africa?[9]

To focus on the distinctiveness of each case of religion or of marriage is to set each apart. By contrast, the epistemological concentration is on each as a case of religion or of marriage—and in turn on religion and marriage themselves as cases of anthropological, sociological, economic, or psychological phenomena. Difference is not to be celebrated but to be overcome.

The hermeneutical approach isolates religion from the rest of life; the epistemological approach connects it to the rest of life. Where the hermeneutical approach "appreciates" religion as religion, the epistemological approach accounts for religion as something else—the only way that it, like anything else, can be accounted for. No more than any other phenomenon can religion generate itself.

The hermeneutical approach finds its advocates among those who cherish the mysteriousness, the inexplicability of religion. The epistemological approach finds its partisans among those who treasure the piercing of veils and the solving of puzzles. The superiority of the epistemological approach might seem obvious to all, but alas it is not.

---

[9] Ibid., p. 43.

CHAPTER NINE

ON "RELIGION" AND ITS DESPISERS

Ivan Strenski

Many Ways to Define "Religion"

Why is the question of the nature of religion an issue at all? Often practical constitutional, civil or judicial contexts call forth definition. When commentators contend as to whether the Heaven's Gate community was a "religion" or a "cult," the context of usage demands a definition. When a federal judge is petitioned by Baptist parents to declare civics classes "religious" indoctrination because they embody the teachings of the "religion" of Secular Humanism, the work of definition must proceed. Or when the Internal Revenue Service is asked to affirm Scientology's exemption from taxation on the basis of its being a religion, definitions are in order.

This is not to say that all demands for definition merit equal attention. Some of the contexts of use of the word, "religion," will be formally trivial and technically uninteresting. I open the Saturday *Los Angeles Times*, turn to the "religion" section, and find before me a massive list entitled "religious organizations." Here, I find everything from "Adventist" through "Baha'i" to "Ramakrishna Mission" and beyond. *These* are what "religions" are. No problem. But am I any the wiser for this ostensive definition of the term? Do I know why the items listed under the "religion" rubric are there, rather than some others. So, before we can ask about the definition of religion in salient senses, we need to eliminate those which are either formally trivial or technically uninteresting. This is also to say that the question of what the definition of religion *is* should really be analyzed as the question of how religion *should be* defined. What then is a salient definition of religion? Conspicuous by their absence from the *Los Angeles Times* list, for example, are entries of Roman Catholic churches! So, this sort of attempt to define religion proves both formally trivial and technically uninteresting. We would learn little by using the *Los Angeles Times* list to guide our thinking about the definition of religion, and indeed, because of the exclusion of Roman Catholics, we even would have been badly misled in our efforts so to do.

There are also other attempts to define religion which might be called "vulgar" because they are commonplace and/or uniformed. Here, we could also include common uses such as religion is belief in god. But again in response to this definition that religion is belief in superhuman beings or gods,[1] the further question may be asked why belief in god should count as a criterion for the use of the term, "religion." After all, there are many sorts of self-described "religious" folk, Buddhists for example, who are not theists.

Such ignorant, trivial or technically uninteresting types of definition are not, however, restricted to uninformed or common usage. They may also be found in the work of high-brow intellectuals, such as in neo-Orthodox Protestant theologian Karl Barth.[2] There, the apparent attempt to define "religion" yields to question-begging sophistic play. For Barth, "religion" is a kind of sin: it is humanity's attempt to grasp the (ungraspable for Barth) divine. Thus Barth says, that the religions are "attempts by man to justify and sanctify himself before a willfully and arbitrarily constructed image of God."[3] Or, in a passage that has become classic: "Religion is unbelief. Religion is a concern—the concern, one must say straightaway—of the Godless human being."[4] Put in other terms, Barth laments the gradual emergence of religion as "an independent known quantity alongside revelation" until at last "religion is not to be understood in terms of revelation but rather revelation in terms of religion."[5] Or, as Garrett Green notes in his defense of Barth: "The theological task at hand is therefore to establish the priority of revelation over religion without denying the religious nature of revelation."[6]

But in these ways Barth simply *evaluates* "religion," instead of *defining* it. Giving away the apologetic game, Barth later confuses the issues, despite assurances from Green, that "*the Christian religion is the*

---

[1] E. Thomas Lawson and Robert N. McCauley, *Rethinking Religion* (Cambridge: Cambridge University Press, 1990).

[2] For an interesting but perverse discussion of Barth on religion see Garrett Green, "Challenging the Religious Studies Canon: Karl Barth's Theory of Religion," *The Journal of Religion* 75 (1995), pp. 473-86.

[3] Karl Barth, *Church Dogmatics*, vol 1-2 edited by G. W. Bromiley and T. F. Torrance, translated by G. T. Thomson and Harold Knight (Edinburgh: T. & T. Clark, 1956), p. 280.

[4] Green, "Challenging the Religious Studies Canon," p. 480.

[5] Ibid., p. 478, citing Barth, *Church Dogmatics*, vol 1-2, p. 291.

[6] Ibid., p. 479.

true religion" (emphasis original).[7] Now Green immediately tries to qualify this apparently imperialistic Christian move, by arguing that Barth is only speaking in a pickwickian (or ironic/insincere?) sense about a "true" religion. Thus Christianity is only the "true religion" in the sense that humans are "justified sinners." This is at best to say that if Christianity is the "true" religion, it has nothing to do with the qualities of Christians or the institution called Christianity, but is solely dependent upon divine election and grace. Christianity is subject to divine judgment just like any other religion.[8]

Green's attempt to save Barth from exposing his imperialist intentions will, however, not do, since when confronted with religions of grace like Japanese Pure Land Buddhisms, Jodo and Jodo Shinshu, Barth declines to allow that they may qualify as "true religions"— even in the pickwickian sense that Christianity can. And why? Because they fail to be religions shaped by revelation; they fail to identify with the name of Jesus:

> Through the grace of God there are human beings who live by his grace. Or, stated concretely: through the name Jesus Christ there are human beings who believe in this name. To the extent that this is the self-understanding of Christians and of the Christian religion, it can and must be said of it that it and it alone is the true religion.[9]

Thus, since Christian religion is the only religion "*bound to God's revelation*"[10] in Jesus, it alone can be true. Thus after pages and pages of Green's labored exegesis of Barth, and after all the wriggling over Barth's dialectics, we are back where we started with Barth's original position! The man is indeed as vulgar an apologist as it seemed from the beginning. Religion is unbelief. I am frankly offended by this stunning display of bad faith, initiated by Barth's tortured dialectic and Green's defense of so transparent a piece of sophistry.

To see the Barthian plot exposed, all we need to do is ask some straightforward "Says-who?" questions of the "religions." Do the other religions think they are trying to grasp what to Barth's mind they are incapable of grasping? I hardly think so, since many of the great religions, such as Theravada Buddhism or the many schools of Vedanta, have sophisticated accounts of the limits of ordinary

---

[7] Green, "Challenging the Religious Studies Canon," p. 477, citing Barth, *Church Dogmatics*, p. 280.

[8] Green, "Challenging the Religious Studies Canon," p. 482, citing Barth, *Church Dogmatics*, pp. 326, 329.

[9] Green, "Challenging the Religious Studies Canon," p. 482, citing Barth, *Church Dogmatics*, p. 346.

[10] Green, "Challenging the Religious Studies Canon," p. 482, citing Barth, *Church Dogmatics*, p. 329 (emphasis original).

knowledge and human abilities—often long in advance of anything developed by Christian theologians. Do they feel that their religions are products of human construction in Barth's sense? Not as far as I know. People these days should surely know that Muslims are abundantly clear as to the divine origins of the Koran; Hindus see the Vedas as originating from beyond the human realm; the Buddhist dharma is likewise something transcending humankind and its history. Do they too not feel that revelation favors them rather than the Christ? Does the question even need to be asked? Do they even accept the ideal of revelation assumed by Barth as the measure of the ultimate worth of a religion? They do not—at least while remaining what they are. The parochialism and abject ignorance of advocates of the Barthian position is not only embarrassing, it is offensive to the dignity of the spiritual and religious lives of literally billions of fellow human beings. Thus, there is arguably more intellectual integrity in ordinary usage of a daily newspaper like the *Los Angeles Times*, than there is in the polemics of the leading Christian theologian of the twentieth century. So, let me return to ordinary usage for the moment.

The Wisdom of the Vulgar

In ordinary usage, and even for those who people our law offices, judicial courtrooms, legislative houses, public and parochial schools and such, there is no problem about identifying or listing the "religions," or for that matter even giving a formal definition of religion—and this without Barthian sophistry. The particular wisdom of ordinary usage lies in its reflecting a deep feature of the world in which we live. Thus, just as "everyone knows" what religion is, so also do we all know what "art," "politics," "language," "nation," "race," "sex," "privacy," "economics"—all the commonplaces of our culture—are. Part of what it is to live at our time and in our place is that "we" all assume insuperable authority to discourse on what these things are. We need no experts to tell us what is "art"; we just need to introspect. Our confidence—absolute or relative, well-founded or not—arises from the fact that these commonplaces are some of the larger categories which make up our lived-in world. As historic and civilizational creations, "we" are the kind of people who assume the reality of a world carved up along the lines represented by these sorts of distinctions—whatever the ultimate merits of this way of "cutting up the pie" are. What we are as a civilization in fact is the result of our having marked certain boundaries, featured certain things as different and others as the same—"church" versus "state," "politics" versus "economics." These distinctions simply make up our system of cultural *a prioris*. They constitute what we bring to our encounter with the world as surely as in other times and in other places others would take for granted notions like *gens, yajña, artha, dharma, li,* and such.[11]

In this sense of "religion" as a cultural apriori, it is probably already too late, and in any event beyond human will or effort, to reverse the segmenting of the human realm into one in which "religion" will occupy a space alongside politics, art, economics and the like. When Israelis speak of "religious" versus secular Jews, when the PRC along with many other nations establish ministries of religious affairs, when politicians, church-folk and scholars quarrel over whether Auschwitz-Birchenau should be classified as a "religious" site or museum site, when Pro-Life forces declare the "sacredness" of life, it is much too late to close the barn door on that wayward nag, "religion," now in full gallop down our cultural freeways. "Religion" is now, and for the foreseeable future will be, one of the ways people divide and categorize human experience, institutions and history. Moreover, if we are to believe political scientists like Harvard's Samuel Huntington in his recent book, *The Clash of Civilizations and the Remaking of the World Order* as well as Susanne Hoeber Rudolph and James Piscatori's work on the emergence of religion as one of the bases of "transnational civil society,"[12] it is not only too late to purge "religion" from our conceptual vocabularies, it is uncannily ill-timed too. Thus, far from being minor perturbations of our old political orbits, the new religiously informed conflicts and associations show the way forward to a new world of global conflict and co-operation based in part on religious identification.

This view of "religion" as a cultural *a priori* puts the question of the definition of religion into a context with questions we might also ask regarding the definition of "art," "politics," "language" and so on. If then we ask about the definition of "religion" we are asking a question like what is the definition of, say, "art." In this case, we are just as likely to get answers as satisfying or frustrating about the definition of "art" as for "religion." The lords of the theory class might profitably reflect on their irrelevance to cultural creation and cultural understanding at the level of mass human existence.

---

[11] To prove this we only need to refer to a nearly three decades old masterpiece of historical inquiry, Michel Despland's *La Religion en occident* to help us unravel the centuries old historical genesis of the term "religion."

[12] Susanne Hoeber Rudolph and James Piscatori (eds.), *Transnational Religion and Fading States* (Boulder, Colorado: Westview Press, 1997).

Toward a Theory of Religion: Becoming a Religion

Where then do I stand on this issue? Given the fact that religion is one of those larger social realities which exist beyond anything intellectuals control, how should we use, understand or conceive religion? One way to articulate a positive view would be to begin by opposing my approach to one which I feel manifests most of the errors afflicting the way we deal with this issue of defining religion.

I find myself particularly uncomfortable with the ways the matter of the definition of religion is often discussed, particularly by voices raised in the pages of MTSR (*Method and Theory in the Study of Religion*) among those I would call the NAASR (North American Association for the Study of Religion) group—Gary Lease, Russell McCutcheon and Tim Fitzgerald. I am "uncomfortable" with their work because of the nihilistic polemic which it embodies. I believe it is alternately an exercise in naivete, bad faith, or ignorant mischief, or indeed all of the above. They desire simply to dissolve the study of religion into cultural studies; the NAASR "gang" really wants to eliminate the study of religion from higher education—something Lease has already succeeded in doing by playing a part in the demise of an admittedly batty department of religious studies at the Santa Cruz campus of the University of California over a decade ago. Insofar, therefore, as these writings are taken seriously as representing anything more than the opinions of an inbred clique, their implementation would be a disaster for the study of religion.

These are strong charges. So let me defend them one at a time. Having done so, I will then show how much of my approach can be understood as a systematic negation of the theoretical efforts of the NAASR group. Tim Fitzgerald's writings can be cited as a *locus classicus* of the NAASR gang's approach, given not only its appearance in MTSR, but also his prominent place on the program of the 1997 NAASR annual meeting. I shall refer to Fitzgerald's lead article in a recent number of NAASR's own house organ, *Method and Theory in the Study of Religion*, "Critique of 'Religion' as a Cross-Cultural Category."[13]

Fitzgerald's Manifesto

Fitzgerald has many things to say in this programmatic piece, but for present purposes I will concentrate on those matters bearing on

---

[13] Timothy Fitzgerald, "A Critique of 'Religion' as a Cross-Cultural Category," *Method and Theory in the Study of Religion* 9/2 (1997), 91-110.

the definition and theory of religion. First, Fitzgerald believes that "religion" is "inadequate" as an analytic notion; it is "virtually useless as a cross-cultural analytic concept."[14] By this, he means that religion is not a distinct category of culture; it "picks out nothing distinctive and it clarifies nothing."[15] Second, Fitzgerald wants nonetheless to "represent and re-represent" what he takes to be the "important" work done by scholars in religious studies departments. Finally, Fitzgerald decries the complicity of the study of religion and the concept of religion in programs of (yawn) colonial domination. The problems generated by the concept of religion are not the result of some sort of "category mistake" or logical mishap, says the author. The currency of the term "religion" is a sinister "form of mystification generated by its disguised ideological function."[16]

Before beginning my critique of Fitzgerald, I must point out that his article seems less an argument than a litany of assertions and insinuations. It is a manifesto, a laundry list of misdirected complaints. I think this becomes clear when we note that where we expect reasoned polemic, we instead find additional declarations and further assertions, often made by appeal to their apparent self-evidence. Thus, Fitzgerald bares his post-structuralist breast and indicts "religion" for being "too deeply embedded in a legitimation process within western societies...to be successfully liberated from the semantic hold of liberal ecumenical theology."[17] A tall and fundamental claim in Fitzgerald's polemic to be sure. But what evidence does Fitzgerald give for this? None. He feels that it is sufficient to "suggest" as much and "argues" no further.

Perhaps most damning of all is that Fitzgerald flunks the "compared to what?" test. That is to say that throughout the entire discussion of analytic inadequacy, uselessness and such of "religion," Fitzgerald offers no standard of comparison by which we might judge his criticisms. I mean, is "religion" analytically useless in the same sense and in the same degree as, say, the terms "literature," "art," "culture" and such? On the face of it, I see no reason to single out "religion" *a priori* for being any more or less analytically useful than any of these other equally commonplace terms. Why light upon "religion" for failing to pick out a distinctive feature of culture, any more than, say, thinking that "culture" itself does? Are Fitzgerald's memories of the ideological baggage weighing down

---

[14] Ibid., p. 91.
[15] Ibid., p. 93.
[16] Ibid., p. 91.
[17] Ibid., p. 95.

"Kultur," "cul-chah" (as in "cul-cha, dahling"), "Zivilisation" or
"Civilisation" (as in "Mission civilsatrice") so dim? Why does "religion" uniquely fail to name a distinctive sub-category of culture
when one must assume, due to lack of comparative comment, "art"
does? Given this way of proceeding, why should not we just see
Fitzgerald's piece as a manifesto for a kind of prejudice? Fitzgerald
seems to answer by saying that his "argument" is that

> The study of cultures as institutionalized values and their relation to
> power, including the institutionalized values of our own academic
> praxis, is more likely to be sensitive to our own mystifying objectifica-
> tion of our own and other cultures than the present uncritical (sic) tra-
> dition of comparative study of religion. Indeed "religion" is part of
> our cognitive imperialism.[18]

Perhaps close reading of the literature on "culture" or "Kultur" and
its relation to colonialism might change Fitzgerald's mind?[19] The
problem is of course that Fitzgerald risks no "argument" at all; it is
just a flat assertion of prejudices, a fashion statement, a manifesto.

Fitzgerald's Manifesto "Cui Bono"?

If Fitzgerald's piece is then a manifesto, we should not be asking
questions about the intellectual merits of its absent arguments, but
about its political purposes. What Fitzgerald really wants is to de-
stroy religious studies. He tries to do this in effect by retrospectively
disinheriting the theologically-motivated and theologically-informed
Liberal Protestant ancestors of the study of religion as well as any of
their (knowing or unknowing) theological heirs.

First, Fitzgerald insists on dropping the term "religion"—what to
the Liberal Protestants was the key term of their intellectual vocabulary. Ironically, in their common attack on the discourse on "religion" of the liberals, Fitzgerald and the NAASR group also hop into
bed with Karl Barth and his right-wing theological crowd.

Second, Fitzgerald insists furthermore on the lack of reference of
the term, "religion"—especially the absence of transcendent reference. If the Liberal Protestants were about anything, they were certainly about a theological backdoor attempt to bring "God" back
into public discourse by means of a loaded and ultimately transcendent notion of religion. For them, religion was the *fact* of humanity's

---

[18] Ibid., p. 96.
[19] George W. Stocking, Jr., "Franz Boas and the Culture Concept in Historical
Perspective," in George W. Stocking, Jr, *Race, Culture and Evolution* (New York: Free
Press, 1968), pp. 195-233.

real relationship with God. To assert the reality of religion was to them to assert the reality of God.

Fitzgerald might have made an intellectual contribution had he written in the late Victorian period—a time when "religion" had something of the special ideological content which Fitzgerald senses. For them, "religion" was indeed essentially and necessarily good, apolitical, interior, theistic, spiritual and non-material and so on. But this sense of religion, even given its embrace by Eliade, is no longer what matters in religious studies—even though it lingers on. I certainly have been one of its most vociferous critics.[20] Significant in Fitzgerald's attacks upon these key features of the (theologically informed and motivated) study of religion inaugurated by the Liberal Protestants of the late nineteenth and early twentieth centuries and continued among crypto-theologians like Eliade, is Fitzgerald's failure to distinguish them from such anti-theological students of religion like other NAASR types, Donald Wiebe or Luther Martin, or from others like Jacob Neusner, Ninian Smart, Jonathan Z. Smith or myself for that matter. By failing to do so, Fitzgerald in fact indicts all of religious studies. So, while there is merit in showing where today's studies of religion depart (and ought to depart) from the basic theoretical assumptions of these Liberal Protestant theological ancestors, to banish the memory of these ancestors totally is to call for the elimination of the study of religion itself. This is really what Fitzgerald is about.

Now some so-called students of religion still hold onto these old theological principles of Liberal Protestantism, and I share Fitzgerald's indictment of them and their cryptic theological agendas hiding beneath the term "religion." But there is no practical or theoretical reason to indict non-theological studies of religion simply because they continue to use the term as well. Would Fitzgerald deal similarly with those colleagues of ours who march under the banner of "philosophy" because they persist in using a term long since out of joint with its original uses? So, if Fitzgerald wants to purify the lines of inheritance by calling attention to their crypto-apologetic efforts, that is fine and dandy with me. The problem with Fitzgerald is that he not only wants to throw out the baby with the bathwater, but to rip out the plumbing from the wall as well! This is unnecessary. The modern study of religion does not depend upon theological commitments—and Fitzgerald's belief that it does does not con-

---

[20] Ivan Strenski, "Lessons for Religious Studies in Waco?" *JAAR* 61 (1993), pp. 567-74.

stitute an argument in his own behalf. Even though the theologians continue to try to overwhelm religious studies, we are not "conceptually or institutionally dominated" by theology, as Fitzgerald blithely asserts—again without benefit of argument.[21]

The study of religion is not alone in the academy in striving to fight off being co-opted by its well-meaning ideological fellow-travelers. The modern study of religion struggles with theology in the same way today as sociology does with its fervent social activists, the way economics does with the legions of conservative market orthodoxy, the way political science departments do with the overwhelmingly liberal political commitments of its faculty, the way ethnic studies programs are under pressure to advance social and political agendas proper to certain elements of our "minority" communities. The entire university is under this self-censoring, corrupting partisan ideological pressure to serve the interests of the most powerful segments of their natural constituencies. Christian students want us to reassure them that Jesus is Lord, that God's in his heaven and all's right with the world. A great pity however is that other religious minorities are no different: they want their visions of reality legitimized by the affirmation of the academy. The enlightenment ideal of neutral inquiry, however much despised by post-structuralists like Fitzgerald, is still a radical principle, well worth the fight to preserve. It is this kind of populist political corruption of our duty to be even-handed in pursuit of the truth which represents the real danger to the intellectual integrity of the humanities, religious studies included—and not the language of "religion" however much it may have had a Liberal Protestant pedigree.

The modern study of religion does not suppose the reality of a transcendental referent of the term, "religion," any more than the study of art or literature requires that we believe in muses! The study of religion has been about the study of human phenomena for generations. Nor does the study of religion require a univocal referent—some "thing" called "religion"—anymore than the study of economics requires the existence of a "thing" called "The economy," anymore than the study of art demands the existence of a single "thing" called "art," and so on. Although Fitzgerald panics when he has to deal with the idea of "family resemblances," all sorts of scholars have learned to live with ambiguities, with fuzzy logics, if you will, and furthermore to produce rich scholarship despite the

---

[21] Timothy Fitzgerald, "A Critique of 'Religion' as a Cross-Cultural Category," p. 97.

absence of "clear and distinct ideas" in their conceptualizations or concrete foundations under their feet. In fact, where is Fitzgerald's evidence that good work in the humanities needs to meet his requirements? Who are his heroes? Does Fitzgerald really think the epigones of cultural studies, the Derridas of this world, represent any kind of improvement over what has gone before? What kind of work would Fitzgerald hold up as indicative of the benefits of the standards he praises?

Two Cheers for Autonomy

Now since both Fitzgerald and I have passed over the matter of a univocal sense of "religion" as important in matters bearing on a theory of religion, I would like to take it up now. Like many other disciplines, the study of religion depends upon there being some, however rough and ready, referent to a term like "religion." Is there art history without some sort of shared sense, however open and subject to constant revision, of what art is? Is their political science without some agreement about what politics is, and so on? Once again however we must wonder why Fitzgerald makes an exception for religion. Why does he require more of religion than he does of any other of the great segments into which the human world is, however temporarily, divided? So, while the Liberal Protestants were mistaken (as far as I believe the requisites of a "science of religion" are concerned) in identifying the referent of "religion" with a transcendent person or thing, they were right in expecting that the term "religion" would both be analytically useful and have a referent or family of referents. I believe that the Liberal Protestants were correct in building science of religion upon the assumption of there being some sort of referent, however loosely we might now demarcate that class of referents according to contents that shift with different contexts of time and space.

I say this because by assuming there to be this "thing," it let them focus on subjects, events, times and places which otherwise would never have been seen in such illuminating ways. For all their failings, the Liberal Protestants are to be admired for pressing on with the job of constructing a science of religion—however we have had to revise it in subsequent years—rather than to make matters of so-called "method and theory" the stuff of the study of religion. Was it not better that the early Liberal Protestant buddhologues mistakenly tried to force the Buddha onto a Procrustean bed fashioned in the image and likeness of Jesus than perhaps passing over the Buddha entirely? Likening Buddhism to Protestantism and Hinduism to

Roman Catholicism has generated numerous errors. But had they not been compared at all as religions, they would never have forced us to revise and define the nature of their relationship more subtly. The study of religion has made mistakes, and will make more, and sometimes because of assuming a theologically grounded notion of "religion," but Fitzgerald has not shown that we can proceed to understand anything without making assumptions and mistakes, or that his subsumption of religion to some generic "culture" cum "values" cum "power" will be as fruitful as the comparative study of religion has been. I know, however, that we know a great deal more than ever before about other people because our intellectual ancestors chose to look at them through the lens of "religion." A bird in the "hand" of "religion" is worth far more than the flock supposedly fluttering around Fitzgerald's "bush." In this sense, that the official academic journal of NAASR should be *Method and Theory in the Study of Religion*, rather than a journal about "religion," is a telling enough symptom of the malaise afflicting both Fitzgerald and some of his NAASR colleagues. Do they imagine that one day a Prince Charming of theories of religion will arrive to fulfill their theoretical dreams of a scientific study of religion? Do they imagine that if they wait just a little longer this Prince Charming of theories will win the day and lay before them a way of doing the study of religion so superior to whatever has come before that all will bow down in acknowledgement of his lordship? Fond hope. Let me instead "suggest," *pace* Fitzgerald, that an addiction to criticism and a fear of risking a notion of religion or a method of doing the study of religion—which one day may have to be revised or falsified—keeps the likes of Fitzgerald idling their intellectual engines.

A final measure of either the naivete or stupidity of this extreme eliminationist position is Fitzgerald's endearing hope that he will have graduated to the land of analytic utility in dumping religion for such paragons of clarity and analytic power as "culture" and "values."[22] Russell McCutcheon even proposes that we replace "religion" with a barbarism of remarkable infelicity—"authorizing practices."[23] That these are better able to provide the kind of cross-cultural power and universality not possible with the term, "religion" is ludicrous. Fitzgerald complains that "religion" is disqualified as a cross-cultural comparative notion because of its western origins. But, how could he overlook the fact that terms like "cul-

---

[22] Ibid., pp. 96, 105.
[23] Russell McCutcheon, personal correspondence, July 1996.

ture" and "value" are just as much originated in the West as is "religion" and are far vaguer to boot? In fact the only way to make
these vague notions, "culture" and "value" informative is to qualify
them specifically—as political, artistic or yes, even religious. We
can point out and contrast, for example, to good effect the "esthetic" versus the "religious" *values* of, say, forms of kitsch or popular
art. Does it not clarify matters greatly to observe, for example, that
while cheap Hindu religious posters may have low "esthetic" to
"economic" value, they may nonetheless have highest "religious"
value? And, only an ignoramus would not know why and how this
were so: calling such a poster "religious" makes it perfectly clear
(and perfectly effective for the purposes of singling out a distinct
use) that such a poster serves the purposes of worship of a god or
goddess, devotion to a life defined by absolute valuations or meditation upon a transcendental realm. So much for Fitzgerald's belief
that dissolving religion into culture and value achieves anything
useful in cultural analysis.

One can only assume that Fitzgerald's inability to appreciate why
it might be useful in understanding people to separate out—although not absolutely—their religious versus their esthetic attitudes
and behavior indicates to me Fitzgerald's tone deafness to religion
combined with an allergic reaction against anything called "religion." This is why one can say that he repeatedly flunks the "compared to what" case, and rather simply carries on a vendetta against
religion. If this is not true then why is he not even-handed in his
treatment of all our categories of inquiry? For surely what he claims
to be true of "religion" is true in equal measure of all the central notions of the humanities and human sciences. What is so precise and
analytically powerful about terms such as culture, society, art, literature, politics and such? "Religion" fits right in with this vocabulary
of rough and ready conceptual language. No better, no worse.
Fitzgerald simply does not like "religion."

This is so, one must surmise, because Fitzgerald, McCutcheon
and others are just unwilling to accept any kinship with at least the
liberal Jewish and Christian theologians, who in their own blunder-
ing and often insincere ways—as I have amply indicated in my critique of Barth, no liberal to be sure—nonetheless invented a remarkable discipline—the study of religion. In this sense, I would
reaffirm my place in the lineage of the kind of religious studies orig-
inally practiced by the Liberal Protestants—but as their radical re-
former, their loyal opposition. Fitzgerald and many in the NAASR
crowd are so embarrassed by this potential affiliation that they need
to cut themselves off, root and branch, from the founders. But in

doing so, Fitzgerald and the NAASR crowd either imagine that they can do without lineages or in time will adopt another.

Getting On with the Job

This then brings me to part of my paper where I shall argue for a certain articulation and identification of the referent of the term, "religion." Here is why I believe in the future of "religious studies," and in doing so why I think something going by the name "religion" is a most fascinating and challenging area of study.

Consider some events which we generally pass over without duly appreciating what they may portend in terms of the nature of the larger ontological categories into which the human realm is segmented.

Let us consider a relatively uncontroversial example, but one with ever increasing importance in today's post-Cold War world of mass communication and globalization. How are we to look on the reinvigoration, for example, of Muslim identity in the "modern" world? Yes, "it" has always been there—at least in theory, like the common "Christian" identity of masters and slaves in the American South—but it has not been, for all that, an actualized mode of identification. What then has happened when Egyptians, Nigerians, Pakistanis, Turks, Indians, Indonesians, Iranians, Bosnians and Louis Farrakhan—all living, for example, in metropolitan Chicago—come to think of themselves primarily as Muslims and begin to act accordingly for what they define as their common interests? They need not abandon their various and often antagonistic national identities in the process. But they see themselves as being somehow strongly bonded with these one-time enemies, strangers or indifferent neighbors. They assume a whole constellation of understandings and intimacies which marks the boundaries of "us" against some other "them." This "something" in the case I use here is what I mean by "religion." The nature of mutual identification consists in a whole universe of shared beliefs and practices bearing on the transcendent and worshipful god, Allah; they share rigorous moral norms and social institutions which single them out as devoted to giving a certain kind of absolute or transcendent meaning to their lives. And, what matters above all—they embrace this meaning.

Now although this identification may look like others we may want to name—economic, cultural or political, for instance—something else is going on besides the pursuit of economic gain, political power or the colorless activity of making "culture." These identifications are clearly not ethnic either, given the vast and obvious differences in the constituent groups mentioned. What draws these folk together across national, ethnic, class, and other boundaries is their *religion*. They are drawn together for common worship of a common transcendent god; they aspire eventually at least once in their lives to do pilgrimage to Mecca; they bow in prayer daily and voice the same beliefs; they pledge themselves to (at least a family of) legal and institutional restraints. They, in short, share a common religion.

Consider a second, somewhat unfamiliar, example. What precisely has transpired in terms of cultural or social ontology when out of the existence of a few beliefs about the nature of human history and knowledge propounded by Auguste Comte and which we call "positivism," there comes to be a social institution, still found today in Brazil, called the Church of Positivism? I answer that a "religion" *has come to be*. This Church is defined by social institutions, actual buildings and physical property, a clergy, a set of sharply defined beliefs, a program of prescribed rituals, a group of adherents. Perhaps some, like Fitzgerald, might want to call this a "cultural," "social" or "affinity" group because it has a collective nature organized around certain shared interests. Or, because issues of power arise here as they do in every human group, we might call this a "political" society? Or, because the architecture of the churches tends to a highly refined standard, we might say that this is a society which patronizes art. But, if we are willing to grant any or all of these possible descriptions, why not call it a "religion"? Why not do so especially when adherents of this church are doing something special, and not other things? The things that they do are not primarily economic activities like an "investment club" might do. They spend their time publically professing dedication to lofty and transcendent ideals— not to scanning the *Wall Street Journal*. Although they do politics, that is to say, although they may endorse candidates or vote as a block in elections, they themselves do not enter their church's name on a ballot. Likewise, this church is not an arts organization: they subordinate the utility of their architectural creations to the purpose of reinforcing the belief and values which they profess, rather than making architecture an end in itself. Thus, in something like the Church of Positivism, there is a special mode of social organization—something with distinguishable functions of ritual worship, personal edification, spiritual culture and not simply esthetic, political or generically social—but some rather peculiar form of social organization which can interestingly be called "religion." Although I have selected the unusual example of the Brazilian Church of Positivism, I am prepared to make the same sort of argument for other social "things" we now call "religions." All of the seven separate dimen-

sions of religion laid out by Smart may exist independently or in relation to other social formations. But when they are clustered into
an interactive social complex in some sort of tension with other sub-
systems of a given society, we have what is usefully called a "religion."

Let me finally introduce a fourth and final example to see how
"religion" emerges, but here in the case of something ceasing to be a
"religion." Thus, obversely, what has been *eliminated* when Yoga becomes nothing more than another member of the suburban diet and
exercise industry? What has transpired when Yoga loses its metaphysics, its projection of a transcendent world, its lineages of teachers, its sacred language and cosmology, its elaborate rituals, or when
it retains some of these in corrupted or ignorant form, such as the
practice of some health and fitness yoga instructors to ape Hindu
manners and language? I think that at least one of the more informative things we can say is that yoga in this context has ceased
being a "religion."

We can also observe similar changes of social ontological conditions in the realm of politics. What has transpired, what has been
lost when, say, the British Liberal Party became little more than a
debating society or gentleman's club? What happened when it faded
away at the turn of the century, only to be re-invented as a political
entity in the 1980's, later to be merged into the Alliance? I would
say that as we can see things ceasing to be religions, in the case of
the old British Liberal party we witnessed an organization ceasing to
be political. What also for the passings to and fro between politics
and religion, in particular, of the Rosicrucians or Masons in its
many national forms such as the Franc-Maconnerie?

Given these examples of my cross-culturally comparative use of
"religion," how is this language then "analytically useless," to echo
Fitzgerald? Indeed, contrary to what Fitzgerald asserts (but never
proves) "religion" makes an excellent comparative notion in understanding the cases I lay out. For yoga and positivism are not just any
kind of generic cultural phenomenon; nor are they particular phenomena of, say, a distinctly political, musical, artistic or economic
sort. What is so terribly imperialistic about calling them then "religion"? In their concern with serious, even transcendent issues and
experiences, in their absolutism, in their interrelation of doctrines,
rituals, social institutions, ethical schemae and the like, what else
should they be called?

What I aim to underline in my examples is that the main item miss-
ing in almost all definitions (or attempted eliminations) of religion is
an appreciation of religion as a compound, complex and dynamic his-

torical and social reality. Religions are peculiar types of social realities which come and go, pass and linger. As social realities, there is nothing particularly mysterious about them. Ninian Smart's view of religions as being composed of "dimensions" comes closest to the view I wish to elaborate, and indeed is one of the main inspirations of it.

Let me now advance a few theses in connection with my view of "religion." First, I shall invoke a principle of relative autonomy: "religion" names (and should name) a special mode of human social activity and organization, but no more or less so than "art," "politics" and the like. This means that "religion" is relatively thing-like, such that it makes sense to speak adjectivally of "religious" institutions like the Sangha along the same lines as it does to speak of "political" institutions like "kingship." When I say that this autonomy is "relative" I mean therefore that the Sangha may well play roles we could call "political," such as in the recent "troubles" in Sri Lanka or during the Viet Nam war, just as the kingship, say, of Ashoka as Chakravartin or Louis XIV as Most Catholic Monarch could as well have been said to have been "religious."

Second, religions are compounds. By this I mean that we should only speak of a "religion" as a substantive where we can say that simpler cultural units have "crystallized" into a unity of some sort. There is no end to our speaking of this or that as "religious"—in the adjectival sense—as "religion-like" or as "suggesting aspects of a religion," and so on. But we should only speak of a substantive, "religion," when we can say that a certain level of cultural coherence has occurred. Thus, today among some of our African-American neighbors the feast or ritual of Kwanzaa is celebrated, much as the Lupercal or Kalends were celebrated in ancient Rome. While recognizing these as festivals, rites or ceremonies, I would only want to speak of a distinctly African-American "religion" in connection with Kwanzaa, if it were compounded with other features or "dimensions" as Smart has discussed. To wit, does a church, order, lineage or society begin to form around Kwanzaa? Is there a priesthood or other ritual institutionalizations associated with it? Does Kwanzaa call forth dogmas or an ethical code or become the venue of particular kinds of special experiences? If these should begin to happen, then I think we would have the right to speak of Kwanzaa being or becoming a religion. However, on their own, not linked with these other "dimensions," they are just part of the extravagant flourishing of unrooted cultural forms that come and go with vicissitudes of human history.

In my view, a "religion" is that social entity which comes into being when diverse or dispersed cultural forms are brought under the command and control of an overarching system. Theravada Buddhism, for example, is not simply the adherence to the Four Noble Truths or the Eightfold Path. The "religion" of Theravada Buddhism is not just a matter of ideas and ethics, as our nineteenth century predecessors felt; it is those together with the institution of the Sangha, the rich yogic experiential life of meditating monks, the cycle of calendrical rites, the veneration of relics and construction of stupas, as well as the cult of the devatas.

A "religion" is moreover all of these dimensions taken together with other features in a condition of dynamic interaction. The dimensions of Buddhism, like the "texts" of post-structuralism referring to other texts, "refer" to other dimensions of religion. One dimension takes its meaning and purposes from others within the Buddhist constellation. Rituals such as monastic begging reinforce *dogmas* of selflessness and detachment. Experiences of emptiness resonate with vows of poverty and material simplicity, with the refined austerity of the shaven head of the bhikkhu, with purity of some of Theravadin architecture such as in the simple white stupas seen everywhere in these countries.

Just how these aspects or dimensions become associated is still largely unknown. But we can get some idea of how and perhaps why "religions" came into being from considering some well understood features of the evolution of Christianity such as Peter Brown discusses in a recent work.[24] The short answer is that religions are voracious and somewhat imperialist social formations which "accrete" elements from their environment. Consider sacredness as a prime example. In the ancient world (as indeed it seems today among the devotees of the New Age), sacredness was deployed everywhere—in the sun and moon, in tree and plants of special kinds, in rocks, springs and mountains—in short in any place the spiritual imagination of people wanted to locate or find the sacred. What "religions" tend to do is co-opt, concentrate, monopolize or take command of undisciplined growths of spirituality, and in doing so link them systematically with other of what Smart calls the "dimensions." For these early Latin Catholics, the sacredness imputed to these diverse forms came under the command of the high God. Only He is sacred. Either the worshippers of the sun are wrong in calling the sun sacred, or if it is sacred, it is only so because of the One God. He

---

[24] Regarding the origin of Catholic cults of relics as replacements for non-Christian nature worship, see Peter Brown, *The Rise of Western Christendom* (Oxford: Blackwell, 1996), pp. 108-11.

then demands certain ethical and ritual behaviors, calls forth architectural forms, and inspires certain transcendent experiences—in
short is linked to all the range of phenomena described by Smart in
his talk of the "dimensions" of religion.

Why?

In conclusion, I believe that it is worthwhile and especially compelling today to speak of these clusterings of phenomena as relatively distinctive, and as "religions." These social formations have been
recognized historically as unusual, distinctive and special. A world
organized around such units as Christendom, the Dar al-Islam, the
people of Israel, the Buddhashasana and so on, differs from one organized around nation-states or multinational corporations—despite
their sometimes religious character. Indeed, one of the puzzles of
contemporary life is to understand how the organization of peoples
into nation-states and/or corporations articulates with the way people increasingly identify themselves today *transnationally* as Jews,
Buddhists, Christians, Hindus and so on—either over against their
national identities or in some combination with them. Susanne
Hoeber Rudolph argues that "modern social science did not warn
us that" these transnational identifications would arise.

> Instead it asserted that religion would fade, then disappear, with the
> triumph of science and rationalism. But religion has expanded explo-
> sively, stimulated as much by secular global processes—migration,
> multinational capital, the media revolution—as by proselytizing acti-
> vity. Contrary to expectations, its expansion has been an answer to
> and driven by modernity. In response to the deracination and threats
> of cultural extinction associated with modernization processes, reli-
> gious experience seeks to restore meaning to life. [25]

Now it has been the argument of my paper that we cannot even
begin to come to terms with these curious and troublesome modes
of identification if we continue to insist on eliminating "religion"
from the options available. On the face of it, at the very least, people
are identifying themselves in ways which are not strictly speaking
only ethnic, political, economic and so on, but as belonging to something in tension with these "secular" identifications—something referring variously to absolutes and transcendence rather than to prag-

---

[25] Susanne Hoeber Rudolph "Introduction: Religion, States, and Transnational
Civil Society" in Rudolph and Piscatori (eds.), *Transnational Religion and Fading States*,
p. 1.

matics and compromise. I must confess not knowing why they do so. But, their doing so strikes me as intensely interesting—so much so that it is worth setting aside as a field of definite study. I have always thought that the career of science to which I am above all committed called me to try to make sense of the world, and not to wish it were otherwise than it is.

CHAPTER TEN

WHAT ON EARTH IS RELIGION?

James Wiggins

In his *Confessions* St. Augustine remarked that he knew what time is—until someone asked him. He demonstrates the difficulty by a verbal exercise that suggests that past, present and future are ephemeral and that the reality of time is mysterious, indeed. At this time in my life, after many years of teaching in the field of the academic study of religion, I have a similar difficulty regarding the question of what religion really is. My dismay and discomfort have grown as I have sat down on four previous occasions with every intention to write this reflection piece. Each time I have hit a wall comprised of additional questions and uncertainties. One solution to this dilemma would be to hope that nobody ever again asks me the question and that the editors of this volume would forget ever having asked me to contribute to it. That might enable me to avoid further consternation. However, given that I have been a professor in a department of religion in a university for thirty-five years, and will be for a while longer, I rather imagine that I shall yet again hear the question. And I will, doubtless, be made aware yet again, as I try to respond to it, how uncertain I am regarding what to say in response. And it is in fact also embarrassing to be in this predicament in contrast to colleagues who work in other areas of study who seem to have a firm hold on the subjects that they study and teach.

It is not that I am unaware of at least some of the history of attempts to define religion. Some purchase on the project has been made through the insights offered by thinkers of many different stripes—philosophers, sociologists, anthropologists, psychologists, philosophers, poets, and even theologians and some scholars of religion are among those who have worried the question. And I am aware that there is a near consensus among scholars in the field that the term "religion" is a product of the academy, a term created to facilitate a conversation regarding what we intend to study from our several different perspectives and out of our many approaches or methods. I have been very influenced by the approach referred to as "History of Religion," which has helped us identify certain constituent dimensions of religion: myth, ritual, belief, ethics, etc. But, knowing at least that much, about which I am capable of expounding for long periods of time *ad nauseam*, and about which I have written on several occasions in the past,[1] I still hear the haunting question: what really is religion?

In my scholarly work of the last several years I have tried to make virtue of the fact of diversity,[2] a phenomenon that more and more sensitive people recognize to be characteristic of every aspect of life in the world. The more value people place on an experience, a person, a relationship, an idea—the more diverse seem to be our ways of expressing its meaning and significance. For example, recent efforts to universalize the notion of "human rights" have come forcefully up against the realities of what anthropologists have long tried to teach us about cultural relativism. What is accepted as a human right in one culture is not always so accepted in others. Then what? Shall one culture and its values be forced upon all others by any means available? The histories of imperialism and missionizing certainly offer their respective cautionary tales regarding the price of those strategies. Military, economic, ideological power create forms of "might" that are often marshaled to try to impose "right" upon recalcitrant others, but even if relatively successful in the short term, these efforts rarely survive long-term. The sun long ago sat on the British Empire, as it has sooner or later upon every previous other political empire, whether occidental or oriental, and the jury is out on whether the widely celebrated and cherished democratic capitalism will last indefinitely.

The time has arrived on the world historical scene and within the shores of these United States when the conventional notions of what count as "religion" simply must become more expansive and elastic than ever before in human history. No longer will it suffice in our efforts to understand and define religion to confine our attention to only the multiple and millennia-old religious traditions that still in the eyes of many people, including some scholars, are the only legitimate embodiments of religion: ones like Hinduism, Buddhism, Confucianism (perhaps), Shinto, Judaism, Christianity and Islam. At this moment five years have elapsed since the siege on the compound near Waco, Texas, by the forces of the United States government. The Branch Davidians challenged the official consensus re-

---

[1] During the decade of the 1980's I was invited on several occasions to write on the subject "religion," and related issues, for a number of publications. At that time I suffered little reticence on the subject and attempted to be quite definite in what I wrote.

[2] Cf. my *In Praise of Religious Diversity* (New York: Routledge, 1996).

garding what legitimately counts as "religion" and men, women and children paid with their lives. So the conflicts between Hindus and Sikhs, Hindus and Muslims, Jews and Muslims, Catholics and Buddhists, Catholics and Protestants are not just barbarous events in far off India, or Pakistan, or Vietnam, or Ireland. The reality of diversity and the obligations attendant to determining how to live within that reality are now to be found in most of the cities and many of the towns and villages of these United States of America. The USA is now the site not only of European immigrant religions but also of many other flourishing diaspora religious traditions that also originated in other cultures and that must themselves now learn how to accommodate to and acculturate themselves in a context in which freedom of religious expression and affiliation is constitutionally guaranteed and vigorously defended. And the one thing clear about this necessity is they will be different in this context than they were where they originated. But then what on earth is religion if it can shift its shape, change and adapt in such extensive ways?

In a recently broadcast interview played on National Public Radio, a devout Sufi Muslim who daily works in the streets of Cairo attempting to communicate his religious views contrasted his understanding of religion with his understanding of the dominant Sunni tradition in Egypt. The Sufi teacher said, "The essence of religion is love, piety, mercy and forgiveness." That's all he said. No requirement of doctrinal purity; ritual participation recommended, but surely to be misleading in some ways; no elaborate ethical code being expounded—in short, few of the elements that many scholars insist must be emphasized to have a "complete" religion. It is my growing suspicion that many people for whom "religion" is experientially alive and well would in large measure agree with the Sufi teacher.

Further, I suspect there to be a clue in this about how little influence the academic study of religion appears to have exerted on the practice of religion around the world. I have had the great good fortune in my professional contacts in this field to be personally acquainted with many, many scholars who have devoted themselves to the academic study of religion. And in my teaching in a research university during most of that same period after I completed my own graduate studies, I have by now taught thousands of students in elementary, introductory courses to sophisticated Ph.D. courses. Only rarely have I become aware of our work as scholars in this field having any appreciable direct influence on the conduct and practice of institutional religion. The few exceptions to that comment have most frequently emanated from the work of either Biblical studies or from some novel theological offering. But then it must be noted that many scholars of religion express doubts about whether Biblical studies or theological studies, at least as they are sometimes conducted from a confessional faith perspective, rightfully belong in the academic study of religion.

Of course it may matter very little that discernible influence on the practice of religion emanates from the study of religion in the academy. After all, we seek to understand "religion," not to practice it. We declare interest in seeing the world as it is, not in changing it. And it is conceivable, even if quite unlikely, that many practitioners and devotees within religious traditions have a deep and sophisticated understanding of religion, but nonetheless demonstrate little or no evidence of that understanding in their practices.

These latter considerations lean directly into the issue of the relationship between what people think and believe, on the one hand, and what they do and how they behave, on the other hand. The idealist strand in philosophical thinking in the west has long championed the view that theory, insight, and understanding are the grounds and bases for genuinely ethical actions. People should think before they act. They should consider the grounds upon which they are standing before they make a move. So deeply entrenched is this tradition of thinking in most of us that we often take for granted the accuracy of the priority of theory before action. But, alas, much of the rest of the world proceeds quite differently—people act and then, perhaps, become reflective about what kind of understanding they were enacting. Thinking and understanding in this case come *ex post facto*—if at all. Further, even if the conventional notion of the priority of thinking over action is accepted, there remains the intractable problem of inconsistency between what people say they believe and how they choose to act.

Perhaps a partial account for the distance between religion on the ground and the study of religion in the classroom lies in the temptation of scholars to oversimplify the very complex phenomena of religion. We who are deeply invested in the academic study of religion often regard the efforts of scholars outside the field, whose specialties fall in sociology, anthropology, history, psychology, et al., as "reductionistic." Their accounting for only one or just a few dimensions of religion, as if that were sufficient to achieve understanding of religion is severely criticized as deficient and inadequate. But suppose it were the case that in different ways we who are engaged in the academic study of religion fall into similar predicaments and inadvertently become reductionists ourselves? I have been challenged by Paul Tillich to reconsider some of these things as I have worked on this piece. I refer to his book *What is Religion?*

From his cryptic assertion that religion is to be understood as ultimate concern in relation to Ultimate Reality (the Unconditional),
Tillich draws some very trenchant observations. He argues that
"every statement about the Unconditional must necessarily appear
in the form of paradox. Aesthetic and logical paradoxes are in principle resolvable...But the paradox of the Unconditional is not resolvable."[3] He continues: "...a philosophy of religion which stands apart
from the religious reality is as absurd as an aesthetic unrelated to the
actual world of art."[4] I am proceeding on the assumption that what
holds for a philosophy of religion holds no less for any other approach or method that intends in its productions to take religion seriously. But, alas, it is far from clear that many scholars in the academic study of religion actually intend to take religion seriously.
Would most of us in the field recognize a religious event, were one
to occur directly before us? Tillich judges that many attempts to get
at "religion" have failed precisely because they have reduced it to
one or another autonomous subjective function of human beings.
The net result of that reductive move is to create what is really a
derogatory term; "religion" comes to indicate "that inferior quality
within religion which consists in its failure to go beyond the subject
(human beings)."[5] The point is clear. Humans are necessarily and
without remainder complicit in the appearance of religion in the
world, but if only what humans contribute to that process is the sole
focus of scholarly attention, then an inadequate and false understanding of religion must inevitably result. Might it be the case that
at least some scholars committed to the academic study of religion
have led themselves and their students to the same dead end, even
though we are very astute in identifying the ways in which scholars
working in other fields have falsified religion?

So the challenge seems to be how we humans who exercise our
vocation as professors of religion, especially in this Enlightenment-
fevered western tradition, can at once retain our place in the academy and simultaneously avoid falsifying the very thing we intend to
elucidate. Our linguistic forms and subject-object modes of thinking
pull us in certain directions; our intuitions, and, sometimes, our experience draw us in another. Coupled with the paradox imposed by
"religion," i.e., when you objectify it you almost certainly do not

---

[3] Paul Tillich, *What is Religion?*, in an essay entitled "The Conquest of the Concept of Religion in the Philosophy of Religion" (New York: Harper & Row, 1969),
p. 123.
[4] Ibid., p. 123.
[5] Ibid., p. 127.

have it within your intellectual nets, is the deep ambivalence imposed within us by the distance imposed between our experience and our difficulties in thinking and speaking out of that experience.

And yet, the story of every religious tradition is in some measure the story of such efforts and the difficulties against which every such effort sooner or later encounters. We cannot speak adequately of these matters and yet speak apparently we must. All such efforts will be marked by tentativity and will be susceptible to constant revisitation and correction in light of new experience and in response to conversation with others engaged in attempting to articulate their ever expanding experience. But such conversations must also provide a place for those of us engaged in the academic study of religion, if only because we are those who have contributed to the emergence of "religion" as a concept and as multiple theories. We need such conversations to test theories and to harvest the testimonies of those engaged in the practice of religion on the ground. Both will benefit from such engagements and both, with a bit of generosity of mind and heart, will have great opportunities to learn from each other.

That every religion fails in some respects is a given; that every scholarly effort to understand religion is deficient in some respects is self-evident. But, perhaps even more important is the lesson that taken together all the religious traditions about which we are able to learn anything at all constitute what Jacob Neusner has named—"humanity's heritage of aspiration...a vision of what we are and what we can become."[6] Every such mapping activity, from the most soaring assumptions of transcendence to the radically secularized post-modern insistence that surface is all that humans have available, and every permutation between them—all express the human need and desire for meaning in our lives.

Of the making of books there was for millennia no end in sight. In these days of the electronic revolution and postmodernist assertions that the book is closed, the verdict is out in some unprecedented ways. But given the affinity of many religious traditions with texts and books, it seems highly likely that books will remain staples in both the practice and the study of religious traditions for some time into the future. The study of religion spawns many books aimed at expressing insight into the beliefs, practices, and actions of adherents

---

[6] Jacob Neusner, "Why Study Religion?" a lecture sponsored by the Religious Studies Program of the University of Wyoming, April 7, 1997, p. 8 of the text from the Internet.

of one or several religious traditions. Against the grain of what I have presented throughout this essay, Daniel Pals in his *Seven Theories of Religion*[7] concludes that the authors of the theories that he examines–Tylor\Frazer, Freud, Durkheim, Marx, Eliade, Evans-Pritchard, and Geertz–in fact share a definition of religion. It is this: "religion consists of belief and behavior associated in some way with a supernatural realm, a sphere of divine or spiritual beings."[8] Such a consensus, assuming it can be established, surely demands careful consideration, given the eminence of the scholars whose theories are examined by Pals.

It must be acknowledged that listening to the people who self-identify as being religious is one of the virtues of the theorists whom Pals cites. That is to say that in ordinary language, the kind that finds its way into dictionary definitions, almost anywhere one looks one finds reference to "a system of beliefs and practices relative to superhuman beings."[9] Many scholars find this definition too restrictive, however, precisely because of reference to "superhuman beings." In excluding such phenomena as political and socio-economic systems from the definition it seems to confine religion to those institutionalized forms borne by the major religious traditions, excluding even Buddhism due to its "atheism." But surely much disagreement remains among scholars in the larger field of the academic study of religion.

So we come in the end to the place of our beginnings. What on earth is religion? We often seem to get further in our efforts to say what it is not than we do in our saying what it is. We who spend our lives studying religion know full well that there is an important distinction between what we do in our teaching and scholarly work and what people do who are identified as being "religious." The lure of somehow saying more than "religion is not this and is not that" calls forth many responses. And every serious response is worthy of being extended the most generous attention we can give it. For professors and students alike the journey of exploration of the question is likely more significant and meaningful than would be any place of arrival. And it keeps "religion" lively, both as studied and as lived, never to be satisfied with any resting place, as if it were final. Kafka long ago saw this when he wrote in one of his parables that "our destination is away from here."

---

[7] *Seven Theories of Religion* (New York: Oxford University Press, 1996).
[8] Ibid., p. 270.
[9] Jonathan Z. Smith (ed.), *The Harper Collins Dictionary of Religion* (San Francisco: HarperCollins, 1995), p. 893.

CHAPTER ELEVEN

FROM THE LEXICAL TO THE POLYTHETIC:
A BRIEF HISTORY OF THE DEFINITION OF RELIGION

Brian C. Wilson

Throughout my graduate education in Religious Studies, my in-structors continually impressed upon me the impossibility of defining "religion." Indeed, its indefinability was almost an article of method-ological dogma. When seminar conversations inevitably came around to the question of definition, students were often politely re-ferred to Max Weber's *Sociology of Religion* and his famously cautious approach to the definitional problem. "To define 'religion,' to say what it *is*, is not possible at the start," Weber argued: "Definition can be attempted, if at all, only at the conclusion of the study."[1] Thus it came as somewhat of shock when I later encountered those in the field who just as vociferously argued the opposite, contending that Weber's definitional strategy made little sense either method-ologically or pedagogically. As one scholar of religion put it, "if in principle we cannot determine what religion is, then we cannot de-termine what it is not, and if this were the case there would be no point in studying it."[2] And further, if "religion" corresponds to no definable object of study, how then can we justify an autonomous field devoted to "religious" studies?

Such is the on-going definitional debate in the academic study of religion. Regardless of where one stands in this debate, however, it is obvious that defining religion has been, and still is, one of the more popular pursuits in the field—a fact attested to by an abundant liter-ature on the subject. During the last hundred years or so, dozens, if not hundreds of proposals have been made, each claiming to solve the definitional problem in a new and unique way. Needless to say, no one definition of religion has garnered a consensus, and the defi-

---

[1] Max Weber, *The Sociology of Religion* (Boston: Beacon Press, 1991), p. 1.
[2] D.H. Freeman, *A Philosophical Study of Religion* (Nutley, NJ: Craig Press, 1964), p. 1. The same point is made in Hans H. Penner and Edward A. Yonan, "Is a Science of Religion Possible?" *Journal of Religion* 52:2 (1972), pp. 107-33; Charles Vernoff, "Naming the Game: A Question of the Field," *Council on the Study of Religion: Bulletin* 14 (1983), pp. 109-13.

nitional enterprise, as well as the debate over the very need for definitions, continues in full vigor.

I, myself, am in two minds about the definitional debate: I understand the methodological attractiveness of working with an explicit definition of religion, but I also understand the difficulties in formulating one that is even marginally adequate. Nevertheless, I have found that the study of the definitional enterprise in general is immensely interesting, and I feel that regardless of where one stands in the definitional debate, the historical development of definitions of religion demands more systematic study than it has received hitherto. Even a cursory review of the literature, for example, reveals that, formally at least, the definition of religion has developed considerably over the last hundred years. Such formal development did not occur spontaneously, but was driven by those issues and ideologies being argued over in the field at large. An awareness of the formal development of definitions of religion thus provides an important perspective on the historical development of the field as a whole—a perspective which, pedagogically at least, could prove to be quite valuable.

In this chapter, therefore, what I wish to do is to provide a brief historical overview of the definitional enterprise in the academic study of religion. Obviously an exhaustive history would require book-length treatment, and what follows is perhaps elliptical in the extreme. However, it is, I feel, a necessary prolegomena to such a future study. Perhaps one of the reasons why the history of the definitional enterprise remains relatively neglected within the academic study of religion is because the field has failed to develop any kind of uniform formal categories for dealing with definitions of religion. In the following pages, therefore, I present a brief historical overview organized with an eye towards highlighting and labeling formal developments in the definition of religion.[3] I hope this overview will serve not only as an introduction to the range of definitional possibilities for religion, but that it will also facilitate further attention to the history of the definitional enterprise in general.

---

[3] For formal philosophical approaches to definition, see Richard Robinson, *Definition* (Oxford: Oxford University Press, 1954); Alex C. Michalos, *Principles of Logic* (Englewood Cliffs, NJ: Prentice-Hall, Inc., 1969), pp. 379-91; Irving M. Copi, *Introduction to Logic* (London: The Macmillan Company, 1971), pp. 89-120; Joannes Augustinus Maria Snoek, "Classification and Definition Theory" in his *Initiations: A Methodological Approach to the Application of Classification and Definition Theory in the Study of Rituals* (Pijnacker: Dutch Efficiency Bureau, 1987), pp. 25-56; "Definition" in Robert Audi (ed.), *The Cambridge Dictionary of Philosophy* (Cambridge: Cambridge University Press, 1995), pp. 185-86.

Lexical and Precising Definitions of Religion

Until the early modern period, the evolution of the definition of the word "religion" was largely an unconscious process, the result of a spontaneous social consensus. Philosophers call definitions that develop in this way *lexical* definitions.[4] Lexical definitions tend to be vague and elastic, partaking of the semantic slipperiness of everyday speech. In terms of the word "religion," for example, at any one time and within any given population, it has had a range of meanings, with old meanings often overlapping new meanings.[5] Moreover, lexical definitions of religion, as far as these can be inferred, have tended to be constructed through denotation; that is, the class "religion" was implicitly defined by simply pointing out members of the class (e.g. religion is Judaism, Christianity, Islam, etc.).[6] Even today, most scholars continue to work from just such lexical definitions of religion.

Beginning with the Enlightenment, however, some scholars have taken the effort to preface their studies with a consciously constructed and reasoned definition of religion. Such definitions attempt to make lexical definitions more precise—hence the name *precising* definitions.[7] Unlike lexical definitions, precising definitions represent a conscious construction of a definition in order to create a community of discourse. Typically, construction of precising definitions is accomplished through connotation, not denotation. In the case of religion, this means that the class "religion" is constructed by indicating the characteristic or characteristics that each member must have to be included in the class (e.g. Judaism, Christianity, Islam, etc. are religions because they share characteristics x, y, z, etc.). Precising definitions, therefore, are necessarily theoretical, based as they are on ei-

---

[4] For discussions of lexical definitions, see Robinson, *Definition*, pp. 35-58; Michalos, *Principles of Logic*, pp. 382-83; Copi, *Introduction to Logic*, pp. 99-100.

[5] For general overviews of the developing definition of religion from Antiquity to the modern period, see W. Warde Fowler, "The Latin History of the Word 'Religio,'" *Transactions of the Third International Congress for the History of Religions* II (1908), pp. 169-75; Wilfred Cantwell Smith, *The Meaning and End of Religion* (New York: Macmillan, 1962); Leopold Sabourin, "What is Religion?" *Religious Studies Bulletin* 1:3 (1981), pp. 58-66; Benson Saler, "*Religio* and the Definition of Religion," *Cultural Anthropology* 2:3 (1987), pp. 395-99; Ernst Feil, "From the Classical *Religio* to the Modern *Religion*: Elements of a Transformation Between 1550 and 1650," in Michel Despland and Gerard Vallee (eds.), *Religion in History: The Word, the Idea, the Reality* (Waterloo, Ontario: Wilfrid Laurier University Press, 1992), pp. 31-44.

[6] For a discussion of denotative vs. connotative definitions, see Michalos, *Principles of Logic*, pp. 388-89 and Copi, *Introduction to Logic*, pp. 107-14.

[7] For a discussion of precising definitions, see Copi, *Introduction to Logic*, pp. 100-101.

ther a descriptive (analytic) or explanatory (synthetic) theory.[8]
Depending on the theoretical basis of the definition then, we can
speak of *analytic* and *synthetic* precising definitions.

Perhaps one of the earliest precising definitions of religion can be
credited to Edward, Lord Herbert of Cherbury (1583-1648).[9]
Distressed by Europe's continuing religious strife and convinced of
God's universal benevolence for humankind, Herbert argued that all
religions are true at some level. To prove this, Herbert maintained
that all religions could be boiled down to five universal characteristics: (1) the belief that there is a Supreme Power external to the
world; (2) that this Power is to be worshipped; (3) that worship consists not in outward ceremony, but in piety and holiness; (4) that sin
can be expiated; and (5) that there are rewards and punishments
after this life.[10] Of course, these five characteristics represent
Herbert's attempt to create a new universal religious system and
their selection was driven by *a priori* assumptions about what constitutes religion. Nevertheless, Herbert claimed that it was by close
"dissection of, and inspection into religions" that the five "Common
Notions" of religion were discovered.[11] Along with forming the core
of Deism, therefore, the five characteristics can also be seen as an
early attempt at an analytic precising definition, that is, a definition
based on an analytic or descriptive theory of religion.

Lord Herbert of Cherbury had the confidence to frame an analytic precising definition of religion due to the Enlightenment's ideology of universalism. It was not until the development of evolutionary
theory in the 19th century that the next major step in the formal development of precising definitions of religion occurred. From Herbert's time on, increasing ethnographic evidence from the non-west-
ern world made it clear that there were systems of belief and
practice among the "primitive" peoples of the world that did not fit
into a Deistic scheme or its equivalents. Logically, there were two
ways of dealing with this: either violate the spirit of Enlightenment
universalism and admit that there were cultures that lack religion.

---

[8] For a discussion of analytic vs. synthetic definitions, see Michalos, *Principles of
Logic*, pp. 384-87. See Peter B. Clarke and Peter Byrne, *Religion Defined and Explained*
(New York: St Martin's Press, 1993) for a clear discussion of the difference between
descriptive and explanatory theories.

[9] See Peter Byrne, "Religion and Religions" in Stewart R. Sutherland (ed.), *The
World's Religions* (London: Routledge, 1988), pp. 3-28, pp. 15-16.

[10] Lord Herbert of Cherbury, *De Religione Gentilium* (1663), quoted in Eric J.
Sharpe, *Comparative Religion: A History* (La Salle, IL: Open Court Press, 1986), p. 16.

[11] Herbert, *De Religione Gentilium* (1663), quoted in J. Samuel Preus, *Explaining
Religion: Criticism and Theory from Bodin to Freud* (New Haven: Yale University Press,
1987), p. 29.

Or, "religion" itself could be redefined with fewer characteristics, dropping out those characteristics that "primitive" religions did not seem to share with Christianity, Judaism, Islam or the other "world religions" (e.g. the Judeo-Christian ethical code, belief in post-mortem punishment, etc.). Abandoning such characteristics, how-ever, seemed to entail a debasement of the "world religions," placing them on a level with "primitive religion." Evolutionary theory, how-ever, solved this problem by positing the "world religions" as more highly evolved forms of "primitive religions," thus acknowledging a connection between them while simultaneously maintaining their as-sumed hierarchical relationship.

Although perhaps not the first precising definition based on evolu-tionary theory, by far the best known is the classic minimal defini-tion of the anthropologist E. B. Tylor (1832-1917). According to Tylor, religion is "a belief in Spiritual Beings."[12] Tylor interpreted the available ethnographic evidence to show that prior to the devel-opment of the complex systems of beliefs and practices lexically called religion, human beings had a notion of non-material entities or spirits, a notion that arose naturally through an interpretation of dreams. It was this concept of "spiritual being" that connected all religious systems, since it was out of this rather undifferentiated no-tion that the concept of deity arose. Indeed, according to Tylor, if one were to posit a unilinear evolution of religion from spirit wor-ship or "animism" through polytheism to monotheism, the one characteristic that remained constant—at least at some basic struc-tural level—was a belief in spiritual beings. For this reason, a belief in spiritual beings could serve as a structural marker for all religious systems regardless of where they were on the evolutionary scale.[13]

---

[12] E. B. Tylor, *Primitive Culture: Researches into the Development of Mythology, Philosophy, Religion, Language, Art, and Custom* (London: John Murphy, 1903): Vol 1, p. 424.

[13] According to Hans G. Kippenburg, Tylor's model for the definition of religion was based on "the comparative anatomy founded by Charles Darwin a few years earlier. Even before Tylor this model had been introduced into the study of soci-eties. In this way, certain elements in the history of mankind, which retained an identical structure despite increasing differentiation, were supposed to be identifi-able. Just as the number of vertebrae always remains the same in more and less de-veloped mammals, the belief in souls was held to be a constant in the development of religion. In this sense the soul remains a constant element throughout the history of religions. Its development is identical with the increase of complexity of a given structure." (Hans G. Kippenburg, "Rivalry Among Scholars of Religion: The Crisis of Historicism and the Formation of Paradigms in the History of Religions," *Historical Reflections* 20 (Fall 1994), pp. 377-402, p. 380). In terms of the creation of an analytic definition of religion, this approach has something in common with con-temporary cladistics in biology.

Importantly, behind Tylor's definition was not simply an analytic theory, but a synthetic or explanatory theory as well. According to Tylor, a belief in spiritual beings was not only a "marker" for all religious systems, but it was also from this simple belief that all the characteristics of religious systems such as myth, doctrine, ritual, ethics, etc. developed. Tylor's definition, therefore, was not only descriptive of the genus *religion*, but it also contained a capsule genetic explanation for the speciation and evolution of all religious systems. In this sense, Tylor's definition functioned both as an analytic *and* a synthetic precising definition of religion.

Not surprisingly, Tylor's minimal definition of religion quickly attracted criticism, primarily in terms of its analytic adequacy. Tylor believed that his precising definition of religion held up well when compared to the lexical definitions of his day. The emphasis on spiritual beings, Tylor believed, could accommodate deity in all its forms. Nevertheless, scholars such as J. G. Frazer (1854-1951) criticized the definition because it cast too wide a net, bringing under the rubric "religion" those systems of beliefs and practices that Frazer believed should be considered "magic." Religion, Frazer argued, evolved out of magic, but the two systems of beliefs and practices were nevertheless fundamentally different. This opened an exceedingly long-lived debate concerning the difference between magic and religion, a debate that has lasted to this day.[14] As interesting as this debate is, however, it was the opposite critique that Tylor's definition did not cast its net widely *enough* that ultimately had the most impact on the development of new precising definitions of religion. Such a critique came from the pen of another anthropologist, R. R. Marett (1866-1943).[15]

According to Marett, Tylor's minimal definition of religion was in error since examples existed of societies that had systems of beliefs and practices that were obviously religious (lexically speaking), but which did not involve anthropomorphic spiritual beings. In such societies, belief and practice centered around an undifferentiated belief

---

[14] See Eric J. Sharpe, *Comparative Religion: A History* (La Salle, Illinois: Open Court, 1986), pp. 87-94. For more recent discussion of the difference between magic and religion, see Jack Goody, "Religion and Ritual: The Definitional Problem" *The British Journal of Sociology* 12:2 (June 1961), pp. 142-64 and H. S. Versnel, "Some Reflections on the Relationship Magic-Religion," *Numen* 38:2 (1991), pp. 177-97.

[15] For general discussions of R. R. Marett, see Sharpe, *Comparative Religion*, pp. 65-71; Kippenburg, "Rivalry Among Scholars of Religion," pp. 381-82; E.E. Evans-Pritchard, *Theories of Primitive Religion* (Oxford: Oxford University Press, 1980), pp. 32-37.

in supernatural power. The belief in supernatural power, Marett argued, predated that of the belief in spiritual beings, which was simply the next evolutionary step. In 1900, in a paper entitled "Preanimistic Religion," Marett essayed his own minimal definition of religion as "a belief in supernatural power."[16] Again, as with Tylor's, Marett's definition was both analytic and synthetic in intent. According to Marett all religious systems embodied at some level this simple belief and thus, "belief in supernatural power" was a good marker for all religious systems past and present. And this, in turn, was precisely because all religious systems in all their complexity found their ultimate causal origin in the belief in supernatural power. Although formally Marett's precising definition was little different from Tylor's, it would nevertheless serve as the catalyst for the next step in the formal development of precising definitions of religion.

Real, Substantive, and Functional Definitions of Religion

According to Hans G. Kippenburg, Marett's preanimism was wildly influential in the first decade of the new century and represented the closest the field has ever come to reaching a consensus on a precising definition of religion.[17] The consensus, if it existed at all, did not last long. For Marett, the origin of the belief in supernatural power was due to a powerful emotional experience—an experience logically prior to belief. Marett, however, left the nature of the experience uncertain, and because of this, it was unclear whether Marett would have claimed that the experience itself was somehow inherently religious.[18] It was at this point that Marett's anthropological theory of the origin of religion intersected with the European theological tradition associated with the thought of Friedrich Schleiermacher (1768-1834). Schleiermacher stressed the primacy and self-authenticating nature of religious experience.[19] Followers of Schleiermacher, therefore, did not hesitate to claim that the powerful experience indicated by Marett was transcendent in origin and completely *sui generis* in

---

[16] This article was reprinted in R. R. Marett, *The Threshold of Religion* (New York, 1919). See also R. R. Marett, "The Tabu-Mana Formula as a Minimum Definition of Religion," *Archiv für Religionswissenschaft* 12 (1909), pp. 186-94.

[17] Kippenburg, "Rivalry Among Scholars of Religion," pp. 382-86.

[18] Evans-Pritchard, *Theories of Primitive Religion*, p. 33.

[19] Friedrich Schleiermacher, *On Religion: Speeches to Its Cultured Despisers* (London: Kegan Paul, 1893). For a good discussion of Schleiermacher, see Walter H. Capps, *Religious Studies: The Making of the Discipline* (Minneapolis: Fortress Press, 1995), pp. 13-18.

nature. Accordingly, the theologian Rudolph Otto (1869-1937) argued for an even more radical precising definition of religion than that proposed by Marett. For Otto, religion was not simply a *belief* in supernatural power, but a completely unique experience of that power, an experience that could be approximately characterized as *mysterium tremendum et fascinans*.[20]

Some scholars of religion, however, were unwilling to make this complete definitional leap from belief to experience. If Schleiermacher represented one European intellectual tradition in which religion sprang from a *sui generis* experience of the transcendent, there was another intellectual tradition that questioned the reality of such experiences altogether. Beginning with the works of David Hume (1711-1776), but perhaps culminating in the psychology of Wilhelm Wundt and Sigmund Freud, this other tradition ascribed "religious" experience to human origins, and explained it away as simply another order of human emotion.[21] For these scholars, there was no such thing as a *sui generis* "religious" experience—only experiences religiously interpreted. It was true, as Marett had contended, that a powerful experience causes religion, but only in the sense that such experiences provoke the human imagination to invent an explanation for its origin, hence the (mistaken) belief in supernatural power.

Differences over how far Marett's minimal definition of religion could be pushed served to crystallize tensions between those scholars who sought transcendental explanations of religion and those who sought naturalistic explanations. In a sense, Marett's definition brought to the fore a different kind of definitional debate—a debate that had been latent in the academic study of religion from its beginning. Harking back to Aristotle, philosophers have traditionally recognized the difference between real and nominal definitions.[22] The lexical and precising definitions we have been dealing with up to this point are classified as nominal definitions. Nominal defini-

---

[20] Rudolf Otto, *The Idea of the Holy: An Inquiry into the Non-Rational Factor in the Idea of the Divine and Its Relation to the Rational* (London: Oxford University Press, 1950). Such definitions were also associated with Nathan Söderblom and Geradus van der Leeuw (see Kippenburg, "Rivalry Among Scholars of Religion," pp. 382-84). For a good discussion of Otto, see Capps, *Religious Studies*, pp. 20-25. For a recent call for a return to a definition of religion based on religious experience, see Karal R. Wernhart, "'Religious Beliefs per se'' —a Human Universality," *Anthropos* 81 (1986): 648-52.

[21] For discussion of Hume and Freud, see Preus, *Explaining Religion*. For a discussion of Wundt, see Evans-Pritchard, *Theories of Primitive Religion*, pp. 37-38.

[22] For a discussion of the difference between real and nominal definitions, see Robinson, *Definition*, pp. 149-92; Michalos, *Principles of Logic*, pp. 379-81; Audi, "Definition," pp. 185-86.

tions are constructed more or less by an empirical process of affixing a name to an object or class of objects. A real definition, on the other hand, is a "specification of the metaphysically necessary and sufficient condition for being the kind of thing a noun...designates."[23] In other words, real definitions are constructed by signalling the metaphysical essence of an object or class of objects. Of course, if one does not believe in a metaphysical reality, then real definitions are *ipso facto* impossible.

For most of the history of the study of religion in the West, real definitions of religion have generally been assumed to be possible. Only in the modern period, when materialist philosophies came to be taken with increased seriousness, could real definitions of religion be dismissed as meaningless. With Marett's precising definition of religion, the debate over the proper nominal definition for religion collided with the debate over the real definition of religion. Whether one was willing to make the definitional leap from belief to experience corresponded to some degree with whether one believed in a metaphysical reality or not. Those who held a positive real definition of religion tended to embrace definitions of religion such as Otto's, while those who held a negative real definition of religion preferred definitions such as those of Marett and Tylor which allowed for naturalistic explanations of religion. In time, the tensions wrought by Marett's preanimism forced the creation of yet a third approach to the study of religion in which one remains neutral in regard to real definitions of religion. For those who embraced this third approach, the goal of the academic study of religion would always remain primarily descriptive, not explanatory. And when it came to the metaphysical reality of religion, one was to practice *epoché*, that is, the suspension of judgement in regard to real definitions of religion.[24]

Despite the articulation of this neutral position, however, the debate over the real definition of religion remained acute during the first decades of the century. The rancor generated by this debate was especially problematic since the academic study of religion was then struggling to establish itself as an autonomous field of study. Fortuitously, there soon began during this period a new wave of theorizing which would culminate in the formulation of new precising definitions of religion—precising definitions that would neatly avoid the question of real definitions altogether. Functionalism was the

[23] Audi, "Definition," p. 186.
[24] For a discussion of the concept of *epoché*, see G. van der Leeuw, *Religion in Essence and Manifestation*, translated by J. E. Turner (London: George Allen and Unwin, 1938), p. 646 (note 1) and p. 683.

basis of this new theorizing, and its promoters promised that it would bring new insights into the origin and persistence of religion. The most important of the functional theories of religion were those derived from the social functionalism of Emile Durkheim and the psychological functionalism of Bronislaw Malinowski. Ironically, both scholars were firmly committed to negative real definitions of religion.

In *The Elementary Forms of the Religious Life*, Emile Durkheim worked through a series of precising definitions of religion. At the beginning of that work, Durkheim used Marett's preanimism theory and definition as a starting point.[25] Durkheim, however, was most emphatically not one of those scholars willing to make the definitional leap from belief to experience. Religious beliefs were indeed the consequence of a powerful experience, although there was nothing supernatural about this experience. It was simply the natural result of certain extreme social situations ("collective effervescence").[26] Importantly, such experience led not only to a belief in supernatural power, but to a complete division of the world into those things that are associated with this power ("the sacred") and those things that are not ("the profane"). Indeed, Durkheim used this dichotomy as the basis for his own minimal precising definition: religion is a "division of the world into two domains, the one containing all that is sacred, the other all that is profane."[27] Durkheim's minimal definition is both analytic and synthetic in intent: not only can all religions be identified as such by their division of the world between sacred and profane, but it is out of the idea of the "sacred" that all the beliefs and practices characteristic of religion (lexically defined) subsequently develop.

In a sense, Durkheim's minimal precising definition of religion could be seen as nothing more than a more sophisticated restatement of Marett's preanimism. However, Durkheim went beyond Marett in that he was interested not simply in what religion was, but in what religion did. Religion, Durkheim surmised, would not have survived and become such an integral part of human society if it did not contribute to the integrity and survival of society. Religion, in other words, must have some social function. Accordingly, Durkheim amended his precising definition of religion to read: "A religion is a unified system of beliefs and practices relative to sacred

---

[25] Kippenburg, "Rivalry Among Scholars of Religion," pp. 384-85.
[26] Emile Durkheim, *The Elementary Forms of the Religious Life* (New York: The Free Press, 1965), pp. 230-32.
[27] Ibid., p. 52.

things, that is to say, things set apart and forbidden—beliefs and practices which unite into one single moral community called a Church, all those who adhere to them."[28] Formally, this represented a new kind of precising definition, a definition that emphasized not only the substantive characteristics of religion (a "system of beliefs and practices"), but also its characteristic social function (the "beliefs and practices...unite into one single moral community called a Church, all those who adhere to them").

Since its introduction, Durkheim's functional theory of religion and the definition based on it have proven exceedingly popular.[29] Even after both the data and the evolutionary presuppositions behind Durkheim's (and Marett's) recovery of the historical origins of religion came under fire, Durkheim's insight into the functionality of religion still remained compelling. Indeed, in time, the functional characteristics of religion came to be seen as fundamental, and gradually one sees a shift away from definitions of religion that stress the combination of substantive and functional characteristics to those that emphasize purely functional characteristics alone.[30] In other words, any system of beliefs and practices that promotes social unity could be viewed as a religious system, regardless of the specific content of the beliefs and practices.[31] It did not matter whether such traditions contained elements of the supernatural or depended on some kind of transcendent referent. Indeed, Durkheim himself argued that the value of such functional definitions of religion was that they allowed space for traditions such as Buddhism, which, while clearly a religion lexically speaking, nevertheless does not pivot on "the idea of gods and spirits."[32]

---

[28] Ibid., p. 62.

[29] For an excellent discussion of the development and subsequent influence of Durkheim's definition of religion, see Brian Morris, *Anthropological Studies of Religion: An Introductory Text* (Cambridge: Cambridge University Press, 1990), pp. 106-40.

[30] For discussion of the shift from substantive to functional definitions of religion, see Peter L. Berger, "Sociological Definitions of Religion" in *The Scared Canopy: Elements of a Sociological Theory of Religion* (Garden City, NY: Doubleday & Co., Inc, 1969), pp. 175-77 and Robert A. Segal, "Anthropological Definitions of Religion," *Zygon* 20:1 (1985), pp. 78-79. For a general discussion of substantive vs. functional definitions of religion, see Karel Dobbelaere and Jan Lauwers, "Definitions of Religion—A Sociological Critique," *Social Compass* 20 (1973/4), pp. 535-51.

[31] For a recent version of a purely socio-functional definition of religion, see Loyal D. Rue, "Redefining *Myth* and *Religion*: Introduction to a Conversation," *Zygon* 29:3 (1994), pp. 315-19.

[32] Durkheim, *The Elementary Forms of the Religious Life*, pp. 37-57. For a critique of Durkheim's interpretation of Buddhism, see Marco Orru and Amy Wang, "Durkheim, Religion, and Buddhism," *Journal for the Scientific Study of Religion* 31:1 (1992): 47-61.

Perhaps just as importantly, the de-emphasis of belief in the transcendent as a *sine qua non* characteristic of religious systems seemed to render controversies over the reality of the transcendent, not to mention real definitions, far less relevant to the academic study of religion. Moreover, socio-functional definitions of religion helped to deflect attention away from real definitions in another way. Fueled by evolutionary theory, early anthropologists and sociologists, including Durkheim, were intensely interested in discovering the historical origins of religion. In time, however, both evolutionary theory and the quest for the historical origins of religion fell into disrepute. Functionalism and functional definitions served to shift attention away from the discredited quest for the historical origins of religion, placing emphasis instead on explanations of the persistence of religion. As a consequence, attention was also diverted away from potentially divisive questions about the *ultimate* origins of religion, thus forestalling debates about the real definition of religion.

A similar shift to purely functional definitions can also be noted with those definitions based on the psychological function of religion. One of the clearest statements of psychological functionalism comes in the work of Bronislaw Malinowski.[33] For Malinowski, religion was "intrinsically although indirectly connected with man's fundamental, that is, biological, needs."[34] Malinowski said "indirectly" because religion, with its systems of belief concerning supernatural powers and deities, functioned to relieve the psychological anxiety that comes with "the curse of forethought and imagination, which fall on man once he rises above brute animal nature."[35] Specifically, religion helped human beings deal with a "range of anxieties, forebodings and problems concerning human destinies and man's place in the universe."[36] Ultimately, religion is that which "is largely concerned with the sacralization of the crises of human life," especially the "supreme crisis," death.[37] In short, for Malinowski, those systems

---

[33] For a good discussion of Bronislaw Malinowski's work and influence, see Morris, *Anthropological Studies of Religion*, pp. 148-49. For recent examples of Malinowski's influence on the definition of religion, see E. R. Goodenough, "A Historian of Religion Tries to Define Religion," *Zygon* 2:1 (1967), pp. 7-22 and Ward H. Goodenough, "Toward an Anthropologically Useful Definition of Religion," in Allan W. Eister (ed.), *Changing Perspectives in the Scientific Study of Religion* (New York: John Wiley & Sons, 1974), pp. 165-84.

[34] Bronislaw Malinowski, "The Role of Magic and Religion" in William A. Lessa and Evon Z. Vogt (eds.), *Reader in Comparative Religion: An Anthropological Approach* (New York: Harper & Row, Publishers, 1979), pp. 37-45, p. 45.

[35] Ibid., pp. 37-45.

[36] Ibid., p. 45.

[37] Ibid., p. 46.

of beliefs and practices which served to ameliorate the greatest and most intractable problems of human existence could rightly be called religion.

As with Durkheim's definition of religion, Malinowski's definition was formally a precising definition with both substantive characteristics (systems of beliefs and practices) and functional characteristics (the psychological function of anxiety reduction). As happened with socio-functional definitions, however, there seems to have been a gradual shift away from a substantive/functional precising definition to a purely functional definition. Such purely psycho-functional definitions maintained that any system of belief and practice that addressed humanity's fundamental existential concerns was *ipso facto* religion, regardless of the content of those systems. Perhaps the most famous formulation of a purely psycho-functional definition was that of Paul Tillich, who maintained that "[r]eligion, in the largest and most basic sense of the word, is ultimate concern."[38] Although Tillich constructed his definition in response to theological currents somewhat removed from those in the academic study of religion, nevertheless, purely psycho-functional precising definitions of the "ultimate concern" variety became at least as popular as socio-functional definitions in the academic study of religion from the late 1950s on.[39] Again, as with purely socio-functional definitions of religion, purely psycho-functional definitions of religion de-emphasized the transcendent as the *sine qua non* of religion and de-emphasized the quest for the historical origins of religion, thus helping to deflect attention away from divisive questions about the real definition of religion.

---

[38] Paul Tillich, *Theology of Culture* (London: Oxford University Press, 1983), quoted in Capps, *Religious Studies*, p. 34.

[39] For examples of "ultimate concern" definitions, see J. M. Yinger, *Religion, Society and the Individual: An Introduction to the Sociology of Religion* (New York: Macmillan, 1957), p. 9; Robert. N. Bellah, *Tokugawa Religion: The Values of Pre-Industrial Japan* (New York: Free Press, 1957), p. 6; Hideo Kishimoto, "An Operational Definition of Religion," *Numen* 8 (1961), pp. 236-40; J. Paul Williams, "The Nature of Religion," *Journal for the Scientific Study of Religion* 2:1 (1962), pp. 3-17; Robert D. Baird, "Interpretative Categories and the History of Religions" in James S. Helfer (ed.), *On Method in the History of Religions* (Middleton, Conn.: Wesleyan University Press, 1968), pp. 17-30; E.H. Pyle, "In Defence of 'Religion'," *Religious Studies* 3 (1968), pp. 347-53; Frederick Ferré, "The Definition of Religion," *Journal of the American Academy of Religion* 38 (1970), pp. 11-16; Frederick J. Streng, "Studying Religion: Possibilities and Limitations of Different Definitions," *Journal of the American Academy of Religion* 40:2 (1974), pp. 219-37; Morton B. King, "Is Scientific Study of Religion Possible," *Journal for the Scientific Study of Religion* 30:1 (1991): 108-13.

Monothetic and Polythetic Definitions of Religion

Throughout the second half of the twentieth century, purely functional definitions of either the socio-functional or psycho-functional type have continued to be extraordinarily popular. They have dominated, in fact, much of the discourse of the academic study of religion.[40] Indeed, certainly the best-known definition of religion to come out of the 1960s—that of Clifford Geertz—was essentially an ambitious attempt to combine social function and psychological function into a single precising definition of religion. According to Geertz, religion was "(1) a system of symbols which acts to (2) establish powerful, pervasive, and long-lasting moods and motivations in men by (3) formulating conceptions of a general order of existence and (4) clothing these conceptions with such an aura of factuality that (5) the moods and motivations seem uniquely realistic."[41] Again, as with other purely functional definitions, religion was simply "a system of symbols," the content of which was relatively unimportant. What was important was that these symbols functioned to establish a "general order of existence," or, in Geertz's terms, a "world view." World views in turn served to establish an "ethos," "powerful, pervasive, and long-lasting moods," which ultimately functioned to promote both psychological and social integration.

Despite their popularity, purely functional precising definitions were not immune to criticism. Some called into question the analytic adequacy of purely functional definitions because they failed to correspond to most lexical definitions of religion. For example, some religions (lexically so-defined) work against social cohesion or seem to undermine psychological well-being.[42] Are millenarian movements, then, not to be classified as religious because they function to

---

[40] A point made by Robert W. Friedrichs, "The Functionalist Paradigm Dominating Social Scientific Study of Religion and a Structural Alternative," *Council on the Study of Religion: Bulletin* 13 (Fall 1982), pp. 1-5.

[41] Clifford Geertz, "Religion as a Cultural System" in *The Interpretation of Cultures* (New York: Basic Books, 1973), pp. 87-125, p. 90.

[42] For such critiques see Allan W. Eister, "Religious Institutions in Complex Societies: Difficulties in the Theoretic Specifications of Functions" *American Sociological Review* 22 (1957), pp. 387-91; Richard Machalek, "Definitional Strategies in the Study of Religion," *Journal for the Scientific Study of Religion* 16: 4 (1977), pp. 395-401, p. 399; Murray L. Wax, "The Paradoxes are Numerous," *Zygon* 20:1 (1985): 79-89. It is interesting to note that the socio-functional definitions that became most popular were those that emphasized religion's positive role in social cohesion, and not those, à la Marx, that emphasized religion's negative function as "ideology": see, Stephen J. Casey, "Definitions of Religion: A Matter of Taste?" *Horizons* 11:1 (1984), pp. 86-99. For a discussion of Marxist definitions of religion, see Gregory Baum, "Definitions of Religion in Sociology" in Mircea Eliade and

disrupt the social order? Are authoritarian "cults" not to be classified as religious if they function to disrupt one's psychic integrity? To fix on *positive* functions alone as the defining factor for religion seemed to entail normative judgments that were hardly appropriate for an objective field of study. On the other hand, some scholars took the opposite tack, contending that purely functional definitions were actually too undiscriminating when judged against lexical definitions.[43] While purely functional definitions made space for non-theistic Buddhism, Confucianism, etc., they also allowed for all sorts of systems of beliefs and practices not normally (i.e. lexically) deemed religious to be labeled as such. Such problematic "religions" ranged from Marxism to nationalism to big league sports.[44]

In addition to the analytic critiques, purely functional definitions of religion were also open to criticism of their synthetic adequacy. Since the 1960s, functionalism in general has come under attack because of its limited explanatory power.[45] Functions, it is argued, are side-effects and can never account for the origins of any substantive phenomena. Functions may select for certain substantive phenomena according to a kind of "natural selection," and therefore functionalism might account for the persistence and development of certain cultural, social, or psychological structures, but this again does not account for the origins of any of these structures. In terms of religion, the functional utility of theological or cosmological ideas, rituals, ethical schemes, etc. could never account for how these beliefs and practices came about in the first place. Functional theories may

---

David Tracy (eds.), *What is Religion? An Inquiry for Christian Theology* (New York: The Seabury Press, 1980), pp. 25-32, pp. 30-32.

[43] Machalek, "Definitional Strategies in the Study of Religion," p. 398, and Baum, "Definitions of Religion in Sociology," pp. 28-29.

[44] Indeed, such functional definitions had the decided Cold War utility of classifying Marxism as a religion; see, for example, Werner Cohn, "Is Religion Universal? Problems of Definition," *Journal for the Scientific Study of Religion* 2:1 (1962), pp. 25-35 or Philip E. Devine, "On the Definition of 'Religion,'" *Faith and Philosophy* 3:3 (1986), pp. 270-84. For a critique of the notion of sports as religion, see Joan M. Chandler, "Sport is Not a Religion" in Shirl J. Hoffman (ed.), *Sport and Religion* (Champaign, Illinois: Human Kinetics Books, 1992), pp. 55-62.

[45] For example, see Robin Horton, "A Definition of Religion, and its Uses," *Journal of the Royal Anthropological Institute of Great Britain and Ireland* 90 (1960), pp. 201-26; P. Worsley, "Religion as a Category" in Roland Robertson (ed.), *Sociology of Religion: Selected Readings* (Baltimore, MD: Penguin Books, 1969), pp. 221-35; John Y. Fenton, "Reductions in the Study of Religions," *Soundings* 53:1 (1970), pp. 61-76. For more recent critiques of the explanatory nature of functionalism, see the articles "Religion, Explanation of" and "The Study of Religion" in Jonathan Z. Smith (ed.), *The HarperCollins Dictionary of Religion* (San Francisco: HarperCollins, 1995), pp. 894-97 and pp. 909-17, respectively.

account for the persistence of these substantive characteristics of religion, but they can never explain their origins.

In response to these and other critiques, a few investigators in the 1960s chose to return to substantive precising definitions à la Tylor or Marett. Anthropologists such as Horton, Goody, Spiro, and Swanson all embraced definitions that specified a belief in "spiritual beings" or, in Spiro's less tendentious phrase, "superhuman beings" as the *sine qua non* of religion.[46] This in turn spawned a relatively small but vigorous research tradition that took as its starting point such precising definitions of religion.[47] Not surprisingly, the same critiques that were leveled at Tylor's and Marett's definitions have been revived as well,[48] although the counter-arguments have changed somewhat. For instance, when it was pointed out that the minimal definition of religion as "belief in superhuman beings" excluded certain non-theistic traditions, some, most notably Spiro, frankly admitted that perhaps "religion" is not a category universal to all human cultures. The "criterion of cross-cultural applicability," according to Spiro, "does not entail...universality."[49] As a consequence, Spiro argued that some lexically-defined religions in which superhuman beings do not figure, such as Confucianism, should simply not be classified as religion.[50]

---

[46] Horton, "A Definition of Religion, and its Uses"; Jack Goody, "Religion and Ritual: The Definitional Problem" *The British Journal of Sociology* 12:2 (June 1961), pp. 142-64; Melford E. Spiro, "Religion: Problems of Definition and Explanation" in M. Banton (ed.) *Anthropological Approaches to the Study of Religion* (London: Tavistock Press, 1966), pp. 85-126; G. E. Swanson, "Experience of the Supernatural" in Roland Robertson (ed.), *Sociology of Religion: Selected Readings* (Baltimore, MD: Penguin Books, 1969), pp. 237-52.

[47] See, for example, W.D. Hammond-Tooke, "Is There a Science of Religion?" *Religion in Southern Africa* 3:1 (Ja 1982), pp. 3-17; Hans H. Penner, *Impasse and Resolution: A Critique of the Study of Religion* (New York: Peter Lang, 1989); Pascal Boyer, *The Naturalness of Religious Ideas: A Cognitive Theory of Religion* (Berkeley: University of California, 1994); E. Thomas Lawson and Robert N. McCauley, *Rethinking Religion: Connecting Cognition and Culture* (Cambridge: Cambridge University Press, 1996). For a critique of the last two studies, see Stewart Elliott Guthrie, "Religion: What Is It?" *Journal for the Scientific Study of Religion* 35:4 (1996), pp. 412-19. For a critique of Guthrie's own theory and definition, as presented in *Faces in the Clouds: A New Theory of Religion* (Oxford: Oxford University Press, 1993), see Edward A. Yonan, "Religion as Anthropomorphism: A New Theory that Invites Definitional and Epistemic Scrutiny," *Religion* 25 (1995), pp. 31-34.

[48] For example, Murray L. Wax, "Review of *Religion: An Anthropological View*," *Journal for the Scientific Study of Religion* 2:1 (1962), pp. 112-13 and Werner Cohn, "Is Religion Universal? Problems of Definition," *Journal for the Scientific Study of Religion* 2:1 (1962), pp. 25-35.

[49] Spiro, "Religion: Problems of Definition and Explanation," p. 91.

[50] Ibid., p. 94. Others, however, in order to preserve the universality of religion, have proposed substantive precising definitions based on other substantive characteristics perceived by their authors to be universal. Peter L. Berger, for example, has

In terms of synthetic critiques, the revived substantive precising definitions were just as vulnerable as when they were first proposed. As with Tylor's and Marett's formulations, these revived substantive precising definitions were at some level claims to be capsule explanations of both the origin of "religion" as well as the diversity of "religions." However, as observed above, the evolutionary presuppositions that allowed Tylor and Marett to claim that they had recovered the historical origins of religion had been discredited. Therefore, while these revived precising definitions still claimed to encapsulate the origins of religion, the origins referred to were ontogenic, not phylogenic. In other words, research shifted from the historical origins of religion to the recurrent origins of religion, especially as they were thought to be found in psychological development and in the very structure of human consciousness. Cognitive anthropologists, for example, argued that the human mind was predisposed to acquire certain kinds of "mental representations," including the idea of "superhuman beings."[51] Of course, whether this insight into the ontogenic origins of religion can be extended to account for the development of all religious systems remains to be seen. Research along these lines still remains largely undone.

It should also be said that the return to substantive precising definitions, with all their implicit claims about origins, revived the debate over real definitions of religion. The research tradition discussed above, for example, was strongly committed to a negative real definition of religion or what Peter Berger called "methodological atheism."[52] It was perhaps for this reason that not all of those who rejected purely functional definitions of religion were willing to return to substantive precising definitions. Some, especially religious studies scholars committed to "methodological agnosticism,"[53] advo-

---

suggested belief in a sacred cosmos is a universal substantive characteristic of religion ("Sociological Definitions of Religion" in *The Sacred Canopy: Elements of a Sociological Theory of Religion* [Garden City, NY: Doubleday & Co., Inc, 1969], pp. 175-77).

[51] See, for example, E. Thomas Lawson, "Defining Religion...Going the Theoretical Way," chapter four in this volume.

[52] Berger, *The Sacred Canopy*, pp. 100, 180. Indeed, it is perhaps from the re-introduction of substantive precising definitions in the 1960s that we can trace the origins of the contemporary "reductionism debate." For more on the reductionism debate, see Thomas A. Idinopulos and Edward A. Yonan, *Religion and Reductionism: Essays on Eliade, Segal, & the Challenge of the Social Sciences for the Study of Religion* (Leiden: E.J. Brill, 1994).

[53] Methodological agnosticism is the position that one must always hold open at least the *possibility* that the transcendent exists. For discussions of methodological agnosticism, see Ninian Smart, *The Phenomenon of Religion* (New York: The Seabury

cated instead a return to purely analytic precising definitions—but analytic precising definitions constructed according to a new model. This new model was based on the concept of *polythetic* or "family resemblance" classes.[54]

Up to this point, the precising definitions that we have been discussing have been based on a set of *sine qua non* characteristics (e.g. Herbert's Deism) or a single *sine qua non* characteristic (e.g. Tylor's "spiritual beings" or Tillich's "ultimate concern"). Under such definitions, systems of beliefs and practices must have all the characteristics (or the one characteristic) in order to qualify as a religious system. Definitions that are based on a set of *sine qua non* characteristics or a single *sine qua non* characteristic are called *monothetic* definitions. Polythetic definitions, on the other hand, are more flexible because they are based on relative instead of absolute identification. A polythetic definition of religion is based on a set of characteristics, only some of which a system must have in order to be counted as a religion. Say, for example, we are comparing four distinct systems of beliefs and practices. System 1 contains characteristics a, b, and c; system 2 has characteristics b, c, and d; system 3 has characteristics c, d, and e; and system 4 has characteristics d, e, and f. No one of these systems of beliefs and practices is identical to another, but they all have some characteristics in common with some of the other systems. In other words, while not identical, they nevertheless share, to use Wittgenstein's phrase, a "family resemblance."[55] If we define religion to mean any system that contains some—but not necessarily all—of the characteristics (a, b, c, d, e, f...etc.), this then is a polythetic definition of religion.

Press, 1973); Donald Wiebe, "Is a Science of Religion Possible?" *Studies in Religion* 7:1 (1978), pp. 5-17; Karel Werner, "The Concept of the Transcendent: Questions of Method in the History of Religions," *Religion* 13 (1983), pp. 311-22; Michael Pye, "Religion: Shape and Shadow," *Numen* 41 (1994), pp. 51-75.

[54] For discussions of polythetic classification schemes, see Rodney Needham, "Polythetic Classification: Convergence and Consequences," *Man* 10:3 (September, 1975), pp. 349-69 and especially Snoek, "Classification and Definition Theory," pp. 25-56. The language of monothetic vs. polythetic is borrowed from biological taxonomy (see Snoek, p. 30).

[55] The first explicit articulation of this definitional model is generally credited to Ludwig Wittgenstein in his *Philosophical Investigations*, translated by G.E.M. Anscombe (Oxford: Oxford University Press, 1953), p. 32e. One of the earliest proposals of a family resemblance definition of religion is found in Ninian Smart, "Numen, Nirvana, and the Definition of Religion," *Church Quarterly Review* 160 (1959), pp. 216-25. It is interesting to note that Smart proposed his family resemblance definition of religion in the context of a critique of lexical adequacy of Otto's experiential definition of religion. Recently, Smart has renewed his call for family resemblance definitions of religion in "Theravada Buddhism and the Definition of Religion," *Sophia* 34:1 (1995), pp. 161-66.

CHART 1
POLYTHETIC DEFINITIONS

Open or Fully Polythetic (Family Resemblance) Definitions

Religion 1 = A + B + C characteristics
Religion 2 = B + C + D characteristics
Religion 3 = C + D + E characteristics
Religion 4 = D + E + F characteristics
...etc.

Prototypical Polythetic (Family Resemblance) Definitions

Prototype Religion = A + B+ C + D+ E + F + G characteristics
Religion 1 = C + D + E + F characteristics
Religion 2 = B + D + F + G characteristics
Religion 3 = A + B + C + D + E + F characteristics
Religion 4 = C + E + G characteristics
...etc.

In practice, there are two ways of constructing polythetic defini-tions.[56] In the example above, the definition is an *open* or *fully* poly-thetic definition. It is "open" because no one member of the class "religion" contains all the characteristics (a, b, c, d, e, f...etc.). In some cases, one of the members of the class *does* contain all the char-acteristics and functions as the "prototype" for all the other mem-bers of the class. Polythetic definitions that are constructed in this way are called *prototypical* polythetic definitions. The two types of polythetic definitions are summarized in chart one above.

As with any other definition of religion, polythetic definitions, too, are not without their critics. For one thing, how does one go about selecting the set of characteristics that form the basis for polythetic classification? In prototypical polythetic definitions, this problem is solved since one religion is taken as "an ideally clear case of reli-gion" against which all other systems of beliefs and practices are

---

[56] See W. P. Alston, "Religion" in Paul Edwards (ed.), *Encyclopedia of Philosophy* Volume 7 (New York: The Macmillan Company & The Free Press, 1967): 140-45.

compared.[57] This in itself presents two problems. First, what is the minimum number of characteristics that a system must share with the prototype religion in order to be classified as a religion? And second, will not the choice of a prototype religion bias the definition in such a way that it becomes invincibly ethnocentric?[58]

It has been suggested that a possible response to these critiques is to adopt a completely open polythetic definition of religion.[59] With an open polythetic definition of religion, it does not matter much where one starts, since it is assumed that no one example of religion will contain all the characteristics, and thus no one example of religion would become normative. Nevertheless, the question then becomes where does one stop the definitional chain? Since membership in the class "religion" can be conferred on a system of beliefs and practices based simply on its sharing one or two characteristics with any other member of the class, the class is then infinitely expandable. As with purely functional definitions, open polythetic definitions could be used to place almost any system of beliefs and practices under the rubric "religion." In the end, if prototypical polythetic definitions are too exclusive and tend towards ethnocentric bias, the opposite is true of open polythetic definitions since they tend towards an indiscriminate universalism. Despite these criticisms, however, polythetic definitions of religion have become increasingly popular—so popular in fact that it has recently been observed that "practically every introductory textbook on religion is testimony" to the popularity of polythetic definitions of religion.[60]

---

[57] The quoted phrase is from Alston, "Religion," p. 142. For a clear endorsement of a prototypical polythetic definition, see Benson Saler, "Cultural Anthropology and the Definitions of Religion" in Ugo Bianchi (ed.), *The Notion of "Religion" in Comparative Research* (Rome: "L'Erma" di Bretschneider, 1994), pp. 831-36. Perhaps the best known prototypical polythetic definition of religion is Ninian Smart's dimensional approach; see, for example, Ninian Smart, *Worldviews: Crosscultural Explorations of Human Beliefs* (New York: Charles Scribner's Sons, 1983).

[58] For the critique of prototypical polythetic definitions on the grounds of their inherent ethnocentricism, see William Herbrechtsmeier, "Buddhism and the Definition of Religion: One More Time," *Journal for the Scientific Study of Religion* 32:1 (1993), pp. 1-18; Timothy Fitzgerald, "Hinduism and the 'World Religion' Fallacy" *Religion* 20 (1990), pp. 101-118; Donald Wiebe, "Benson Saler, 'Conceptualizing Religion'," *Numen* 42 (1995), pp. 78-82; Stewart Elliott Guthrie, "Religion: What Is It?" *Journal for the Scientific Study of Religion* 35:4 (1996), pp. 412-19.

[59] For discussion and endorsement of open polythetic definitions, see Jonathan Z. Smith, *Imagining Religion: From Babylon to Jonestown* (Chicago: University of Chicago Press, 1982), pp. 1-18; W. Richard Comstock, "Toward Open Definitions of Religion," *Journal of the American Academy of Religion* 52:3 (1986), pp. 499-517; Bertel Wahlstrom, "The Indefinability of Religion," *Temenos* 17 (1981), pp. 101-15; Jacques Waardenburg, "In Search of an Open Concept of Religion," in Despland and Vallee (eds.), *Religion in History*, pp. 225-42.

[60] Herbrechtsmeier, "Buddhism and the Definition of Religion," p. 6.

Conclusion

As we have seen, a variety of definitions of religion have appeared in the literature of the academic study of religion over the last hundred years or so. Despite their diversity, however, these definitions can be reduced to a few formal categories as summarized in chart two below. Again, it is not my belief that such formal analysis and classification will instantly produce a consensus on a definition of religion, nor do I think it will convince those not already so-inclined that a definition of religion is truly necessary. Nevertheless, such formal analysis is useful for at least two other reasons.

CHART 2
FORMAL POSSIBILITIES FOR THE DEFINITION OF RELIGION

I. Real definitions of religion
   a. Positive vs. negative real definitions of religion.
II. Nominal definitions of religion.
   a. Lexical definitions of religion.
   b. Precising definitions of religion.
      i. Analytic vs. Synthetic precising definitions.
      ii. Substantive vs. Functional precising definitions.
      iii. Monothetic vs. Polythetic precising definitions.

First, formal analysis of definitions of religion gives us a useful starting place for the evaluation of new definitions of the same formal type. Recently, for example, Brian K. Smith offered a new precising definition of religion based on the functional characteristic of "canonicity." According to Smith, the *sine qua non* charcacteristic that all religions share is "a canonical source—whether it be a text or set of texts, an oral tradition of a myth or set of myths, the pronouncements of the founder, or any other functional equivalent (i.e. any other absolutely authoritative source for legitimation)."[61] Smith's formulation is definitely one of the most original definitions of religion to be proposed in years, and yet, formally, it is simply another example of a purely functional precising definition of religion. As such, it is open to the same kinds of analytic and synthetic critiques to which all formally-equivalent definitions are subject. In order to

---

[61] Brian K. Smith, "Exorcising the Transcendent: Strategies for Defining Hinduism and Religion," *History of Religions* 27 (1987), pp. 32-55, p. 53.

most effeciently build on past scholarly effort, therefore, perhaps the first step in evaluating new definitions of religion should be submitting them to formal analysis and critique.

The second reason formal analysis of definitions of religion is important is because it contributes to a fuller "second-order" understanding of the field as a whole. As stated in the introduction, I feel the history of the definitional enterprise has been unduly neglected, partly because the field has failed to develop any kind of uniform formal categories for dealing with definitions of religion. This is unfortunate since, as we have seen, many of the issues that influence the construction and popularity of certain forms of definitions have also driven the development of the academic study of religion at large. In this chapter, I have had space to touch on only a few of these issues, e.g. Enlightenment universalism, evolutionary theory, and, especially, the debates over the real definition of religion. Undoubtedly, a much more thorough investigation is in order. However, if the categories I have proposed in this chapter prove useful for developing a more sophisticated history of the definitional enterprise and facilitate the teaching of that history, then I will consider it successful.

CHAPTER TWELVE

THINKING RELIGION

Charles E. Winquist

...while there is a staggering amount of data, of phenomena, of
human experiences and expressions that might be characterized in one culture or another, by one criterion or another, as
religious—*there is no data for religion*. Religion is solely the creation of the scholars study.
—Jonathan Z. Smith.[1]

For my purposes, religion will mean orientation—orientation
in the ultimate sense, that is, how one comes to terms with the
ultimate significance of one's place in the world.
—Charles H. Long.[2]

Probity

The field of the study of religion does not have clearly defined
boundaries or methodologies that are universally acceptable or
applied. Instead, the field has emerged out of a complex of related
disciplines primarily from the human sciences that through their
diverse applications have made the field responsible to a wide
range of phenomena. There is no simple agreement as to what
should be studied as religious phenomena or whether there are
methods of interrogation that are specific to the field.

The dissolution or relativizing of dominant religious and philosophical ideologies through the globalization of the field is a dis-
persion of formal unities that had at one time been unexamined
and considered self-evident. In a postcolonial world the *natural attitude* is denaturalized and is now representative of specific cultures,
classes and interests.

The field of religion presents itself as a heterogeneous field of
incorrigibles, positivities, empiricities and multiplicities without a
unifying discipline that we can fall back upon for orientation and

---

[1] Jonathan Z. Smith, *Imagining Religion: From Babylon to Jonestown* (Chicago: University of Chicago Press, 1982), p. xi.
[2] Charles H. Long, *Significations: Signs, Symbols, and Images in the Interpretation of
Religion* (Philadelphia: Fortress Press, 1986), p. 7.

familiarity. Students of religion must now ask whether they can endure the phenomenality of experience without the protection of a theological pretext. We may need an ideology critique before we can probe the matter hidden in the data or repressed through a methodological voluntarism. The only claim that is self-evident is that the data of consciousness is the data of consciousness. We certainly need an on-going critique of our own thinking if that thinking is the production of the sense of *religion*. This is why J.Z. Smith argues that for the student of religion, "self-consciousness constitutes his primary expertise, his foremost object of study."[3] We need to hesitate before accepting easy definitions of our interpretive work or easy definitions of religion because the field of data as a whole resists assimilation into all but the most minimal definitions. We must be both tentative and heuristic. To maintain a probity in thought we should make the heuristic assumption that our speeches on religion are addressed to its cultured despisers. That is, we may have to think under conditions not of our own choosing if we want to avoid begging the question of the meaning of religion. It would appear that in the contemporary period the conditions of intelligibility are secular and fully inscribed on a plane of immanence. References to transcendence must at least be indexed on a plane of immanence. Even if the world is *not* all that is the case, it is the world that we know. Anything that is *other* will have to be *other* in the world if it is to be knowable. Theology in this context is a self-consciousness or a thinking about thinking that is not in any way artificially restricted. Theology is in this context a thinking religion.

In other words, the expertise in self-consciousness that Smith demands of the student of religion is a consciousness of consciousness, a thinking about thinking. It would thus appear that the first interrogation of the meaning of religion is epistemological. We have to access and assess the epistemic status or function of the figurations that we use in the assemblage of data that we are calling religious. We have to decide why we are calling any particular datum religious. This designation is a product of our thinking. If we start in the scholar's study and in this case the study of Charles H. Long, the minimal definition of religion is *orientation* but this minimal definition is conditioned by the unconditional formulation of *orientation in the ultimate sense*. The logic of thinking about religion is a logic of ultimate sense.

---

[3] Smith, *Imagining Religion*, p. xi.

If we accept the word *logic* as a notation for gathering and assemblage, the words that stand out as unexplained are *ultimate* and *sense*. They may be imbricated in such a way that they will have to be thought together. That is, it may be that the logic of sense is implicated in what is meant by ultimacy. This would have to be determined by deciding whether there is a meaning to sense that is more than our conscious rationality and this would have to be decided within the domain of that conscious rationality. Can consciousness designate a realm that is other than itself and does that realm have any affinity with what consciousness designates as ultimacy?

As we learned from neo-orthodoxy *and* its talk of God, *ultimacy* has to do with what is *wholly other* from ordinariness. I am suggesting that we can only know this as an epistemic rather than a metaphysical consideration. We stay within the realm of the ordinary to talk about what it is not. We cannot escape from the realm of sense. Thinking *religion* is about thinking even if it includes talk of God. There are certain points of intersection between the study of religion, philosophy and theology and they all have to do with what is meant by thinking.

This is an inheritance of the *Age of Reason* or, more specifically, the *Enlightenment*. If Descartes' *cogito* is emblematic of a shift to philosophies of consciousness from philosophies of being, the field of religious studies and the disciplines that contribute to the field are still very much, even after the hermeneutics of suspicion, the linguistic turn in philosophy and deconstructive postmodernism, indebted to the attitude of the *Enlightenment* in the making of sense. As J. Z. Smith very clearly writes, "*the academic study of religion is a child of the Enlightenment*. This intellectual heritage is revealed in the notion of generic religion as opposed to historical believing communities....[R]eligion was domesticated; it was transformed from *pathos* to *ethos*....It was this impulse, this domestication, that made possible the entrance of religious studies into the secular academy. But the price of this entry, to reverse the Steppenwolf formula, is the use of our mind."[4]

The generic concept of *religion* is not innocent of the genealogy of its origination in the Enlightenment. All was not clear and distinct in Enlightenment thinking. There were precursor shadows in Enlightenment epistemologies that are not terribly unlike problematics that have come to mark postmodern sensibilities. There was

---

[4] Ibid., p. 104.

never a simple empiricism that could ground a simple correspondence theory of truth. Descartes' reason was complicated by the division of ideas into those which are innate, adventitious, or factitious. Locke's *Ideas* are incorrigibles that like his predecessor Duns Scotus's *haecceities* or, now, Gilles Deleuze's *singularities*, are points of emission rather than points or things that one can get under, around, or behind. Bishop Berkeley's radically empirical claim that *"esse* is *percipi"* exfoliated into a theological idealism. David Hume acknowledges that the idea of *necessary connexion* required for causal explanation is the result of the habit of a belief associated with the probable intelligibility of the experience of constant conjunction. Kant inscribed and reinscribed processes, which Derrida now calls *différance* and he called the transcendental imagination or schematism of the pure concepts of the understanding, into the First and Third *Critiques*, fissuring the phenomenal from the noumenal world and generating a notion of the sublime which cannot be sublated under epistemic categories or assimilated into objective discourse.

It appears that critical philosophy has subverted a simplistic understanding of thinking and *a fortiori* a simplistic understanding of thinking *religion*. We cannot understand religion without understanding thinking. Paradoxically, it may be that postcritical thinking needs to invent more refined and exact concepts to be distributed across experience to understand the inexactness of thinking experiences.

Marking the Field

Wherever we are we are always in the middle of culture. That is, we begin in the middle and crawl back through the culture as we constitute a sense of a beginning or crawl forward in constituting the sense of an ending. These beginnings or endings are fictive productions of heuristic strategies since we are in fact always in the middle. First principles or beginnings are always belated and endings or purposes are afterthoughts, that is, thoughts after the ending.

We are still in the middle and I think we need a method that does not resist staying in the middle. Peregrinations, wanderings, erring, the carnivalesque are possible images for a nomadic thinking that does not become ideologically rooted in a simplistic notion of Enlightenment truth. In *Epiphanies of Darkness*,[5] I suggested an

---

[5] Charles E. Winquist, *Epiphanies of Darkness: Deconstruction in Theology* (Philadelphia: Fortress Press, 1986), pp. x-xii.

image drawn from the work of Gilles Deleuze and Felix Guattari for rethinking the sense of a root so that we are no longer supporting a system but are instead experimenting with the soil of cultures in their diversity, intractability and heterogeneity. Their image is of a rhizome. A rhizome is a plant that matures underground and becomes more substantial when its stems spread underground in starts, false starts and blockages. The rhizome is elaboration in itself. Stems reach out that can intertwine other stems. Lines stop/start, intersect, and we have different modalities for argument and thinking. The field of the study of religion, in contrast to some of its contained and intersecting disciplines, is a field of rhizomorphic experimentation. There may be times when this is a stroll; but, I certainly do not want to preclude rigor from this field of experimentation. There are other times when thinking is a vigorous interrogation. New and rigorous concepts can be created and exacting questions can be formulated as part of the on-going experiment.

The spreading of the rhizome from its starting point of growth can be the work of description but in my own work it is primarily a work of interrogation. The question, a refracted and minimalized question from theology, that I most often ask in the introduction to religions and cultures is: "How does this culture, peoples or individuals thematize and articulate what is real and important for them?" The question is not value neutral but the theological turn does not become vastly intrusive or sometimes even evident until the question is radicalized into formulations such as "What do we take seriously without any reservation?" or "What is that than which nothing greater can be thought?" or "What is our ultimate concern?" Cultures or religions have not always radicalized this question, but they do give evidence of some hierarchical structure or else we cannot approach them in the study of religion. A culture's or community's sense of what is real and important does not exhaust religious meaning, but the interrogation of these values at least give us a place to start. If religion is not implicated in a sense of importance then there is the question of why we would be interested in it all.

The word that keeps appearing and also subverts the minimalism I am trying to describe is *sense*. There has been mentioned the sense of a beginning, the sense of an ending, the sense of importance, the sense of reality and orientation in an ultimate sense. What insists on itself is the notion of sense. And, in every case I am talking about the production of sense that entails a logic of sense.[6] Giving sense to meaning is more than a signifying practice although it is implicated in signifying practices. Deleuze notes four dimensions to propositional thinking—denotation, manifestation, signification, and sense.[7] Sense is what he calls *"the expressed of the proposition...*an incorporeal, complex, and irreducible entity, at the surface of things, a pure event which inheres or subsists in the proposition."[8] Sense does not exist without a proposition but neither is it identical with it. Following Husserl, Deleuze writes that "[s]ense is that which is expressed."[9] It is the event that is always already possible.

It is not that sense exists and we find it. Thinking is making sense. It is an event that is implicated in denotation, manifestation and signification. Its sense is in excess of the signifying practice. Deleuze refers to sense as extra-being, *aliquid.*[10] It is not that we get behind, around, or below the proposition. There is a singularity to sense. There is a certain impassibility to sense that is implicated in its genesis. Transcendental criticism that attends to sense replaces the old metaphysical Essences with sense and becomes properly genealogical in its method.

What is striking is that sense as expression-event is a becoming that is located on surfaces. The transcendental field is a surface for a genealogical interrogation that asks after the conditions that make thinking possible. The plane of immanence is unrestricted and thus the surface is what is profound. The metaphor of depth gives way to complexity, the complexity of surface arrangements, appearances, phantasms. The logic of sense is a reversal of Platonism. Concepts of extremity are not held captive by a notion of transcendence. God must be fully incarnate and thus fully secular. It is not surprising that Deleuze wrote that "it is our epoch which has discovered theology...Theology is now the science of nonexisting entities, the manner in which these entities—divine or antidivine, Christ or Antichrist—animate language and make for this glorious body which is divided into disjunctions."[11] Thinking the surface can be theological although we don't always recognize

---

[6] I will be referring particularly to the work of Gilles Deleuze in thinking the notion of a logic of sense. See Gilles Deleuze, *The Logic of Sense*, translated by Mark Lester with Charles Stivale (New York: Columbia University Press, 1990).

[7] Ibid., pp. 12-19.

[8] Ibid., p. 19.

[9] Ibid., p. 20.

[10] Ibid., p. 31.

[11] Ibid., p. 281.

it as theological. Even *thinking religion* doesn't always recognize when it is theological.

Problematizing the Field: Surfaces and Objects

I am certainly suggesting that work within the field of the study of religion will require interrogative strategies and that we will try to develop heuristic structures to anticipate the intelligibility and sense of the experience under question. There is along side of this work another characteristic of our studies that I want to bring to some accounting. That is that the nature of the surfaces and sometimes objects or practices of religious experience approached through the criteria of what is valued as real and important within a culture are often those surfaces, objects or practices that defamiliarize us with the ordinariness of our experiences. Not only do we interrogate what we have gathered as data but the adequacy of our interpretations and orientations is itself interrogated by the data.

The surface of experience, the plane of immanence, is highly variegated. It is populated by heterogenous singularities and other constructs, expressivities, that make sense and implicate thinking beyond its immediate perspective and particularity. Parables and paradoxes, myths and legends, texts and rituals, buildings and beliefs, all populate this surface along with the rest of what we call the world. Julia Kristeva draws particular attention to certain beliefs, *doxa*, that are part of the formulations within the habit of thinking that resist symbolization and resist assimilation into what Lacanians would call the symbolic realm. If these beliefs are in the modality of certainty, she calls them *protodoxa*. "The fundamental protodoxa is obviously *Being*, the irreducible archontic position."[12] These protodoxic modalities of belief are singularities that are not themselves assimilable into the rest of the habit of thinking but yet are a condition for thinking. When Paul Tillich writes that God is Being-itself is he saying that God is a protodoxic modality of belief within Christian thought? Is the *brahman* a protodoxic modality of belief in Indian spirituality? If her formulation makes sense then there is a sense in which protodoxic modalities of belief don't make sense. In the study of religion there may be a "staggering amount of data" that can be understood as *protodoxa*.

That is, this data can resist interpretation and understanding. Its

---

[12] Julia Kristeva, *Revolution in Poetic Language*, translated by Margaret Waller (New York: Columbia University Press, 1984), p. 35.

simple presence theologically complicates the secular world. Sometimes there are fissures or discrepancies in the material that suggest to us that maybe something else is going on other than what we are seeing or other than the witness that is presented to us. A form of skepticism that is not a nihilism can be a respect for the data.

Problematizing the Field: Frames and Subjects

One of the most important shifts facing the study of religion is the rejection of the ontotheological frame for the hermeneutical process within the field. What is being rejected is the possibility of finding a first, an irreducible principle, upon which everything is based and from which everything can be derived. If this rejection is credible and compelling then what is radically changed is the status of "foundational" concepts in the formation of discursive practices. This does not mean that we cannot speak of subjectivity, objectivity, ontology, or even God; but, it does mean that these concepts have been defamiliarized when shifted into a differential frame that is other than the ontotheological tradition. In particular, we cannot begin by granting special privilege to discursive formations that reside outside of the specific text production of our inquiry and are not subject to the genealogical analysis that can come by reflecting the text back on itself.

The death of God, the closure of the book, the end of history and the dismantling of a centered and unified subject are not *desiderata* of postmodern thought but are the problematic of this thinking. We cannot will away the historical and cultural witness of our time although we can always challenge the adequacy of interpretive formulations of where we stand. We can question whether we are making sense.

Has too much importance been assigned to the loss of the unified subject or the disassembling of other fundamental concepts? Certainly, if it can be otherwise. What is at stake in this question is whether there is an epistemological framework that can both authenticate itself and be used to restore or rehabilitate the speculative thinking of the ontotheological tradition. If not and there is no proper domain for metadiscourses, then we are always working in an hermeneutics of suspicion.

There is a problem of representation—the secondariness of primary presentation. The legacy of the nineteenth-century traditions of suspicion is the radicalization of Kant through Marx, Nietzsche and Freud. The phenomenality of experience is not innocent.

Strategies

I do not think that we can go on with business as usual and write monumental history as if the problem of representation were not a serious historiographical problem with diverse manifestations and implications. We have failed to grasp the conditions under which we think if we seek for an essence rather than a sense of religious particularities. But, we have also failed to grasp the conditions under which we think if we prescind from thinking the transformational impact of protodoxic modalities on the ordinariness of life.

We have to experiment with thinking. A possible model of descriptive sensibility is the evenly hovering attention of psychoanalysis with attention to trifles, incongruities, resistances. Attention to the structures of everyday life or Foucault's genealogical analyses are moves toward a radical empiricism. These are all moves that are reading against the grain of the totalization of principles of explanation or interpretations. We have to respect the data by making accommodations to theory hard for ourselves.

A different type of strategy is the fashioning of levers of intervention. This is always an experimental work that is itself a text production that is also parasitic on an existing text or corpus of texts. Forcing the juxtaposition of dissimilar figurations or the elaboration of unassimilable ideas is a metonymical strategy that changes the tone of a discursive practice without necessarily changing any of the elements in the discourse. The emphasis here is on style, rhetoric and the theatrics of theological reflection bearing on the study of religion.

I want to suggest that what we need is a complementarity of strategies both of description and intervention just as we need diversity in the selection of what is to be studied and how our interests are defined. This is an affirmation not of relativism but of minimalism. The irony is that there is a richness to the minimalist affirmation. The trifles, the little things begin to matter. We can try to make sense with style, make things more beautiful. The field of religion must take as its responsibility and as part of its theological task the enduring of the phenomenality of experience.

SELECT BIBLIOGRAPHY

Anderson, Benedict. *Imagined Communities: Reflections on the Origin and Spread of Nationalism.* London: Verso, 1991.

Arnal, William E. and Michel Desjardins (eds.). *Whose Historical Jesus? Studies in Christianity and Judaism,* No. 7. Waterloo, Canada: Wilfrid Laurier University Press, 1997.

Asad, Talal. *Genealogies of Religion: Discipline and Reasons of Power in Christianity and Islam.* Baltimore: Johns Hopkins University Press, 1993.

Becker, Gay. *Disrupted Lives: How People Create Meaning in a Chaotic World.* Berkeley: University of California Press, 1997.

Bell, Catherine. *Ritual Theory, Ritual Practice.* New York: Oxford University Press, 1992.

Bianchi, Ugo. *The Notion of "Religion" in Comparative Research: Selected Proceedings of the XVI IAHR Congress.* Rome: L'Erma di Bretschneider, 1994.

Boyer, Pascal. *The Naturalness of Religious Ideas: A Cognitive Theory of Religion.* Berkeley: University of California Press, 1994.

Burkert, Walter. *Creation of the Sacred: Tracks of Biology in Early Religions.* Cambridge: Harvard University Press, 1996.

Capps, Walter H. *Religious Studies: The Making of a Discipline.* Minneapolis: Fortress Press, 1995.

Castelli, Elizabeth A. and Hal Taussig (eds.). *Reimagining Christian Origins: A Colloquium Honoring Burton L. Mack.* Valley Forge, PA: Trinity Press International, 1996.

Chidester, David. *Savage Systems: Colonialism and Comparative Religion in Southern Africa.* Charlottesville: University Press of Virginia, 1996.

Clarke, Peter B. and Peter Byrne. *Religion Defined and Explained.* New York: St Martin's Press, 1993.

Davidovich, Adina. *Religion as a Province of Meaning: The Kantian Foundations of Modern Theology.* Minneapolis: Fortress Press, 1993.

Despland, Michel and Gerard Vallee (eds.). *Religion in History: The Word, the Idea, the Reality.* Waterloo, Ontario: Wilfrid Laurier University Press, 1992.

DiCenso, James J. "Religion as Illusion: Reversing the Freudian Hermeneutic." *The Journal of Religion,* 71/2 (April, 1991), pp. 167-79.

———. "*Totem and Taboo* and the Constitutive Function of Symbolic Forms." *Journal of the American Academy of Religion* LXIV/3 (Fall, 1996), pp. 557-74.

Fishbane, Michael. *The Kiss of God: Spiritual and Mystical Death in Judaism.* Seattle: University of Washington Press, 1994.

Fitzgerald, Timothy. "Hinduism and the 'World Religion' Fallacy." *Religion* 20 (1990), pp. 101-18.

———. "A Critique of the Concept of Religion." *Method & Theory in the Study of Religion* 9/2 (1997), pp. 91-110.

Green, Garrett. "Challenging the Religious Studies Canon: Karl Barth's Theory of Religion." *The Journal of Religion* 75 (1995), pp. 473-86.

Guthrie, Stewart. *Faces in the Clouds: A New Theory of Religion.* Oxford: Oxford University Press, 1993.

———. "Religion: What is It?" *Journal for the Scientific Study of Religion* 35/4 (1996), pp. 412-19.

Harrison, Peter. *"Religion" and the Religions in the English Enlightenment.* Cambridge: Cambridge University Press, 1990.

Hood, Ralph W., Jr. (ed.). *Handbook of Religious Experience.* Birmingham, Alabama: Religious Education Press, 1995.

Ingold, Tim (ed.). *Key Debates in Anthropology.* London: Routledge, 1996.

Kippenburg, Hans G. "Rivalry Among Scholars of Religion: The Crisis of Historicism and the Formation of Paradigms in the History of Religions." *Historical Reflections* 20 (Fall 1994), pp. 377-402.

Lawson, E. Thomas and Robert N. McCauley. *Rethinking Religion: Connecting Cognition and Culture.* Cambridge: Cambridge University Press, 1990.

Lease, Gary. "The History of 'Religious' Consciousness and the Diffusion of Culture: Strategies for Surviving Dissolution." *Historical Reflections/ Reflexions Historiques* 20/3(1994), pp. 453-79.

Lincoln, Bruce. *Authority: Construction and Corrosion.* Chicago: University of Chicago Press, 1994.

———. "Theses on Method." *Method & Theory in the Study of Religion* 8/3 (1996), pp. 225-27.

McCutcheon , Russell T. "The Category 'Religion' in Recent Publications: A Critical Survey." *Numen* 42/3 (1995), pp. 284-309.

———. *Manufacturing Religion: The Discourse on Sui Generis Religion and the Politics of Nostalgia.* Oxford: Oxford University Press, 1997.

Mack, Burton L. *The Lost Gospel: The Book of Q.* San Francisco: Harper & Row, 1993.

———. "After *Drudgery Divine*." *Numen* 39/2 (1992), pp. 225-33.

———. *Who Wrote the New Testament? The Making of the Christian Myth.* San Francisco: HarperCollins, 1995.

Masuzawa, Tomoko. *In Search of Dreamtime: The Quest for the Origin of Religion.* Chicago: University of Chicago Press, 1993.

Morris, Brian. *Anthropological Studies of Religion: An Introductory Text.* Cambridge: Cambridge University Press, 1990.

Obeyesekere, Gananath. *The Work of Culture.* Chicago: University of Chicago Press, 1990.

Paden, William. *Interpreting the Sacred: Ways of Viewing Religion.* Boston: Beacon Press, 1992.
——. *Religious Worlds: The Comparative Study of Religion.* Boston: Beacon Press, 1994.
——. "Elements of a New Comparativism." *Method & Theory in the Study of Religion* 8/1(1996), pp. 5-14.
Pals, Daniel. *Seven Theories of Religion.* New York: Oxford University Press, 1996.
Patton, Laurie and Wendy Doniger (eds.). *Myth and Method.* Charlottesville: University of Virginia Press, 1996.
Penner, Hans H. *Impasse and Resolution: A Critique of the Study of Religion.* New York: Peter Lang Press, 1990.

Roof, Wade Clark. *A Generation of Seekers: The Spiritual Journeys of the Baby Boom Generation.* San Francisco: HarperCollins Publishers, 1993.
Rudolph, Susanne Hoeber and James Piscatori (eds.).*Transnational Religion and Fading States.* Boulder, Colorado: Westview Press, 1997.
Ruf, Frederick J. *The Creation of Chaos: William James and the Stylistic Making of a Disorderly World.* Albany: State University of New York Press, 1991.

Saler, Benson. *Conceptualizing Religion: Immanent Anthropologists, Transcendent Natives, and Unbounded Categories.* Leiden: E. J. Brill, 1993.
Smith, Jonathan Z. "Social Formations of Early Christianities: A Response to Burton Mack and Ron Cameron." *Method & Theory in the Study of Religion* 8/3 (1996), pp. 271-78.
Stark, Rodney. *Rational Choice Theory and Religion: Summary and Assessment.* London: Routledge, 1997.
Strenski, Ivan. "Lessons for Religious Studies in Waco?" *Journal of the American Academy of Religion* 61 (1993), pp. 567-74.
——. "Between Theory and Speciality: Sacrifice in the 90s." *Religious Studies Review* 22/1 (1996), pp. 10-20.

Wiggins, James. *In Praise of Religious Diversity.* New York: Routledge, 1996.

INDEX OF NAMES

INDEX OF SUBJECTS